Helping College Students

Helping College Students

Developing Essential Support Skills for Student Affairs Practice

Amy L. Reynolds

With contributions from John A. Mueller and Marcia Roe Clark

Foreword by Susan R. Komives

JOSSEY-BASS
A Wiley Imprint
www.josseybass.com

Published by Jossey-Bass
A Wiley Imprint
989 Market Street, San Francisco, CA 94103-1741—www.josseybass.com

Jossey-Bass books and products are available through most bookstores. To contact Jossey-Bass
directly call our Customer Care Department within the U.S. at 800-956-7739, outside the
U.S. at 317-572-3986, or fax 317-572-4002.

Jossey-Bass also publishes its books in a variety of electronic formats. Some content that
appears in print may not be available in electronic books.

Library of Congress Cataloging-in-Publication Data

Reynolds, Amy L.
    Helping college students : developing essential support skills for student affairs practice/
  Amy L. Reynolds; with contributions from John A. Mueller and Marcia Roe Clark.
      p. cm.
    Includes bibliographical references and index.
    ISBN 978-0-7879-8645-2 (cloth)
      1. Student affairs services—United States.   I. Mueller, John A., 1961.   II. Clark,
  Marcia Roe.   III. Title.
  LB2342.92.R49   2009
  378.1'97—dc22
                                         2008032860

Printed in the United States of America
FIRST EDITION
HB Printing   10 9 8 7 6 5 4 3 2 1

The Jossey-Bass
Higher and Adult Education Series

Contents

I dedicate this book to my family—my immediate family, my family of origin, and my family by love. You sustain me every day, especially during the hard times. My mother, Norma S. Reynolds, passed away as I was writing this book. I still miss her every day. I offer this book in her name and her memory.

Foreword

John Lennon frequently said that one of the most meaningful songs he ever wrote and performed was "Help." His lyrics poignantly present both a request based on need as well as gratitude for the role of the helper: "Help me if you can, I'm feeling down / And I do appreciate you being round / Help me get my feet back on the ground / Won't you please, please help me?" (downloaded May 26, 2008, from http://www.lyricsandsongs.com/song/4739 .html). Reminiscent of another Beatles song, "A Little Help from My Friends," one of the early titles Reynolds suggested for this book was "With a Little Help." Challenging the convention that a single counseling course adequately prepares new professionals for the complexities of their roles, she supports the broader notion that helping is a more appropriate skill set for all student affairs professionals, regardless of role. She further asserts that the conceptualization of helping should be broadened. Helping is enacted through advising, supervising, facilitating, and engaging in conflict and crisis management, and it includes group work. Reynolds's thesis seems to be that overarching all these conceptualizations is that helping must be a mind-set, a way of envisioning and enacting student affairs work.

Reynolds proposes that student affairs functional areas can be grouped into four core areas. Professionals in all four areas serve in a helping role and would benefit from developing professional helping skills. These four core areas include the following: (1) counseling-oriented positions, like career and personal

counseling; (2) leadership development and educational positions, such as student activities, fraternity and sorority advising, health and wellness, and residence life; (3) administrative
positions, such as dean of students, judicial affairs, and admissions; and (4) academic affairs positions, such as advising and
academic support services. Blimling (2001b) envisioned these
functional groupings a bit differently when he identified four
communities of practice in student affairs work. He differ-
entiated these communities as either educational (including
student learning or student development functions) or management (including student services and student administration
functions). Whether viewing students as learners or clients
(the educational functions) or as customers or participants (the
management functions), professionals employing helping skills
truly connect with the student and more effectively engage
with their functional roles.

Helping College Students presents a tremendous overview of
the evolution of taxonomies of knowledge, skills, and attitudes
essential for student affairs practice. When Doug Woodard and
I were designing the third and fourth editions of *Student Services*
(Komives & Woodard, 1996, 2003), we felt strongly that professionals needed foundational grounding in the historical, ethical, legal, and philosophical dimensions of student affairs work.
Within the complexities of institutional diversity and student
diversity, professionals must organize the work and functions of
student affairs, engage in strategic planning and finance, manage
information technology, and manage human resources. Further,
professionals must understand the role of theory and research
in shaping intentional practices. They should understand psychosocial, cognitive, and typological perspectives of student
development, identity development, student learning theory,
organizational theory, the dynamics of campus environments,
and how all those theoretical frames combine to work toward
student success. We advanced the essential competencies and

techniques of multiculturalism, leadership, teaching, counseling and helping skills, advising and consultation, conflict resolution, community building and programming, assessment and evaluation, and professionalism.

Reynolds includes many of those competencies in this new conceptualization of the broader construct of helping, but this book makes the important connection of helping skills being essential to working with students in all functional areas and in all educational processes. It reminded me of the African parable that sticks tied in a bundle are unbreakable. Helping skills are not just one discrete set of skills (as perhaps presented in our *Student Services* book); helping skills are (perhaps like multiculturalism) one of the important essential threads that tie the bundle of student affairs functions and processes together to be an essential educational process promoting student learning and development.

The Invitation and the Offer

This book led me to some deep reflections about my own forty-year career in student affairs work as an administrator, educator, and graduate faculty member. I pondered the many contexts in which students presented themselves to me or in which I encountered them. I realized that the helping process was central in all the most developmentally powerful encounters I recalled—from the student leader struggling to resolve a terrible conflict among key members in his student organization to the student accused of plagiarism trying to understand why she had engaged in that action. In all cases I could remember when I felt most proud of my professional behaviors; these moments were cast with the helping focus I tried to bring to the encounter. This helping process is worthy of the exploration offered in this book.

It seems to me the helping process involves someone or a group recognizing that they cannot quite manage something and reaching out to a helper or helpers who willingly join that person or group to assist, empower, inform, advise, or support them. The transcendent power of helping brings people together with care and empathy and, in the context of higher education, creates a student-centered environment that reaches out to students in every possible context to support their learning and development. At its core, the helping relationship is about the invitation or the offer.

In its most transcendent expression, the invitation "Can you help me?" is an invitation into the head and the heart when a person is most open to examination, expresses a need to change, and is willing to risk moving from old ways of being to a new level of perspective or ability. It is an opening to join with another to aid her/him where that person finds a need. Learning to authentically request help is complex. The gendered and cultural dimensions of help seeking are widely researched, and many students may not ever comfortably extend this invitation. The initiative may need to be with the offer instead.

The offer "How can I help you?" demonstrates one's willingness to focus on the needs of another. The offer communicates a commitment to use one's information, skills, time, and attention in assisting another. Authentically initiating the offer demonstrates a willingness to be in relationship with the other person.

Developing a Helping Mind-Set

Helping College Students promotes the centrality of the helping role and importance of the helping process that leads to the development of specific competencies that are enacted by a helping mind-set. Developing this mind-set requires that graduate preparation programs examine how effectively they teach these broader helping skills and that supervisors of new professionals model and expect these approaches to engaging with students. Further, *Helping College Students* calls professionals to acknowledge their advocacy role and helping by acting on behalf of those who have less of a voice in the academy. This kind of advocacy is a social justice commitment to change systems that cause distress and raise barriers for students to succeed personally and academically.

In their provocative *Rethinking Student Affairs Practice*, Love and Estanek (2004) challenged student affairs professionals to develop new mind-sets and engage in new habits of practice as a new way of being in student affairs work. These mind-sets include an assessment mind-set, a global mind-set, an intrapreneurial leadership mind-set, and a future-forecasting mind-set. This book adds a helping mind-set to these capacities. Although some view mind-sets as invisible and subconscious or as fixed and "immutable," Love and Estanek challenge us to realize that "new mindsets can see better or additional ways of serving the needs of students" (pp. 211–212).

Helping College Students is subtitled *Developing Essential Support Skills for Student Affairs Practice*. This book will help the reader understand how all aspects of student affairs practice must be enriched with a helping framework. The book identifies the needs inherent in the diverse contexts of the helper's role. As a superb professional development read, *Helping College Students* provides useful dimensions of multiculturally competent helping, microcounseling, managing conflict and crises, facilitating groups, and supervising. These broad helping skills empower students and their groups to understand themselves better and then act on that insight.

A Final Reflection

Over the years too many professionals have bifurcated professional preparation as being either counseling or administration focused. This book provides a useful bridge promoting a helping mind-set and explores how using helping skills broadens the effectiveness of any professional to engage students, employees, staff, and others in collaborative, supportive ways that empower growth and development.

Susan R. Komives
Professor of College Student
    Personnel Administration
University of Maryland

Preface

Many of us have ideas about books that we want to write. We fantasize about what we want to say and whom we want to reach. The idea for this book lingered for many years, yet it never quite went away. In actuality, the true impetus for writing *Helping College Students: Developing Essential Support Skills for Student Affairs Practice* came from many conversations over the years with faculty members in student affairs preparation programs who felt that the counseling texts available were typically not appropriate for or relevant to training graduate students in their programs.

Although most, if not all, student affairs preparation programs provide specific academic courses to assist new professionals in developing necessary helping and interpersonal skills to more effectively meet college students' needs, many of these courses are modeled on beginning counseling courses for master's-level counseling students. In fact, it is fairly common for student affairs or higher education professionals to be required to take one or two counseling courses alongside graduate students in counseling programs (e.g., counseling psychology, school or guidance counseling). Typically, these courses focus more on clinical and therapeutic issues rather than address the unique helping competencies needed for practitioners working in higher education. Such counseling courses may be interesting and provide important information; however, they often offer far too much traditional therapeutic, perhaps even psychodynamic, content and not enough background on how to address helping issues in a nontherapeutic context. These courses usually emphasize counseling theory at a level that is beyond the scope and type of helping that most student affairs professionals need or use in their daily practice. Learning about Freud in depth and various therapy techniques will not assist the typical student affairs practitioner in comforting or advising a student who wants to withdraw from school because of a death in the family, in understanding and addressing the deleterious group dynamics present in a dysfunctional resident assistant staff, or in challenging student leaders to take more responsibility for their campus groups. The texts used in these counseling psychology and counselor education courses tend to be traditional therapy and microskills texts that provide important information on necessary counseling skills and theories with little to no attention to the unique issues or concerns of student affairs practitioners who need to apply helping skills in specific contexts. Clearly, there is a need for a professional text that addresses helping skills and how to apply them within the higher education setting.

The primary purpose of this book is to examine the specific and unique awareness, knowledge, and skills that are necessary for student affairs and other higher education practitioners to be effective and ethical in their helping, counseling, and advising roles. This book addresses the core assumptions and underlying beliefs that impact the helping, counseling, and advising roles and the skills that are central to higher education. It synthesizes and integrates information from traditional counseling therapy texts and offers examples of how to use such skills within student affairs. A more in-depth exploration of helping and advising, as offered here, will assist professionals in understanding the demands and limits of their work. In particular, student affairs practitioners need helping skills that are relevant and useful for working with students and colleagues (as individuals or in groups) who have been historically underserved and underrepresented in higher education, so this book intentionally and purposefully integrates the latest literature on multicultural counseling. Faculty members and higher education professionals may use this book as a stand-alone text or as a companion text to the more traditional counseling theory and technique books often used in counseling courses. While there are other books that offer more in-depth knowledge about a specific helping skill used in higher education, such as crisis intervention, there are no books that provide a thorough overview of the core helping competencies essential to effective student affairs practice. In addition to serving the needs of graduate students in training, this book can be used as a means of professional development for practitioners at various levels of experience who want to enhance or extend their helping skills.

Audience

This book was written for student affairs and higher education professionals who work on college and university campuses across the country. It was designed to be a practical book that will increase the helping awareness, knowledge, and skill level of the many practitioners working in a variety of positions within student affairs and higher education. This book addresses the unique concerns of all levels of student affairs professionals, from new and entry-level professionals to senior administrators. Professionals may use this book for personal or professional development as an avenue for enhancing their own level of helping competence.

This book may also be helpful for faculty members who want to expand their helping skills to meet the needs of their students in more effective ways. It may also be useful to graduate students enrolled in student affairs, higher education, and related programs. This book may be used as part of a class or training intervention efforts for either graduate students (master's and doctoral level) or undergraduates (possibly peer helpers, resident assistants) who are interested in working in student affairs and higher education. It can also be used for higher education administration or student affairs administration courses that focus on the counseling or helping skills needed by those working in higher education.

Terminology

For this book to be meaningful to its diverse readers, there needs to be an understanding of some of the key terminology used. This is not always easy because many of the relevant terms are similar but may hold different meanings for different readers. There are a variety of terms that can be used to describe student affairs helping roles. In reality, most student affairs professionals are helpers, not professional counselors, so when using the term *counselor*, the intent is to focus on counseling center staff or other personnel who are trained and hired to conduct counseling on campus. The term *adviser* is used to describe those professionals who are academic advisers, while the broader term *helper* is used to connote any student affairs professional who is involved in helping interactions. Whenever possible, exact language that delineates the specific roles involved (e.g., faculty members, student affairs practitioners) is used to avoid any confusion regarding whom is being discussed. The term *student affairs professional* is used when globally discussing members of the student affairs profession.

In addition, the terms *helping, counseling,* and *therapy* are quite similar, and their usage is often determined by the preference of a particular author. It is useful to briefly identify the differences in these terms to solidify their use in the context of this book. The use of the terms *counseling* and *therapy* are often debated even within the counseling field. Parrott (2003) delineates these terms by suggesting that counseling focuses more on prevention, while therapy is more reparative or remedial. So counseling tends to be viewed as less intense and more focused on normal developmental concerns with an emphasis on support, problem solving, and education. Counseling occurs more frequently in educational settings, while therapy often takes place in more clinical settings, such as hospitals or private clinical practices. Finally, counseling is often viewed as more short-term in scope (e.g., weeks or months), whereas it is not uncommon for therapy to be more long-term oriented (e.g., years). Parrott suggests that, unfortunately, the distinctions between these terms are not useful because the lines between them are often blurred.

While there may be professionals on campus who serve as counselors and therapists, typically in student counseling and psychological centers, the term *helper* is more commonly associated with student affairs professionals who work outside these settings. Okun (2002) uses the term *helper* to describe people who assist others in understanding, coping, and responding to problems. She suggests that *helper* is an umbrella term and includes professional helpers, generalist human service workers, and nonprofessional helpers who differ from one another in terms of their formal training on theory and their communication and assessment skills. In her framework, student affairs practitioners would fall largely within the second category of generalist human service workers, whom she characterizes as having specialized human relations training at the college level, a team of colleagues and supervisors to consult with, access to professional development, and more routine and day-to-day contact with their clients (i.e., students). For the purposes of this book, *helping* and *helper* will be the primary terms used. When the role of the counseling center counselor or psychologist is being discussed or counseling theories are being examined, the counseling term will be used to be consistent with the terminology used in such settings.

Overview of the Book Content

This book is divided into two primary sections. The first section identifies the rationale for conceptualizing student affairs practitioners as helpers and details what their roles, responsibilities, competencies, and ethical concerns are. The mental health issues on college campuses and their impact on the environment are also explored. Concrete examples are used throughout the book to make it more meaningful and relevant to student affairs practitioners.

Chapter 1 explores the diverse roles that student affairs practitioners play on campus and how those roles have changed over time. Since helping is an essential part of almost every job in student affairs, this chapter identifies and describes the range of helping behaviors, roles, and responsibilities that practitioners display. Using the Dynamic Model of Student Affairs Competence from Pope, Reynolds, and Mueller (2004), this chapter addresses the helping awareness, knowledge, and skills that student affairs practitioners need to be effective in their work.

Chapter 2 addresses the current status of mental health issues on college campuses. Campuses are witnessing an unprecedented rise in the incidence of serious mental health issues, like depression, anxiety, and substance abuse. All student affairs practitioners interact with and provide assistance for students who struggle with personal issues that affect their ability to succeed on campus. This chapter reviews the current research that examines the mental health issues facing college students and the impact of those issues on college campuses.

Chapter 3 explores the key ethical issues that student affairs practitioners face when in their helping roles. The unique ethical and professional issues facing practitioners who offer support and counsel to college students is described, and suggestions for conceptualizing and addressing such concerns are examined.

Chapter 4 addresses the counseling and helping theories, including their history, key theoretical assumptions, core strategies, and relevance to helping in a higher education context. These theories' strengths and weaknesses are critiqued, and suggestions are made for creating a personal theory of helping that practitioners can use in their interactions with students. This knowledge provides a necessary foundation for the essential helping skills that all professionals need. In considering this chapter, I decided that I wanted it to be written by someone who actually taught counseling theories to graduate students in a student affairs preparation program. John A. Mueller was the first colleague whom I considered because of numerous conversations that we have had over the years about the challenges of teaching such courses. His insight and ability to traverse the fields of counseling and student affairs created an excellent integration of the most relevant counseling theories that will surely assist readers.

The second section of the book examines the essential helping skills that all practitioners need regardless of their specific job responsibilities. In addition, how to incorporate multicultural competence within the helping role is also addressed. Recommendations for the future and how to more effectively and intentionally prepare student affairs professionals to fulfill their role and responsibility as helpers are also explored.

Chapter 5 identifies the specific multicultural awareness, knowledge, and skills that student affairs practitioners require to apply their helping skills to meet the needs of all students more effectively. Best practices and approaches for working across cultures are explored, as are the challenges facing student affairs practitioners in becoming multiculturally competent. Finally, strategies for developing multicultural helping competence are identified.

Chapter 6 specifies the communication and microcounseling skills necessary to be an effective helper, such as active listening and paraphrasing. Concrete examples are used to demonstrate effective ways to communicate and help others. When contemplating how to approach this chapter, I decided that it would also benefit from being written by a faculty member who

had taught a counseling course within a student affairs preparation program. Marcia Roe Clark immediately came to mind
because our previous discussions demonstrated to me that she
was an outstanding teacher who was able to assist her students
in understanding the many challenges inherent in being helpers
on a college campus.

Chapter 7 highlights the specific skills that are needed to
resolve conflicts and address the various crises that can occur on
a college campus. Illustrations are used to explore what to do,
and what not to do, to effectively address these issues.

Chapter 8 addresses the various group situations, from training to providing workshops or advising student groups, with
which student affairs professionals are often involved. This
chapter identifies the stages of group development and how to
effectively work with groups in different contexts. In addition,
the unique group skills needed by student affairs professionals
are explored.

Chapter 9 examines the various supervision and mentoring contexts that student affairs professionals experience and
require their helping skills. Specific skills needed to effectively
work with colleagues and assist them in their professional development are identified, and concrete examples are used to illustrate these skills.

Chapter 10 concludes this book and summarizes the key
points while addressing what the profession needs to do to ensure
that student affairs professionals are adequately prepared to be
helpers and understand their unique role and responsibility on
campus.

Acknowledgments

This book is the result of endless conversations with student
affairs colleagues about the need for a text that adequately
and comprehensively prepares graduate students to face the

challenges of being a helper on a college campus. Whether they want to be helpers or not, higher education professionals are continually placed in that role. In addition, my years as a counseling center staff psychologist have taught me about the increasing (and sometimes furtive) need for student affairs professionals to have adequate awareness, knowledge, and skills as helpers to effectively meet the needs of the countless college students who struggle with psychological, interpersonal, and academic concerns. Over time the need and severity only seem to grow, and many student affairs professionals are unsure of how to best support and assist students. This need has turned into anxiety for many because students' increased mental health issues have led to suicide attempts, interpersonal conflict, and even violence with increasing frequency. Then, of course, there is also the reality that the majority of the time, the helping skills that student affairs professionals need involve less serious psychological issues, like the everyday adjustment, interpersonal, and academic concerns that students face.

That being said, there are many people who have helped with the development of this project from start to finish. This book began as a speck like the one found by Horton in *Horton Hears a Who!* by Dr. Seuss. Horton eventually realized that on this tiny speck there was an amazing village of people who were all committed to the same purpose. I want to take this time to thank all those people who assisted me along the way. First, I want to thank Erin Null, my editor at Jossey-Bass, for her unwavering support and belief in this project. Her attention to detail and access to resources made it so easy for me to do my work. I also want to thank reviewers of this book—Michael Cuyjet, Jane Fried, and Robert Reason—whose helpful suggestions and critiques strengthened its applicability and readability. In addition, I want to thank my very good friends and colleagues, John A. Mueller and Marcia Roe Clark, who have made such vital contributions to this book. Their expertise as preparation faculty who regularly address these issues when teaching graduate students has been essential to making this book relevant and meaningful to the field.

I have spent more than half of my career working in student affairs as a counseling center psychologist and have worked with so many incredible psychologists and counselors who have mentored, motivated, and supported me in my efforts to help college students. I especially want to thank the many colleagues and friends with whom I have worked at the Ohio State University, the University of California at Irvine, the University of Iowa, and Buffalo State College. Add to that the infinite number of student affairs colleagues who have worked in every possible student affairs office and whose first priority has been to be there for students. The names and faces are endless; they are professionals who have inspired me with both their compassion and their skill. Without these many helpers, so many college students would have suffered and struggled alone. With the demanding nature of our work, it is sometimes easy to forget what a difference we make. So I want to acknowledge the many who have made, and will continue to make, a difference.

Of course, it is also important to acknowledge the many students who bring their dreams, fears, joys, and struggles with them and choose to share these precious gifts with us. They are the reason we do what we do. So when we see them smile after facing a chasm of pain, graduate after being near academic termination, fall in love when they were convinced they would always be alone, and persevere when they lacked support and encouragement, it is all worth it. And for those students who have the additional burden of feeling invisible, disempowered, or otherwise oppressed by society, our institutions, other students, and even professionals who lack multicultural insight and competence, I applaud your courage and resilience.

Finally, I am immensely grateful to my family and friends, who always have supported me and cheered me on, especially as I wrote this book. This book took time from them, and they never complained. I especially want to thank Raechele, Justice, and Mandela for their endless love and encouragement. You are the rock and foundation from which my best ideas come.

In this book I humbly share the many beliefs and ideas that I have come to embrace during my work in higher education during the past twenty-five years in hopes that they will help others in doing this very important and often underappreciated work. It is my desire that the suggestions and ideas offered here will encourage everyone who reads the book to expand her/his expectations, energy, and effort to make a difference in the everyday lives of college students.

Amy L. Reynolds
May 2008

About the Authors

Amy L. Reynolds is an assistant professor in the department of counseling, school, and educational psychology at the University at Buffalo. She received her doctorate in counseling psychology from the Ohio State University and has been working in higher education as a psychologist and professor for the past twenty years. Her work as a scholar, teacher, and consultant focuses on multicultural competence in counseling and student affairs as well as college mental health issues. She has published more than twenty-five journal articles and book chapters and has made over thirty-six presentations at regional or national conferences. She is also one of the coauthors of *Multicultural Competence in Student Affairs*, which was published by Jossey-Bass in 2004.

About the Contributors

John A. Mueller is an associate professor in the department of student affairs in higher education at Indiana University of Pennsylvania. He earned his doctorate in higher education at Teachers College, Columbia University, and his MA in counseling psychology from Illinois State University. He has been working in higher education for more than twenty years, with practitioner experience in residence life at four different institutions. His presentations and publications have focused on social identity and multicultural issues. He is a member of the editorial boards for ACPA Books and Media and *The College Student*

Affairs Journal. He is an active member of American College Personnel Association (ACPA), where he has served on the directorate of the standing committee for lesbian, gay, bisexual, and transgender awareness; the core council for member services and interests; the ACPA awards committee; and the 2009 convention planning committee. He also served as a trainer for the association's Cultural Diversity, Campus Violence, and Beyond Tolerance road shows. Mueller is a recipient of ACPA's Annuit Coeptis and Emerging Scholars awards.

Marcia Roe Clark has held faculty positions in student affairs administration at New York University, the University of Massachusetts Amherst, and the University at Buffalo/SUNY, where she developed and taught a course on helping skills for student affairs professionals. She has also served in student affairs administrative positions at Baruch College/CUNY, Virginia Tech, Seton Hall University, William Paterson University, and Marymount College–Tarrytown. She earned her BA (1981) in psychology from Northwestern University, her MS (1985) in student affairs administration from Indiana University, and her PhD (2001) in higher education administration from New York University. She is currently a senior analyst at Eduventures in Boston.

Helping College Students

Part One

Understanding the Helper's Role

Part 1 of this book primarily focuses on understanding the realities of being a helper on a college campus today. Conceptualizing student affairs practitioners as helpers and exploring their roles, responsibilities, and ethical concerns is the cornerstone of this section. Background on the relentless and sometimes overwhelming mental health issues on college campuses and their impact on the campus environment is provided. Concrete examples and illustrations of some of these ethical dilemmas and helping scenarios are offered to further illustrate the realities and to make the text more meaningful and relevant to student affairs practitioners. Understanding the helping theories that are most useful and applicable to student affairs practitioners is an important part of being a helper. Core helping theories and how they can be applied in a student affairs context are explored as a precursor to examining specific and essential helping skills.

Chapter One

Student Affairs
Practitioners as Helpers

Julia had been a graduate residence hall director for all of two weeks when she had her first crisis. One of Julia's residents came down during office hours and reported that her roommate was increasingly withdrawn, staying in bed, and not leaving the room for classes or meals. She had noticed in the bathroom that her roommate was taking some medicine that she thought was for depression. She was afraid to leave her roommate alone and wasn't sure how to help her. And now Julia had to decide what to do.

As the dean of students, Dr. Molina was used to dealing with difficult situations, but this one was harder than most. One of the university's most beloved student leaders had died in a car crash over the weekend, and he had spent the past forty-eight hours with some very emotional students. And now he was about to meet with the student's parents, which made him so sad just to think about. He was going to have to find a way to get through it.

Hamid had been a career counselor for many years, and he loved helping students discover their goals and wishes for their future. However, it seemed as if their stories were becoming increasingly complicated. For example, Ming was an international student from mainland China who was about to graduate but was desperate to stay in the United States by either finding a job or going back to school. As they spoke further, it became clear that this desire had little to do with career issues. Ming was the only son of his mother, who was a single parent. She wanted him to come back home to be with her. Yet his identity as a gay man who was not out to his mother made China the last place he wanted to be.

Advising student government always had its challenges, but this year was more perplexing than most. Marisa, as the adviser of the United Student Government (USG), had noticed that there had been a lot of interpersonal drama going on, more than usual. Gloria, one of the USG vice presidents, was constantly stirring up conflict and pitting one person against another. Initially, it was happening behind the scenes, but now these conflicts were starting to play out during meetings and nothing was getting accomplished. Marisa knew that she needed to intervene but had absolutely no idea what she wanted to say or do.

Marcus was in charge of the academic support center, and it was his job to supervise the student tutors. This was a fun group of students who really enjoyed each other and liked helping others. He met with the students as a group weekly and had noticed that one of his best tutors, Harry, had been calling in sick recently and not doing his best work. One morning when Harry came in late for the second time that week, Marcus went to talk with him. Marcus couldn't help noticing that Harry seemed very hung over. Actually, when he thought about it, he realized that this was not the first time he had seen Harry come to the center that way. What was going on? How could he bring this up with Harry?

Judicial cases were never easy. Every student always had a story to tell, but this one was more troubling than most. A student, Liz, had her residence hall contract terminated after engaging in cutting behavior, which was very upsetting to her suitemates

*and the women on her floor. She was seeking counseling, and
her counselor determined that she was not suicidal; however, the
residence hall staff felt she was creating turmoil in the hall and
had therefore violated her contract. Liz was appealing this action
and looking to the judicial office to resolve the conflict.*

As long as there have been college and university campuses, there have been individuals who have adopted the role of caretaker, helper, and educator. Initially, that role was accomplished by faculty members who, in addition to teaching, provided advice, guidance, and supervision to college students. This was the era of *in loco parentis*, where faculty, and later on student affairs practitioners, adopted parental roles, ensuring the intellectual, social, moral, and spiritual development of their students (Fenske, 1989). Eventually, faculty members, following the model of German research institutions, began to focus more on research and teaching, leaving the out-of-classroom supervision of students to others (Evans & Reason, 2001). Fenske described faculty involvement with students as evolving from complete involvement in every aspect of students' lives to detachment.

Over time students' needs for guidance began to expand beyond the early emphasis on moral and spiritual development. The increasing diversity of the student body, through coeducation, heightened the need for more supervision of student activities (Nuss, 2003). In addition, as the world of work and career opportunities expanded, there was an increased need for experts to assist students in their nonacademic development. The overall growth in enrollment meant it was no longer possible for a president, a few support staff members (e.g., librarian, secretary, treasurer), and a small group of faculty members to run a campus (Gerda, 2006).

The diversification and expansion of colleges and universities led to a need for more resources, more coordination of services, and more specialization to address the mounting demands and concerns. This call for specialized training led to the establishment of student personnel training programs in the early twentieth century (Evans & Reason, 2001). New positions on campuses—such as academic deans, director of admissions, and registrar—helped meet these expanding requirements and demands. Counseling, which was once faculty domain, evolved into a separate professional responsibility (Hodges, 2001). The early deans for men and women, who were primarily responsible for discipline and counseling, were the "first professional ancestors of student affairs" (Gerda, 2006, p. 151). Over the next few decades, even more professional titles and roles began to emerge in higher education—for example, vocational counselor, activities director, adviser, nurse, and counselor (Nuss, 2003). Student personnel work began to focus on expertise, specialization, and organization development, leading to the creation of campus entities to address students' specific needs, which was a digression from the historical model of shared responsibility for student development (Roberts, 1998) first articulated by *The Student Personnel Point of View* (National Association of Student Personnel Administrators, 1937).

Despite the various changes and configurations of the roles and responsibilities of student affairs professionals, the emphasis on the development of the whole person has not wavered. The mission of higher education has always been, at its core, to educate the whole student, not just nourish her/his intellect (Creamer, Winston, & Miller, 2001). In their review of all the major foundational writings of the student affairs profession (e.g., *The Student Personnel Point of View, Tomorrow's Higher Education, The Student Learning Imperative*), Evans and Reason (2001) identified underlying themes that included an emphasis on the whole student in every educational endeavor, respect for individual differences, the importance of the educational environment, and responsibility to society. Further study of a wider range of professional statements and published perspectives from student affairs scholars and pioneers in Saddlemire and Rentz (1986) provide additional evidence regarding the powerful and historical emphasis on the value of holistic education.

Although student affairs professionals have always seen themselves as educators first and foremost (cf. American College Personnel Association, 1996; Lloyd-Jones & Smith, 1954), that educational role, often based in out-of-classroom experiences, has included helping students deal with the emotional demands of academic life and promoting personal development (Creamer et al., 2001). According to C. Gilbert Wrenn (1951), one of the early pioneers of student affairs, student affairs professionals need to address "the basic psychological needs of all young people and the specific needs that are the direct results of the college experience" (pp. 26–27). These basic helping skills are at the core of daily interactions with students. Even as administrators' careers advance and they spend less and less time with students, helping skills remain essential to the roles and responsibilities of all student affairs professionals (Winston, 2003).

The purpose of this chapter is to explore the diverse roles that student affairs practitioners play on campus and how those roles have changed over time. Since helping is an essential part of almost every job in student affairs, this chapter identifies and describes the range of helping behaviors, roles, and responsibilities that practitioners display. This chapter addresses the competence of helping and briefly explores the helping awareness, knowledge, and skills that student affairs professionals need to be effective in their work. Specific examples of the types of helping awareness, knowledge, and skills needed across a wide range of student affairs positions are suggested here. In addition, the challenges and benefits to being a helper, as well as important training issues, are explored.

Helping as Essential for all Student Affairs Professionals

Helping, advising, and counseling skills are critical tools for student affairs practitioners whether they work in counseling-oriented positions like career counseling, leadership development positions (e.g., student activities, Greek affairs, and residential life), administrative positions like dean of students, or academic affairs positions akin to advisement or academic support services (Reynolds, 1995b; Winston, 2003). Helping students is central to the history, goals, and responsibilities of student affairs work, and it is vital that student affairs professionals develop the awareness, knowledge, and skills necessary to assist college students with all aspects of their curricular and extracurricular lives.

Winston (2003) suggests that while most student affairs professionals are not trained as professional counselors and do not have more advanced counseling skills gained through specific academic training and supervised practice, they do need basic helping skills to do their job effectively. Using the language of Delworth and Aulepp (1976), Winston states that student affairs professionals are, in actuality, "allied professional counselors" who must use well-developed and practiced interpersonal helping knowledge and skills. Sometimes they focus those skills on their direct interactions with students, and sometimes, as their career advances and they take on broader responsibilities, they focus those helping skills on staff and faculty members as well as external constituents.

Further indication of the centrality of helping skills in the student affairs profession is found in the *Council for the Advancement of Standards in Higher Education Master's-Level Graduate Program for Student Affairs Professionals Standards and Guidelines*, which identifies individual and group interventions as one of five core areas of study, including the following: (1) student development theory, (2) student characteristics and the effects of college on students, (3) individual and group interventions, (4) organization and administration of student affairs, and (5) assessment, evaluation, and research. This document further states that the components of the college student affairs curriculum "must include studies of techniques and methods of interviewing; helping skills; and assessing, designing, and implementing developmentally appropriate interventions with individuals and organizations"

(Council for the Advancement of Standards in Higher Education [CAS], 2003).

Helping as a Core Competence in Student Affairs

Understanding the core principles, beliefs, knowledge, and skills needed within the student affairs profession has been an important area of exploration and study (Lovell & Kosten, 2000). Waple (2006) and others (cf. Creamer et al., 1992; Pope, Reynolds, & Mueller, 2004; Saidla, 1990; Upcraft, 1998) identified the use of a competency-based approach as a primary emphasis within student affairs preparation programs. Pope and Reynolds (1997) stated that a competence approach is needed for ethical and efficacious practice.

Many scholars have identified concrete competencies that student affairs practitioners need to be effective in their work (Creamer et al., 1992; Creamer et al., 2001; Delworth & Hanson, 1989; Komives & Woodard, 2003; Miller & Winston, 1991; Pope & Reynolds, 1997; Pope et al., 2004). Some of these competencies are described across professional levels—such as entry-level, middle-management, and upper-management (Barr, 1993; Burkard, Cole, Ott, & Stoflet, 2005; Waple, 2006)—while others are behaviorally oriented (Creamer et al., 2001; Pope & Reynolds, 1997). Pope and Reynolds state that despite this extensive attention on competence in the field, there is little consensus about what the core competencies for student affairs practice are.

Pope et al. (2004) introduced the Dynamic Model of Student Affairs Competence (see Figure 1.1), which identified seven core competencies as essential to effective and ethical practice: administration and management; theory and translation; ethics and professional standards; teaching and training; assessment and research; helping and advising; and multicultural awareness, knowledge, and skills. While all professionals develop different levels of proficiency for the various areas, depending

Figure 1.1 Dynamic Model of Student Affairs Competence

Source: R. L. Pope, A. L. Reynolds, & J. M. Mueller. (2004). *Multicultural competence in student affairs*. San Francisco: Jossey-Bass.

Reprinted with permission of John Wiley & Sons. Inc.

on their work responsibilities and personal interests, some basic competence in all seven areas is vital for efficacious practice.

Empirical investigation of the knowledge, skills, and personal characteristics fundamental to the student affairs profession has been ongoing for almost thirty years. In a meta-analysis of twenty-three studies over a thirty-year period, Lovell and Kosten (2000) examined the skills, knowledge bases, and personal traits needed for success in student affairs across all levels of work and found that human facilitation skills, such as counseling and supervision, were crucial. Personal traits, including working cooperatively with others and developing skills in interpersonal relationships, were also viewed as important characteristics for success.

Several recent studies (Burkard et al., 2005; Herdlein, 2004; Waple, 2006) explored the specific competencies that entry-level student affairs professionals need. Herdlein, in his survey of chief student affairs officers, determined that the most essential skills for new professionals were management skills and human relations skills, working with diverse populations, interpersonal and communication skills, caring, empathy, and firmness. Burkard et al., using the Delphi method that included a panel of midlevel and senior-level student affairs professionals, identified thirty-two competencies for entry-level practitioners. Two areas, personal qualities and human relations skills, were established as being particularly essential. Some of these specific skills identified were collaboration, teamwork/team building, training, presentation and group facilitation, counseling/active listening, advising, conflict resolution and mediation, supervision, consultation, and crisis intervention. In addition, important personal qualities that were related to helping skills included oral communication, interpersonal relations, problem-solving abilities, and assertiveness/confrontation. Waple surveyed entry-level student affairs staff to ascertain what competencies they obtained through graduate work and the extent to which they used those skills in their jobs. Effective oral and written communication and problem solving were among the skills acquired at a high level. When examining for congruence between what new professionals were taught and what they actually needed for their work, Waple identified the top areas of congruence as effective oral and written communication, multicultural awareness and knowledge, and problem solving. Other areas important to at least 50 percent of those surveyed included crisis and conflict management and advising student organizations. The only competency area related to helping that was identified as having low congruence, meaning that it was not well developed in graduate preparation programs but was significantly used at work, was supervision of staff.

All these studies challenge how the student affairs profession is preparing and training new practitioners. According to Burkard et al. (2005), professionals are expected to have "counseling skills that extend well beyond the basic skills often taught in graduate programs" (p. 298). Introductory counseling courses typically focus on individual counseling and microskills with little attention paid to more advanced helping skills, such as conflict resolution/mediation, crisis intervention, and group facilitation. These types of skills and others—such as collaboration, consultation, and supervision—are not typically incorporated into graduate training. Increased focus on advanced helping skills is a significant change in what is expected of new professionals and may reflect students' changing needs and demands.

The need for improved helping skills for all student affairs professionals has taken on a level of urgency in recent years as college students have struggled with significant interpersonal concerns, stress, and mental health issues (Benton & Benton, 2006b; Bishop, Gallagher, & Cohen, 2000; Kadison & DiGeronimo, 2004; Kitzrow, 2003; Soet & Sevig, 2006). Extensive research has documented the increased presence and severity of mental health issues that have led to disturbing levels of substance abuse, depression, suicidal and self-injurious behavior, posttraumatic stress disorder, and other serious mental health issues that profoundly affect the campus community (Benton, Robertson, Tseng, Newton, & Benton, 2003; Furr, Westefeld, McConnell, & Jenkins, 2001; Soet & Sevig, 2006; Wechsler et al., 2002). Although the average student affairs professional is not primarily responsible for addressing the mental health needs of college students, these issues inevitably influence every aspect of campus life. Therefore, student affairs practitioners need effective helping and interpersonal skills to understand and support students and, when necessary, refer them for counseling and other human services. Owen, Tao, and Rodolfa (2006) suggested that student mental health issues are no longer the sole responsibility of campus professionals with the titles of *counselor* or *psychologist*. They further emphasized the need for campuses to coordinate and collaborate to address mental health issues on campus more effectively. And while there is debate within higher education regarding how much responsibility colleges and universities must assume for the emotional/mental health and well-being of students (Kadison & DiGeronimo, 2004), there are daily opportunities for practitioners to engage with students as helpers. To contribute to campus initiatives on mental health, substance abuse, and related issues, it is essential that student affairs professionals have well-developed helping and interpersonal skills.

Awareness, Knowledge, and Skills Needed to Be a Helper

Although most student affairs professionals are not counselors and may not possess the skills, experiences, or desire necessary to provide therapy to students, they often offer support and help students with important life decisions on a daily basis. Professionals need to know how to respond to students' real emotional and personal needs and concerns because, regardless of those professionals' level of training and comfort, students often approach them with concerns and issues that require sensitivity and specific communication skills. The visibility of student affairs practitioners on campus often makes them easily accessible and approachable for students with a wide range of problems and concerns (Pope et al., 2004). Knowing when to intervene, how to be supportive, and if necessary, when to refer a student for therapy are just a few examples of the skills that student affairs practitioners need whether they work in residence life, admissions, financial aid, academic advising, or intercollegiate athletics. While specific helping skills will be delineated and explored in later chapters, basic helping skills are briefly reviewed here.

Whether student affairs professionals are viewed as educators or helpers, they must possess important behavioral characteristics, including advising, facilitating, coaching, collaborating, supporting, counseling, motivating, managing conflict, solving problems, advocating, and transforming (Creamer et al., 2001; Rhoads & Black, 1995). Many of these behaviors are integrated into the tasks and responsibilities of student affairs practitioners across the various functional areas. According to Reynolds (1995b), some of the specific helping knowledge and skills needed to work effectively with college students across student affairs functional areas include microcounseling skills (e.g., active listening, empathy, reflection, nonverbal skills, paraphrasing), group skills (e.g., group dynamics, group processes, and leadership skills), conflict and crisis management, problem solving, confrontation, consultation, mentoring, and supervision. These basic helping skills are foundational to developing other competencies within student affairs, such as teaching and training, program development and assessment, and individual and institutional interventions. In addition, there are often interpersonal issues that need attention when implementing workshops, performing exit interviews, and responding to students in distress that require a meaningful level of competence.

As suggested by Pope et al. (2004), incorporating multicultural competence into any exploration of competence is essential. Not only does multicultural competence require a distinct type of awareness, knowledge, and skills needed for effective work in student affairs, it must be integrated into all other areas of competence. Cultural identity, diverse life experiences, and learned stereotypes and assumptions are just some of the dynamics that influence communication and, therefore, the helping process. To be effective and competent helpers, student affairs professionals must be aware of these important cultural influences and be able to apply them across the various functional areas within student affairs.

In addition to these vital helping skills, student affairs professionals need to understand what constitutes a therapeutic or affirming environment for most students. According to Pope et al. (2004), "A therapeutic climate is one in which self-exploration and growth is encouraged and a positive and affirming relationship is developed" (p. 79). Developing a working alliance is a foundational counseling construct when two or more individuals work together to resolve an important issue or concern (Meier & Davis, 1997). This alliance begins with making personal contact and building an interpersonal connection that has the potential to develop into a relationship. The basis for these relationships is empathy, understanding, sharing, encouragement, kindness, respect, warmth, and nonjudgmental acceptance (Okun, 1997). Awareness of important influences on student development, such as the significant relationships students form with staff and faculty, is vital to professionals' ability to be effective helpers.

Student development theories, which are at the core of student affairs training and professional preparation, provide an excellent foundation for understanding student growth and development. The work of Sanford (1967); Blocher (1978); Knefelkamp, Widick, and Parker (1978); and others emphasizes the core developmental issue of challenge and support in our interactions with students. Providing "a proper balance of challenge and support ensures that students are challenged to do their best, yet feel supported enough to make mistakes" (Pope et al., 2004, p. 79). To be an effective helper, a student affairs professional must offer balanced and developmental interventions that truly assist students (Evans, Forney, & Guido-DiBrito, 1998).

Illustrations of Helping Behaviors Across Functional Areas in Student Affairs

The functional areas that constitute student affairs divisions may vary significantly from campus to campus; however, it is still useful to identify some of the opportunities that various programs and departments offer student affairs professionals to demonstrate their helping skills. The various functional areas can be grouped into the following core areas: (1) counseling-oriented positions like career and personal counseling; (2) leadership development and educational positions (e.g., student activities, Greek affairs, campus life, health and wellness, and residence life); (3) administrative positions like dean of students, judicial affairs, and admissions; and (4) academic affairs positions (e.g., advisement and academic support services).

Within the counseling area, the primary focus of the work is helping students address their personal, social, and vocational concerns. This can entail individual counseling, therapeutic and psychoeducational groups, and workshops. All these interventions require a wide range of helping skills, such as microcounseling, teaching, workshop design and delivery, and group intervention skills. Helping can involve assisting students who are struggling with relationship issues, self-esteem, mental health concerns like depression or anxiety, academic and career uncertainty, and overall self-exploration.

Leadership development and educational positions require a wide range of helping skills in both individual and group domains. Group advisement, leadership training, supervision of peer helpers and leaders, and mentoring are just some of the interventions common to these positions. Helping skills are needed for training seminars and workshops, group work, individual supervision, crisis intervention, and conflict resolution. These interventions can focus on resolving conflict between or within student groups, helping student staff develop their skills, or dealing with a crisis, like alcohol poisoning at a student-sponsored event.

The type of helping skills needed for administrative positions are unique and may require using helping skills with faculty, parents, and community members in addition to working with students. The interventions used may include individual meetings with parents, students, and other constituent groups;

conflict resolution meetings; and large group meetings. Group facilitation, individual supervision, conflict management, and crisis intervention are some of the helping skills necessary for administration-related jobs. The content of some of these interventions may include student behavioral issues, parental concerns or disagreement with institutional decisions, or a campus crisis, like the suicide or murder of a student.

Finally, the academic affairs positions that are sometimes situated within student affairs divisions necessitate the use of helping skills in addressing important academic concerns, such as advisement, tutorial services, and working directly with faculty and academic deans. The interventions typically used include individual meetings with students and faculty members and training sessions with faculty members, tutors, or other relevant personnel. Some of the specific skills used in academic-related positions include those microcounseling skills necessary for advising, facilitating training and workshops, and consulting with faculty members. The content of these interventions may focus on properly advising students with significant mental health and personal issues that affect their academics, helping tutors motivate their students, and identifying and implementing policies for dealing with disruptive students in class.

Challenges and Benefits of Being a Helper

There are many challenges and benefits to being a helper on a college campus. Some of the more foreboding challenges arise from the complex ethical and legal realities that exist today on college campuses. *In loco parentis* no longer exists as a formal response to students, and yet it is clear that both legal and moral responsibilities for students' well-being exist beyond the classroom (Nuss, 1998). Campuses have the ability and responsibility to regulate student conduct through established student codes and judicial proceedings. Although most campuses want to provide students with freedom and responsibilities that

enhance their development, significant ethical and legal challenges influence how campuses approach these issues. Federal
and state legislation like the Americans with Disabilities Act,
health privacy through the Health Insurance Portability and
Accountability Act, and educational records privacy through
the Family Educational Rights and Privacy Act provide parameters that influence policy and practice on college campuses.
Decisions like when to deny a student with significant substance
abuse issues access to such services as campus housing or what
to do with suicidal students who are affecting the campus community can be stressful for student affairs professionals. Recent
litigation in Massachusetts and elsewhere highlights the liability
risk that even noncounseling professionals have on college campuses (Benton & Benton, 2006b). Many campuses are actively
working to create policies and practices that empower students
with mental health difficulties yet control the liability and risk
that those issues may place on the institution. Further discussion of relevant ethical issues occurs in Chapter 3.

Other challenges that student affairs professionals face
result from some of the demands that come with being a helper.
According to Corey and Corey (1998), there are two primary
sources of stress for helpers: individual and environmental.
Examples of some of the individual sources of stress include
self-doubt, perfectionistic expectations, emotional exhaustion,
and assuming too much responsibility for those being helped.
Dealing with emotional students—whether they are angry,
depressed, or anxious—can be draining. Setting up appropriate boundaries—especially in demanding positions where one
is not limited to daytime responsibilities, as in residence life
and student activities—is a learned skill. One of the primary
edicts of counseling training is that to be effective, helpers must
know themselves and understand why they chose to be helpers
and what personal issues may sometimes interfere with being
effective (Faiver, Eisengart, & Colonna, 1995; Meier & Davis,
1997). Many helpers are not necessarily good at asking for help

themselves and do not always attend to their own needs and feelings (Corey & Corey). Without proper boundaries and the ability to prioritize self-care, it is possible to burn out, which ultimately means that helping others becomes a stressful burden (Davis & Markley, 2000).

External or environmental factors also contribute to the stress level of being in a helping role. Examples of some of the environmental sources of stress in higher education include too many demands and frustration with a bureaucracy that sometimes gets in the way of helping others. By nature, some of these difficulties are beyond the helper's control, but being successful means learning to deal with them. Sometimes the needs of students, especially those who have mental health or substance abuse issues, seem endless, and when there are not effective institutional policies and practices to address such students' concerns, it often falls on individual practitioners to fill the gap.

However, just as there are challenges to being a helper on today's college campuses, there are benefits as well. The many and diverse ways that student affairs professionals assist college students in developing as human beings, reaching their academic and career goals, and making a difference in the world can be very motivating. Mentoring students and seeing them grow and develop over time, helping students face difficult life challenges like the death of a parent, and advocating for students to ensure that their needs and rights are addressed on campus are just some of the experiences that student affairs professionals may find invigorating and inspiring. Helping others seems to make individuals feel better about themselves, others, and the world around them (Corey & Corey, 1998).

Preparation and Training for Being a Helper

Most, if not all, student affairs preparation programs provide specific academic courses to assist new professionals in developing the helping and interpersonal skills necessary to meet college students' needs more effectively. The expectations of the *Council for the Advancement of Standards in Higher Education Master's-Level Graduate Program for Student Affairs Professionals Standards and Guidelines* (CAS, 2003) and the historical linking of student affairs preparation programs with counseling programs have led many graduate programs to emphasize counseling (Hyman, 1985). At first glance this linkage may provide an ideal union that benefits graduate students in student affairs; however, the actual implementation may not fully assist graduate students in developing their helping skills in ways that will fully benefit them as student affairs professionals.

As mentioned in the preface, many of these counseling courses have been modeled after beginning counseling courses for master's-level counseling students. In fact, it is common for student affairs or higher education professionals to be required to take one or two counseling courses alongside graduate students in counseling programs (e.g., counseling psychology, school or guidance counseling) that focus more on clinical and therapeutic issues rather than address the unique helping competencies needed for practitioners working in higher education. Although these courses may be interesting and provide important information, they often offer far too much traditional clinical content and not enough background on how to be a helper in a nonclinical context. In addition, these courses often emphasize counseling theory at a level that is beyond the scope and type of helping that most student affairs professionals, as "allied professional counselors," use or need in their daily practice. Learning about Freud and related therapy techniques in depth will not assist the typical student affairs practitioner in comforting or advising a student who wants to withdraw from school because of a death in the family, in understanding and addressing the deleterious group dynamics present among a dysfunctional resident assistant staff, or in challenging student leaders to take more responsibility for their campus organizations.

As the study by Burkard et al. (2005) suggested, graduate preparation programs in student affairs may need to reexamine the training they provide in human relations and helping skills. The changing needs of students and the ever-expanding role of student affairs practitioners require a higher level of interpersonal skills and personal qualities to assist professionals in their work with students, parents, faculty members, and administrators at all levels of leadership. For example, interactions with parents are becoming an increasingly common task for student affairs professionals that requires nuanced skills.

Summary

Helping is one of the core competencies that constitute some of the awareness, knowledge, and skills that student affairs professionals need to be effective and ethical practitioners. Although most are not counselors, student affairs professionals "cannot predict or choose when they will be called upon to be helpers; opportunities and challenges are presented daily" (Winston, 2003, p. 501). Therefore, it is essential that their academic preparation and professional development focus on creating and enhancing essential helping skills that allow them to perform all aspects of their work more effectively. This chapter has discussed the role of student affairs on campus and how being helpers has been central to that role from the very beginning; it also made a case for helping as a core competence for all student affairs professionals and identified the benefits and challenges of being a helper.

Chapter Two

Mental Health Needs and Realities on Campus

Mental health issues have become a topic of conversation and concern on college campuses. There has been an increase in the number of books and other professional literature (cf. Benton & Benton, 2006a; Davis & Humphrey, 2000; Grayson & Meilman, 2006; Kadison & DiGeronimo, 2004; Kitzrow, 2003; Soet & Sevig, 2006)—as well as mainstream publications, such as *USA Today, Salon*, and the *New York Times*—that have explored mental health concerns at colleges and universities. High-profile incidents during the past five years, such as the shootings at Virginia Tech and Northern Illinois University and the suicide of Elizabeth Shin at the Massachusetts Institute of Technology, have led to local and national conversations about what can be done to prevent such difficult and traumatic events from occurring on campus.

According to Benton (2006), "College student mental health problems are becoming more common, more problematic and a much larger focus on college and university campuses" (p. 4). And because student affairs professionals are often the individuals on campus who help students address and make meaning of the academic, social, and personal aspects of their lives, practitioners face an enormous challenge in providing support for students and confronting these issues. Levine and Cureton (1998b) reported that student affairs administrators spend increasing amounts of time addressing the needs of troubled students and the myriad concerns they experience, such as substance abuse, disruptive behavior, eating disorders, and suicide attempts. However, it is not uncommon for practitioners, who are helpers and not professional counselors, to feel unsure and unprepared to face students' mental health concerns (Williams, 2005).

The purpose of this chapter is to examine the current state of mental health issues on college campuses. There has been a significant rise in the incidence of serious mental health issues like depression, anxiety, and substance abuse. All student affairs practitioners support and respond to students who are dealing with personal issues that affect them as students and as individuals. This chapter reviews the current research that examines the mental health issues facing college students and their impact on the college campus and identifies some specific concerns that most practitioners face. Specific awareness, knowledge, and skills needed to explore mental health issues are identified, and illustrations are used to demonstrate how these issues may manifest across functional areas. Finally, preparation and training issues for addressing mental health issues on campus are explored.

And while discussions of the shifting demographics of today's college student have become commonplace, rarely do such conversations include how the psychological diversity at colleges is changing as well. Keeling (2000) and others (cf. Kadison & DiGeronimo, 2004; Kitzrow, 2003; Megivern, 2001; Owen, Tao, & Rodolfa, 2006) have emphasized the importance of addressing this diversity to ensure the graduation and success of students with diverse psychological problems and needs. Megivern found that mental health symptoms and problems impair functioning in major life domains—such as family, work, social settings, and school—for many students. Such problems make it difficult for students to integrate academically and socially into our campuses, which Tinto (1987) and Astin (1977) have demonstrated to be essential for college student retention. Keeling warns that one of the biggest impediments to the success of these students is the faculty and staff's prejudices and discom-forts about the students' behavior, communication patterns, and interpersonal styles, which are sometimes disruptive, confusing, and problematic.

Much of this concern, and sometimes fear, expressed by administrators and faculty members results from the widespread data about the increase in prevalence and severity of mental health issues among students (Kitzrow, 2003; Rudd, 2004; Soet & Sevig, 2006). This data suggests that students are using counsel-ing services at a much greater rate and are presenting with more serious emotional, behavioral, and psychological issues (Pledge, Lapan, Heppner, Kivlighan, & Roehlke, 1998). College coun-seling centers have evolved from primarily utilizing a develop-mental approach to address academic and transitional issues to diagnosing and treating significant clinical issues (Hodges, 2001). Results from the 2006 National Survey for Counseling Center Directors report that 92 percent of directors believe that the number of students with significant psychological concerns has increased in recent years (Gallagher, 2006). Most directors are concerned that the increased usage is stretching their staff and the services they provide beyond their available resources; many directors also stated that counselor time increasingly focuses on fewer students with more serious psychological prob-lems. They further report heightened demand for psychiatric ser-vices and crisis counseling on campus. Research indicates that larger numbers of college students are receiving psychotherapy, are taking or have taken psychotropic medicine, or have been in psychiatric hospitals or residential treatment centers (Cooper, 2000). These demands mean that many counseling centers are moving away from their traditional prevention focus that included outreach programs on campus (Hodges, 2001).

Most research examining the mental health trends of col-lege students is based on students who use campus counseling centers and has measured the perspective of either the clients or the counseling center staff. The data, while not generalizable

to all college students, is still quite compelling. Two longitudinal studies—by Pledge et al. (1998) and Benton, Robertson,
Tseng, Newton, and Benton (2003)—provide further support
for the belief that college students' mental health is worsening.
Over a six-year period, Pledge et al. discovered that more serious
difficulties—such as suicidality, substance abuse, depression, anxiety, high subjective rating of distress, and history of psychiatric
treatment or hospitalization—had increased at a higher level
than in previous decades, such as found by Heppner et al. (1994)
and O'Malley, Wheeler, Murphey, and O'Connell (1990).
This is a major shift from the typical adjustment and developmental concerns evidenced by counseling center research from
the 1950s through the early 1980s (Heppner & Neal, 1983).
Reliance on retrospective reflections by counseling center staff
(e.g., Robbins, May, & Corazzini, 1985) weakened the reliabil-
ity and validity of the data gathered, so some researchers (such
as Pledge et al. and Cornish, Kominars, Riva, McIntosh, &
Henderson, 2000) have attempted to gather more objective data
that focused on client distress levels at initial intake interviews.
Overall Cornish et al. and Pledge et al. identified no significant
change in client distress levels over six years. Both studies concluded that the increase of severity may have begun to level off.

Benton et al. (2003) examined client distress levels over a
thirteen-year period by examining the clinician's perspective
at the conclusion of therapy. Results indicated that fourteen of
nineteen client problem areas demonstrated increases across the
designated time period. Six problem areas (depression, developmental, situational, academic skills, grief, and use of medication) showed an increase across all thirteen years, while seven
problem areas (relationships, stress/anxiety, suicidal thoughts,
family issues, physical problems, personality disorders, and sexual
assault) increased only during the past nine years. In the early
1990s, relationship concerns were the most frequently reported
presenting issue; however, since 1994, stress and anxiety have
eclipsed relationship concerns as the most frequent problem.

Benton et al. found that the number of students in their study seen from 1988 to 2001 with depression doubled, those with suicidal thoughts tripled, and those seen after a sexual assault quadrupled. They concluded that client problems are more complex, incorporating traditional student problems, such as developmental concerns and relationship issues, as well as more severe psychological issues, such as depression, suicidal ideation, and personality disorders.

While most studies have focused on the presenting concerns of students using on-campus counseling services, a few studies have examined the needs of a broader sample of college students. The American College Health Association (ACHA) has been collecting annual data on the health, including mental health, of college students since 1998, and the organization's results highlight the significant mental health concerns among all college students and not just those using counseling services. The most recent data, from spring 2006, analyzed the results of over ninety-four thousand students and found that almost 18 percent experienced depression and 12 percent reported being anxious (ACHA, 2006). These students reported that the following concerns affected their individual academic performance: alcohol use (7 percent), depression, anxiety (15.7 percent), relationship difficulties (15.6 percent), stress (32 percent), and sleep difficulties (23.9 percent). Almost 15 percent of students reported being in an emotionally, physically, or sexually abusive relationship. Finally, when examining depression, ACHA found that 13 percent of students stated that they felt very sad, 9.8 percent felt hopeless, and almost 30 percent reported feeling overwhelmed by all they had to do. The ACHA survey also reported that almost 10 percent of students surveyed seriously considered suicide during that year and many more (close to 45 percent) stated that it was difficult for them to function at times. Furr, Westefeld, McConnell, and Jenkins (2001) found an even higher rate of depression (53 percent) and a similar level of suicidal thoughts (9 percent) among college students in their study.

Soet and Sevig (2006), in an effort to increase understanding of the breadth and depth of mental health issues on college campuses, undertook a large study with the general student body at a public midwestern institution. They sampled over nine hundred college students and gathered data on the students' mental health history and current distress and coping. In terms of mental health history, Soet and Sevig found that almost 30 percent of students either had been or currently were in counseling; 8 percent of them reported being in counseling for the first time. The top five psychiatric diagnoses that these students reported were depression, eating disorders, attention deficit/hyperactivity, anxiety, and posttraumatic stress disorder (PTSD). Women were more likely to be depressed and have eating disorders, and lesbian, gay, and bisexual students were three times more likely to report being depressed. In terms of medication use, 14 percent reported taking psychoactive medications at some point, while 6.8 percent were currently using such medicine.

When examining the current levels of distress among the college students, Soet and Sevig (2006) discovered, as expected, that the clinical population (those who had been in counseling at least three years prior) was more distressed and less able to cope. However, of the entire sample, 66 percent reported sleep difficulties, and over one-third stated that they drink more than they should. Over 20 percent reported some history of family abuse, and almost 75 percent stated that they were worried about their ability to succeed in college. Finally, almost one-fourth of the students surveyed identified having suicidal thoughts in the prior two weeks. This study also found important group differences (by gender, race, and sexual orientation) that have implications for the provision of mental health services and outreach efforts. According to Soet and Sevig, this data suggested the "need for student affairs divisions to further engage in research, to examine policies around student mental health, to allocate resources appropriately to mental health units, and to engage in data-based preventive programming and interventions" with the "goal of creating a healthier environment for students" (p. 428).

The evidence regarding the mental health challenges facing college students today is complex and multifaceted. As is often the case, how the questions are asked and whom is being asked is crucial to understanding what the evidence means. In addition to exploring the prevalence of mental health concerns, it is also useful to understand what has contributed to these circumstances that are altering the strategies, practices, and policies used by student affairs professionals. The most basic question that is unlikely to be answered is whether there are actually more students with mental health problems or whether today's students are more likely to participate in counseling or are more comfortable acknowledging they have psychological difficulties (O'Connor, 2001). Benton, Benton, Newton, Benton, and Robertson (2004) suggested several viable hypotheses about the causes of the increase of severity and prevalence of mental health issues on college campuses. Therapists may be more focused on clinical diagnosis than in previous years, thus identifying problems more readily. Students may be more perfectionistic and have higher expectations, and this increased stress has a negative effect on them. Students may procrastinate getting help earlier, when their problems are more manageable, so that by the time they seek out counseling, their concerns are more intense and complicated. Another possible explanation is that students are more comfortable seeking help and are less hampered by societal stigma. (An indication of the comfort that young adults experience regarding mental health issues is the degree to which many of them use psychotropic medications to manage their moods and how often they trade and share their meds with other students who may be suffering from similar difficulties [Harmon, 2005].) If students' families are more dysfunctional or unable to cope or provide appropriate support, students may be more likely to look elsewhere for support and encouragement.

In addition, increases in stress, financial pressure, and parental expectations may push students to seek out additional support to meet their needs. Finally, Benton et al. indicated that a lack of sleep makes it difficult for students to cope effectively with everyday problems.

Kitzrow (2003) suggested that some significant "social and cultural factors such as divorce, family dysfunction, instability, poor parenting skills, poor frustration tolerance, violence, early experimentation with drugs, alcohol and sex, and poor inter-personal attachments may account for some of the increase" (pp. 170–171). In addition, some psychological disorders—including bipolar disorder, depression, and schizophrenia—often manifest themselves in late adolescence and early adulthood, making them more common in a college population. Keeling (2000) offered that "earlier diagnosis and treatment, improved drugs, more reasonable social attitudes toward psychological assistance, disability protections, and the availability of more sophisticated services" (p. 2) also contribute. Increased advertisements on the availability of medication and the popular belief that emotional and behavioral problems are caused by chemical imbalances in the brain have led to increased comfort with and demand for psychotropic medications to solve problems and make people feel better (Alishio & Hersh, 2005). Carter and Winseman (2003) expressed concern that this cultural shift in attitude has caused students to be overdiagnosed and overmedicated. Keeling argues that what on the surface looks like a bad thing (students with more serious psychological issues attending college) is, in reality, an indication that a democratization of higher education has made college more attainable to individuals with significant psychological problems and disorders. What is clear, according to Benton (2006), is that these students may need treatment, medication, consultation, relapse prevention, and support to be successful. And since "student mental health is not the sole responsibility of those with titles such as counselor, psychologist, or advisor" (p. 19), student affairs professionals need to expand their awareness, knowledge, and skills to work with students with psychological difficulties and concerns.

Specific Mental Health Concerns and Issues Facing College Students

Moving beyond an understanding of the prevalence of mental health issues on college campuses, student affairs professionals benefit from specific knowledge about various mental health difficulties and their impact on the college experience. Humphrey, Kitchens, and Patrick (2000) identified significant mental health problems to consider for the twenty-first century, including substance abuse, violent behavior, mood and anxiety disorders, personality disorders, eating disorders, and learning disabilities. Soet and Sevig (2006) suggested that depression, anxiety, eating disorders, attention-deficit/hyperactivity disorder, and PTSD also require practitioners' attention. Grayson and Meilman (2006) provided an in-depth exploration of significant mental health issues, including depression and anxiety, stress, sexual concerns, family problems, sexual victimization, eating disorders, personality disorders, and suicidal behaviors. Osfield and Junco (2006) also identified specific mental health disorders that student affairs professionals are likely to confront as part of their work experience. Specifically, they suggested that various anxiety disorders (like panic disorder, obsessive-compulsive disorder, PTSD, and generalized anxiety disorder), mood disorders (like major depression, bipolar I, and bipolar II), developmental disorders (like autism and Asperger's disorder), and a wide range of personality disorders are present on college campuses. Kadison and DiGeronimo (2004) highlighted depression, sleep disorders, substance abuse, anxiety disorders, eating disorders, impulsive behaviors (including sexual promiscuity and self-mutilation), and suicide as being the most significant psychological issues facing college students. In addition to these general psychological concerns, the experiences of specific groups, like students of color, may create unique psychological issues that influence group members' ability to succeed on campus. For example, research has shown that students of color are at risk for race-related stress due to the additional burden of discrimination and bias (Cress & Ikeda, 2003). Race-related stress has been linked with negative self-esteem, concentration difficulties, and increased risk for mental and physical illnesses, such as depression, anxiety, hypertension, and headaches (Contrada et al., 2001; Landrine & Klonoff, 1996; Lopez, 2005; Utsey, Chae, Brown, & Kelly, 2002; Utsey, Ponterotto, Reynolds, & Cancelli, 2000). Similar issues and concerns exist for students of other underrepresented and underserved groups, such as lesbian, gay, bisexual, and transgender students (e.g., Westefeld, Maples, Buford, & Taylor, 2001). All these psychological and behavioral issues create unique challenges for student affairs professionals and warrant further exploration.

Before reviewing common psychological issues of college students, it is important to make some distinctions regarding how and when to conceptualize these concerns as relevant to the college students with whom we work. First, it is not having a psychological diagnosis itself that is significant but how such issues may influence the students and their immediate community— whether it is in their academic, social, or living environment. Some individuals may be depressed or anxious and have learned to manage their mood disorder through therapy, medicine, yoga, or social support. If their behavior or performance is not a problem, then their diagnosis or mental health history is irrelevant. It is discrimination, based on the Americans with Disabilities Act, to make decisions or act in any way that shows bias toward someone with a mental health difficulty or history (Dickerson, 2006; Kinzie, 2006). However, some students who do not have their psychological health under control will have problems in their lives and may create difficulties for other students. Even then, it is their behavior, not their diagnosis, that is most significant and meaningful.

Delworth (1989) made an important distinction in her Assessment-Intervention of Student Problems (AISP) model that further emphasizes the necessity of having a multidimensional view of students in developing effective and just services and interventions. Her work, along with the work of Brown and DeCoster (1989), offered a perspective to help student affairs practitioners assess and distinguish between those problems that fall within their domain and those that do not. The AISP model identifies problematic students as being disturbing, disturbed, and disturbed/disturbing. The disturbing student is characterized as immature and unable to engage in age-appropriate behaviors, to form relationships, or to function appropriately in the campus environment. For example, the disturbing student may repeatedly violate residence hall policies or overreact to minor problems, or may be unable to maintain the motivation or effort needed to do well academically. These behaviors are often based in the developmental issues many practitioners are trained to recognize and respond to; they are not typically signs of deeper psychological issues. The disturbed student is often described as being "out of sync with other students" (Delworth, p. 5) and may exhibit disturbing and declining behavior patterns that are self-destructive or harmful to others in the community. Examples of disturbed students might be those who are abusing drugs or are depressed, psychotic, or suicidal. The third category is a combination of the disturbed and the disturbing student. These students' disturbing behavior *and* disturbed presentation need equal attention and intervention. For example, according to Delworth, this may be the student who is withdrawn and strange (disturbed) until he drinks, and then he becomes easily agitated and starts a fight with another student or destroys campus property (disturbing). To people without proper training, it may not always be obvious that an individual is disturbed and has underlying psychological issues. However, by identifying the problematic behaviors, it is possible to consult with others and determine the most appropriate and necessary response.

To accomplish this, student affairs professionals need active and collaborative relationships with health staff, counselors, and staff from the students with disabilities office.

While practitioners may not prefer or adopt these terms, such terminology can be a useful heuristic device in distinguishing student behaviors and interventions. These categories help illustrate the differences between the counselor/therapist role and the student affairs helper role (Brown & DeCoster, 1989). The student affairs helper has the knowledge, resources, level of student contact, and skills to respond to and assist students who are disturbing. They may attempt to address the developmental issues or tasks that these behaviors evidence. Counselors or therapists are the more appropriate professionals to respond to the disturbed student whose problems may be deeply rooted and dysfunctional. Conversely, student affairs helpers, because they may be the first to become aware of disturbed students (either through a crisis situation or through day-to-day observations), should be trained on how to assess psychological behaviors and problems that are outside their scope of training and expertise and to initiate consultations and make referrals to professional counselors and therapists as appropriate.

Owen et al. (2006) made a further distinction by describing distressed and distressing students as individuals "who are challenged by significant mental health concerns and whose impairment has the potential to negatively affect the larger college or university community" (p. 16). Through assessment, it is essential to focus on more than just the students who appear to be distressed or are distressing the campus environment. Spooner (2000) urges that campuses explore the possibility of a systemic source for the problem, rather than just assuming that all difficulties come from students. If students experience the campus as being distressing or oppressive in any way, it may either create psychological difficulties or intensify ones that already exist. Spooner further emphasizes the need to take a developmental approach and view "students within the context of life transition rather than from the standpoint of psychopathology" (p. 8). This has become increasingly important as many campuses struggle with policies and procedures regarding students with mental health issues and behavioral problems. As Megivern (2001) suggested, campuses are more focused on the disruptive effect of these students rather than how to retain and support students with mental health issues; her research demonstrates that "mental health is an understudied factor in research on integration and attrition" (p. 213) and warrants much closer examination.

In an effort to increase awareness of some of the crucial mental health issues that many college students face, this chapter briefly reviews several of the most common psychological concerns. It is not possible to address the full range of mental health issues facing college students; that is clearly beyond the scope of this book. However, a brief discussion of several prevalent psychological and emotional concerns of college students will assist student affairs professionals in clarifying what they know and when they might need to seek out additional information and resources to better understand and assist college students. Specifically, the following psychological issues will be briefly explored: mood disorders and anxiety disorders, eating disorders, personality disorders, and substance abuse. While these diagnoses and psychological issues may constitute diverse and discrete categories, it is important to note that many of them coexist within the same person, leading to complications in identification and treatment (Grayson & Cooper, 2006).

According to Benton and Benton (2006b), depression, anxiety, and suicidal ideation are epidemics on college campuses. Robertson et al. (2006) reported that mood difficulties explained 25 percent of the variance in college student learning problems and academic concerns.

There are primarily three mood disorders: major depression, dysthymia, and bipolar disorder. Major depression involves five or more of the following behaviors: decreased interest or pleasure in most activities, reoccurring depressed mood, loss of or decrease in appetite, insomnia or sleeping less, feeling restless or lethargic, confusion, feeling worthless, an inability to think or focus, and recurrent thoughts of death or suicide. Dysthymia involves long-term acute depression that may be less severe than major depression but may still lead to diminished functioning. At times dysthymia appears more like entrenched negativity and pessimistic attitudes than a form of depression. Although students may hide their depressive feelings, often their behavior does change. They don't go out socially, stop participating in their daily activities, and have difficulty enjoying themselves. As devastating as depression can be, it has proved to respond to both treatment and medication, so it is essential that depressed students be identified and encouraged to seek out professional assistance.

Although depression and suicidal thoughts or behaviors do not always occur together, they frequently comingle, making them both more difficult to treat. The increasing frequency of depression leads to heightened lethality and risk of suicide. As mentioned earlier, Benton et al. (2003) found that the number of students seen with depression from 1988 to 2001 doubled and those with suicidal thoughts tripled. The ACHA (2006) survey also found that almost 10 percent of students surveyed seriously considered suicide during that year and many more (close to 50 percent) stated that it was difficult for them to function at times. Furr et al. (2001) found a similar level of suicidal thoughts (9 percent) among college students in their study. Suicide is the second-leading cause of death among young adults in their early twenties, and more individuals die from suicide than all other medical illnesses combined (Kadison & DiGeronimo, 2004). Even more concerning is that approximately one in twelve college students attempt suicide (Kadison & DiGeronimo). There are many known risk factors, such as prior attempts, family history of suicidal behavior, or lack of parental support (Silverman, 2006). Specific signs of suicidal risks include talking about "wanting out" or "ending it all," taking life-threatening risks, or trying to give away belongings. Sometimes suicidal individuals can be treated through outpatient psychotherapy; however, they may need to be hospitalized until they can be stabilized. Because suicidal risk is a very serious matter on college campuses, it is essential that student affairs professionals follow up on reports of students who are depressed, withdrawn, or exhibiting behavioral changes. This means initiating contact, preferably in person, with these students. While there are trained individuals who are more expert at detecting and preventing suicide attempts, it is often the job of the student affairs practitioner to ensure that such students are detected and referred to the appropriate services.

The final mood disorder that is increasingly seen on college campuses is bipolar disorder. This disorder typically involves significant mood swings where individuals are very depressed one moment and overly elated and expansive at other times. The elated behavior can develop into mania, where a student exhibits poor judgment, grandiose thoughts, rapid speech, and impulsive or reckless behavior. If a student is found to be up for days at a time and to have difficulty sleeping or focusing, s/he may be experiencing a manic episode. It is also possible for a student to exhibit a more limited or less intense mania that is not as obvious. Ironically, sometimes individuals do not experience their first manic episode until after they take an antidepressant medication. Again, it is the job of the student affairs practitioner to be the eyes and ears of the counseling center and, whenever possible, to identify these students and refer them for consultation or ongoing counseling. Increasingly, residence hall staff are requiring mental health consultations when students exhibit depressive or suicidal symptoms.

In addition to depression, another common mental health issue among college students is anxiety and stress-related conditions. Anxiety disorders actually encompass a collection of anxiety and stress-related conditions, including panic disorder, generalized anxiety disorder, obsessive-compulsive disorder, and PTSD. Panic disorders involve the sudden onset of acute fear along with intense physiological symptoms. Generalized anxiety disorder is characterized by excessive worry and anxiety, while obsessive-compulsive disorder involves obsessive thoughts or compulsive behaviors that interfere with an individual's functioning. Finally, PTSD, with its accompanying anxious thoughts, is often the result of an acute trauma, such as rape or another type of intense violence. The symptoms of all these disorders present themselves with varying intensity across individuals and situations. Like depression, anxiety is a serious mental health issue and warrants the attention and assistance of a professional counselor. Identifying these students and ensuring that they are referred for ongoing counseling is essential. Sometimes anxiety disorders have a negative effect only on the student and may lead to academic disruption or failure; however, anxiety in its many forms may also cause a disruption in the student's relationships (Kadison & DiGeronimo, 2004).

Eating disorders are also very common on college campuses, especially among young women. While it is difficult to fully and accurately estimate their prevalence because of the large numbers of individuals who never seek out help or who refuse it, one study by Mintz and Betz (1988) reported that almost 60 percent of college women display some type of disordered eating such as excessive dieting or exercising, binging and purging, or overeating. The various eating disorders (anorexia nervosa, bulimia nervosa, and binge-eating disorder) are especially common among eighteen- to twenty-five-year-old women. A growing number of men, especially gay men and some male athletes, are also vulnerable to eating disorders (Kadison & DiGeronimo, 2004). Individuals who engage in eating-disordered behaviors often have body image difficulties and some mood disturbance, which may exacerbate the problem and interfere with treatment. Eating disorders are a serious issue, partially because they have medical- and health-related implications, and student affairs professionals need to increase their awareness and knowledge so they are better able to identify students in distress and assist those students in accessing mental health and medical treatment. The hidden nature of eating disorders and the normalized reality of body image disturbances and poor eating habits among college women make detection difficult; however, eating disorders can be life threatening, and student affairs professionals need to be attuned to their varied and unique presentation.

Personality disorders, while less frequently discussed within the college mental health literature, are still important to mention because they are often challenging to diagnose and even harder to treat within the short-term counseling model common on college campuses. Unlike depression or anxiety, personality disorders are especially resistant to treatment because they are characteristics of an individual's personality and not a transitional emotional state (Rosenstein, 2006). Students with personality disorders often exhibit poor judgment and insight, externalize their problems, engage in impulsive behavior, do not see their behavior as causing any difficulties in their lives, and may have problematic relationships with others, often with intense emotions and drama (Linehan, 1993). Individuals with personality disorder characteristics may create chaos in their social relationships, such as among roommates or within a student organization. A common behavior that may be the result of personality-disordered behaviors is cutting. These individuals engage in self-injurious behaviors, which may involve cutting or burning one's skin or other harmful actions. This behavior is always very alarming to the friends and family who discover it and can cause a lot of controversy when discovered in college, especially within intact groups like roommates or sorority sisters. It is important to realize that while such behavior is serious and harmful, it is typically different from suicidal behavior. Individuals who cut themselves as a way to deal with their emotional and psychological pain do not usually have any desire to commit suicide. Once these behaviors become known, it is important to act and refer the individual to counseling.

Such behavior often has a disruptive effect on the students' relationships and environment. Support for roommates, friends, and others may also be necessary. Unfortunately, many individuals who engage in this behavior are not always receptive to treatment and may cause administrators to make some difficult decisions regarding the consequences of their behavior.

The last psychological or behavioral issue warranting the attention of student affairs professionals is substance abuse. Alcohol and drug abuse is particularly concerning because of their serious consequences, including alcohol poisoning, sexual and physical violence, academic difficulties, unprotected sex, and driving under the influence. While many college students may not be addicted to alcohol and drugs, they often meet the criteria for substance abuse and dependence based on their own self-reports (Kadison & DiGeronimo, 2004). These high-risk behaviors are very costly to the campus environment. Student affairs professionals do not need to typically go looking for individuals with alcohol and drug problems because such substance abuse often leads to academic, interpersonal, behavioral, or judicial difficulties. However, it can be challenging to get these students to openly examine their alcohol and drug use and admit that they might have a problem. So often college students view their substance-abuse-related problems as a natural part of the college experience. Addressing the serious issue of addiction and getting college students to examine their behavior is likely beyond the expertise of student affairs professionals, and such students should be referred to appropriate groups and services on or off campus.

Awareness, Knowledge, and Skills Needed to Address Mental Health Issues

To effectively address the emotional and behavioral issues that college students bring to or experience while on campus, it is important that student affairs professionals develop the requisite awareness, knowledge, and skills. Within the various functional areas of student affairs (e.g., residence life), there are opportunities to explore and respond to mental health issues and their impact on the campus community.

The awareness needed to work effectively with individuals with emotional and psychological issues includes the values, attitudes, biases, and assumptions that influence how student affairs professionals view and relate to others who may be struggling and need assistance. Previous experiences with mental health issues, either personally or with significant people in their lives, can help or harm practitioners' work with others. When student affairs professionals have had positive experiences with these issues, they are more likely to have positive expectations and be less hesitant to directly face students who are struggling. Such positive experiences may include observing how therapy has helped others or supporting others who had mental health concerns. Likewise, negative experiences—such as seeing individuals struggle but not get better, having a friend who committed suicide, or seeing how disturbed individuals can have a negative effect on others—may interfere by creating negative expectations and biases toward counseling or the individuals themselves. These negative assumptions may make it difficult to effectively respond to individuals with mental health concerns. In addition to understanding any biases and assumptions, it is important to realize that the relationships formed with individuals with emotional difficulties can be challenging and draining. Working with students who are continually depressed can make helpers feel powerless and frustrated. Realizing that a student's emotional problems are creating relationship havoc among her friends or members of her student organization is an important insight that will assist practitioners in helping that student. Finally, being aware of one's abilities and limitations in working with others is essential to being an effective helper. It is important for student affairs professionals to realize that if they freak out when learning of a student's suicidal thoughts or eating disorder or if they feel overwhelmed hearing about a student's loss of a parent, then they are likely not the best helpers for those students. Awareness of strengths and weaknesses when it comes to helping others is pivotal to being an effective helper.

Developing a knowledge base is also a crucial part of being able to help others with emotional and psychological concerns. Having specific information about mental health issues, such as knowing that asking about suicide does not make a student more likely to attempt suicide or that there are certain stages to the grief process, can make one a more effective helper. There are many resources, including books and Web sites, oriented toward the layperson that explore and explain the realities of mental health issues in a helpful and affirming manner. Some of these resources include *College of the Overwhelmed* by Kadison and DiGeronimo (2004) and Web sites such as www. campusblues.com, www.ulifeline.org, and www.jedfoundation. org. In the past five years, a new student organization called Active Minds has formed that focuses on increasing awareness of mental health issues among college students. There are now over a hundred college chapters across the country. This organization, which is run by college students for college students, has already amassed a strong organization partially because the need and interest are so great. This organization can be accessed at http://www.activemindsoncampus.org. Other books and Web sites geared toward the general public, such as *Feeling Good* by David Burns (1999) or www.nmha.org, can assist student affairs professionals in understanding how certain mental health issues manifest themselves and the best ways to help others with those concerns. Many college counseling center Web sites offer self-help materials and other resources that can assist students and practitioners in dealing with mental health issues. For example, the Counseling Center Village (http://ccvillage.buffalo.edu) provides a collection of virtual self-help pamphlets from counseling centers across the country. Resources within professional associations like the Commission for Counseling and Psychological Services within the American College Personnel Association or the university and college counseling center section of the counseling psychology division of the American Psychological Association can also assist student affairs professionals in their efforts to be effective helpers. In addition to using these resources to learn about specific psychological problems, like eating disorders or cutting, practitioners must also increase their knowledge about how the environment and external stressors can exacerbate certain problems. Consulting with counselors and psychiatrists on campus or other local resources, like a crisis line or domestic violence shelter, can assist practitioners in doing their job.

Having effective helping and communication skills, as explored elsewhere in this book, is an important first step to establishing the competence to work with college students who are having mental health issues. Once you master those skills—whether it is the ability to build a rapport or make a referral—it won't matter what the particular mental health issue is. Having the basic skills to make an appropriate intervention and establish a trusting relationship will earn you the reputation among students as someone who is easy to talk with and who understands. By being available and approachable, you have set the stage to help students who might otherwise fall through the cracks. In addition to developing specific helping skills, it is important to be aware of when you are in over your head and need to consult with counseling experts on campus. Finally, even when you have the skills to assist students who are struggling, you may not be the ideal person to assist them. If you have a dual relationship with a student (s/he is on your staff or in an organization you advise), others may turn out to be more effective helpers. We do not always have to be the one who provides the assistance; what's most central is that students get the help they need.

Illustrations of Mental Health Issues
Across Functional Areas

To illustrate various ways that student affairs practitioners may work with students with mental health issues, this section examines the different types of situations and contexts in which such interactions occur. Some examples are highlighted here to develop an appreciation of the ways in which emotional and behavioral difficulties often manifest themselves. These examples utilize the conceptualization of the various student affairs functional areas used previously in the book: (1) counseling-oriented positions like career and personal counseling; (2) leadership development and educational positions (e.g., student activities, Greek affairs, campus life, health and wellness, and residence life); (3) administrative positions like dean of students, judicial affairs, and admissions; and (4) academic affairs positions (e.g., advisement and academic support services).

Within the counseling functional area, the primary focus of the work is helping students address their personal, social, and vocational concerns. The challenging part occurs for those individuals who are not trained as mental health counselors (e.g., career counselors). There is often a fine line between career and personal concerns, so professionals who are working with individuals on career and vocational issues may find that students face additional personal concerns that influence their career decision-making process. For example, in the course of exploring how a student feels about her/his major, a student affairs professional with strong helping skills may discover that the student is being sexually harassed by her/his professor. Or when asking a student about her/his career choice, an effective helper may discover that the family is pressuring the student to change majors or that a lesbian, gay, or bisexual student is concerned about the implications of entering a profession that works closely with children. All this additional information, while not seemingly directly related to the task at hand (e.g., choosing a major), may ultimately need to be addressed.

Within the context of leadership development and educational positions, student affairs professionals may learn about students with various psychological or emotional difficulties. These professionals may gather this knowledge by observing students in their groups or in their roles as student leaders or by receiving it from other individuals. Often these conversations occur as a normal part of working together, when a student discloses some private yet important information. However, there are other times when students do not disclose their concerns and the information must be obtained in other ways. If they are highly emotional or not able to perform their expected duties, it may become necessary to gather information from others or intervene more directly. Some practitioners may have to initiate a conversation to address these concerns and ensure that the student is getting the assistance that s/he needs.

Individuals in administrative positions may come into contact with students with mental health issues because they are often the ones who address students' behavioral problems. So it is not unusual for a dean of students, admissions director, or judicial affairs staff member to become aware of mental health issues and their effect on students. The bigger challenge for individuals with this type of disciplinary and decision-making power is to figure out how or when to consider students' mental health and well-being information as being relevant to the situation. Responding to students whose parents have died, interacting with the parents of a student who committed suicide, and hearing the discipline case of an individual with a substance abuse problem are just a few of the situations that occur. It is one thing to complete an administrative task (e.g., making a decision about whether to dismiss a student who attempted suicide) and another to deal with the emotional well-being and humanity of a student who is struggling. Consulting with others, such as those involved with legal counsel or a crisis committee on campus, is a necessary part of dealing with these concerns as an administrator.

Finally, individuals in academic affairs positions may have experiences similar to career counselors. While it may not be the function of an academic adviser or the director of tutorial services to address students' personal and emotional concerns, such issues may still arise because students feel comfortable sharing their feelings or are in crisis. If a student's grades suddenly drop, for example, it would be important to discover what some of the reasons for the change might be. Knowing when to intervene and how far to take the conversation can be challenging. Consultation with other professionals is always an ideal first step.

Benefits and Challenges to Addressing Mental Health Issues

The benefits and challenges to working with students who have mental health issues is fairly similar to the basic advantages and disadvantages of being a helper. The particular challenges include the emotionality of the work and how at times it can be draining and discouraging. Not everyone accepts offers of support, gets better, or succeeds. It is difficult, particularly when a helping relationship is time consuming and demanding, to accept the reality that some individuals are not able or open to getting the help they need. In addition, if practitioners are not able to set proper boundaries, especially in positions like residence life or student activities that require everyday contact with students, those practitioners can become overwhelmed or burned out by some students' constant demand for support and encouragement. Being able to be available and present enough to help others but distant enough to take care of oneself is an ongoing challenge even for counseling professionals. The benefits of helping students are quite obvious. It feels good to help others and make a difference in their lives. It is sometimes hard to understand that other adults in their lives never took the time, or didn't know how, to help them address their emotional and psychological concerns. And sometimes even the smallest intervention can enable students to graduate from college and be successful in their lives; there is no better reward than that.

Preparation and Training for Addressing Mental Health Issues on Campus

Student affairs preparation programs have always emphasized learning about college students as a core part of the curriculum. The philosophy of the student affairs profession and the professional guidelines and standards (e.g., Council for the Advancement of Standards in Higher Education [CAS]) has reinforced the importance of a student-centered and holistic approach. However, this developmental perspective has not necessarily prepared student affairs professionals to deal with the increasingly remedial aspects of their work in addressing the academic, behavioral, and psychological concerns of college students. Both CAS and the Council for Accreditation of Counseling and Related Educational Programs recommend that student affairs preparation programs educate graduate students and new professionals about college students, including human growth and development issues (such as developmental theory), addictions, psychopathology, and the effects of college on students. Student affairs preparation programs often do not address mental health issues in the curriculum; even the typical course syllabus on the American college student makes little mention of mental health issues or disabilities. It appears that much of the education about college students' mental health issues occurs as part of on-the-job training.

If, in fact, as Kitzrow (2003) states, "student mental health is an important and legitimate concern and responsibility of everyone involved in higher education" (p. 175), then more preparation programs and professional development efforts need to fully incorporate these issues into their training efforts. In the past, scant literature supported such training, but several books (cf. Benton & Benton, 2006a; Kadison & DiGeronimo, 2004) have been published in recent years, and the major journals of the profession more regularly include articles on mental health and psychological issues. Most colleges and universities have counseling centers or health centers with psychologists, social workers, or psychiatrists who can serve as natural experts and consultants on campus.

These educational efforts should include outreach and consultation to help erase the many negative perceptions and assumptions that individuals have about mental health issues and counseling. Professional staff members need accurate and up-to-date information about mental health issues, treatment, and such issues' effects on the campus community. Counseling center staff can develop workshops, written materials, and Web sites to inform faculty, staff, and administrators about the psychological difficulties that many students experience. In recent years counseling centers have developed materials to assist faculty and staff in identifying students on campus with possible mental health concerns. This information can assist practitioners in recognizing and referring students who are in emotional distress or have psychological concerns that are interfering with their ability to be successful. Student affairs professionals need to also focus on educating students and "conduct an ongoing education, outreach and advertisement campaign to inform them about mental health issues and encourage them to use the services available to them" (Kitzrow, 2003, p. 177). Students can be an excellent source of information about the mental health and well-being of other students; when they are well informed, they are better able to assist professionals by providing important insight and information.

Benton and Benton (2006b) emphasized that to assist campuses in responding to mental health problems, the following five steps need to occur: (1) help administrators better understand the scope of mental health difficulties on their campus; (2) further administrators' understanding of the related legal and ethical issues; (3) provide theoretical frameworks and practical strategies for developing and delivering comprehensive and integrated services for students with mental health issues; (4) ensure that the theories, strategies, and ideas presented are relevant and useful for their target audience (e.g., faculty, staff, students); and (5) assist administrators in fully understanding the unique concerns and needs of underserved and underrepresented student groups. All these steps require a proactive, coordinated, and intentional educational effort to enhance the services provided to students with mental health issues. Creating a campus community where these services can be effective means developing a culture of cooperation, communication, and collaboration among all aspects of the community. According to Kadison and DiGeronimo (2004), in reality, such efforts will benefit individual students, the whole student body, and the entire college or university.

Summary

Mental health and psychological issues affect all aspects of campus life. They have an impact on students' ability to function, perform and succeed academically, and relate to others (Kitzrow, 2003). Students' emotional and behavioral problems can negatively affect other members of the community, such as their classmates, roommates, and faculty and staff members. Student affairs professionals, who are usually very involved in the daily lives of college students, are often the individuals with the ability to assess and intervene when students are struggling with emotional, psychological, and behavioral concerns. Therefore, it is essential that they have accurate information and the necessary resources to effectively meet the needs of students with mental health issues. This chapter explored some of the specific mental health concerns and issues on campus and suggested some strategies for meeting these students' needs and addressing the larger campus issues.

Chapter Three

Ethical Implications for Helping in Higher Education

Given the complex and multifaceted relationships between students, parents, faculty, staff, the community, and the institution itself, addressing ethical dilemmas and making decisions about ethical concerns has become a core and almost inevitable part of student affairs work (Young, 2001). According to Janosik, Creamer, and Humphrey (2004), "The issue of ethical behavior is at the core of what student affairs professionals do" (p. 356). Whether it is the counseling roots of many student affairs preparation programs or the historical and philosophical emphasis on the whole student, student affairs professionals have often been the voice of ethical reasoning, or the conscience, of their campuses (Brown, 1985; Talley, 1997; Waple, 2006). By being involved with and interacting with students on a daily basis where they eat, live, work, and play, student affairs practitioners often struggle with ethical dilemmas or face ethical challenges (Brown; Janosik, 2007).

The dynamic nature of higher education and society itself has caused the task of addressing ethical issues to become more complex, demanding, and nuanced (Fried, 1997; Pope, Reynolds, & Mueller, 2004). Some scholars have suggested that "environmental changes in the diversity of students, the shifting vision of the campus as community, and the monocultural and linear nature of the theories underlying the student affairs profession require an attitudinal shift in how the student affairs profession addresses ethical issues and their underlying values" (Pope et al., p. 122). This new ethical paradigm needs to incorporate the unique cultural realities and diverse values that students, staff, administrators, and faculty bring to campus (Fried, 2003). As a result of such diverse and dynamic educational environments, ideas about what constitutes an ethical dilemma and how to address ethical concerns in productive and proactive ways are constantly evolving and expanding.

The purpose of this chapter is to explore the key ethical issues that face student affairs practitioners who find themselves in helping roles. Having the tools to handle the complex and challenging concerns that accompany helping in a higher education setting is essential for all practitioners. This chapter describes the unique ethical and professional issues facing practitioners who offer support to college students and suggests ways to conceptualize and address such concerns. Preparation and training issues are also explored, with suggestions for how to focus more attention on these important ethical concerns.

According to Fried (2003), "Ethical beliefs and standards represent a community's most deeply held and widely accepted values" (p. 107). By understanding the broader values and ethical codes of the student affairs profession, it is possible to discern the core beliefs and anticipate the inevitable ethical dilemmas and challenges that will occur on campuses across the country. Over the past twenty years, the literature has extensively explored the theoretical foundations of ethics within student affairs and its implications for practice (cf. Brown, 1985; Canon, 1993; Fried, 1997, 2003; Kitchener, 1985; Young, 2001). Kitchener provided a unifying theoretical perspective on ethics in higher education that continues to be the basis for ethical decision making and professional standards and ethical codes within the field of student affairs. She articulated three levels of ethical inquiry: principles, theories, and codes of conduct. Ethical principles describe the core ideas and ideals about what is viewed as good and ethical behavior. Kitchener suggested five central principles: respecting autonomy, doing no harm, bene-fiting others, being just, and being faithful. Fried (2003) added a sixth principle—veracity or truth telling—as essential to the student affairs profession. These principles provide a framework for identifying and understanding critical ethical issues and making decisions about how to respond.

Ethics in higher education has consisted of applying these principles to specific cases or situations and determining the most ethical response to the dilemma. Inevitably, these ethical principles conflict with each other, and student affairs profes-sionals must determine how to resolve the complicated ethical issues that occur on campus. For example, the presence of credit card companies that solicit students to sign up for credit cards creates an ethical challenge. Tension exists between the prin-ciple of respecting autonomy, or allowing young adults to make their own economic choices and live with the consequences, and the principle of doing no harm when many students do not have the emotional and financial maturity to handle that free-dom and end up in severe debt that may lead to academic with-drawal, depression, and even suicide. Often ethical dilemmas do not have simple solutions, and there are rarely easy answers.

Professional standards and ethical codes have been frequently viewed as the first line of defense in responding to ethical dilemmas (Kitchener, 1985). Both major professional associa-tions within student affairs, the American College Personnel Association (ACPA) and National Association of Student Personnel Administrators (NASPA), have created ethical codes or standards to guide their members, and the larger higher edu-cation community, with the ethical decision-making process (ACPA, 2006; NASPA, 1990). However, many ethical chal-lenges, such as the one previously described, are not specifically addressed in the professional codes. Instead, student affairs prac-titioners often need to extrapolate from such sets of values and struggle with the conflicting ethical principles in the unique con-text of their campus and their job responsibilities.

Despite the challenges, it is essential that professionals read, understand, and implement the ethical codes of the student affairs profession. Such codes are not meant to be rule books to control behavior and provide direction for the sometimes ambiguous parts of student affairs work; rather, they provide the core issues and values that need to be examined as part of student affairs practice. According to Young (2001), because of the evolving and sometimes vague nature of legal and ethical codes, it is essential not to abandon the ethical principles as the foundation for solid ethical reasoning. This means being motivated to do what is right rather than what is required. To behave as ethical professionals, student affairs practitioners need to understand the role of professional ethics and standards in their daily work (Janosik, 2007). Both ACPA and NASPA have created very different types of standards and/or codes through which they influence the thoughts and actions of their members and the profession, and these codes reflect the different values that are at the heart of the two associations (Fried, 2003).

The NASPA Standards of Professional Practice (NASPA, 1990) offer statements on eighteen areas of importance within student personnel work, including conflict of interest, equal consideration and treatment of others, student behavior, confidentiality, representation of professional competence, and campus community. While these standards are more oriented toward effective practices than ethics per se, they include statements on confidentiality and other ethical matters, such as "Members ensure that confidentiality is maintained with respect to all privileged communications and to educational and professional records considered confidential. They inform all parties of the nature and/or limits of confidentiality. Members share information only in accordance with institutional policies and relevant statutes when given the informed consent or when required to prevent personal harm to themselves or others" (p. 1).

The Statement of Ethical Principles and Standards developed by ACPA (2006) provide four ethical standards to guide members in all aspects of their work with colleagues, students, educational institutions, and society. These four standards are professional responsibility and competence, student learning and development, responsibility to the institution, and responsibility to society. Within each standard there are anywhere from five to twenty-eight specific statements. For example, within student learning and development, there are statements such as "Treat students with respect as persons who possess dignity, worth, and the ability to be self-directed" and "Refer students to appropriate specialists before entering or continuing a helping relationship when the professional's expertise or level of comfort is exceeded." In addition, ACPA provides concrete suggestions for resolving ethical misconduct. Although the standards provided by ACPA present a theoretical foundation and are more detailed, both professional associations offer codifications of professional expectations that are meant to encourage ethical behavior and instill it within student affairs professionals.

Having a clear understanding of ethics and the centrality of ethics in practice is essential. Waple (2006), in his study of the skills and competencies required for entry-level student affairs work, found that knowledge of ethics was attained through professional preparation programs from a moderate to high degree and was viewed as the third most important area of competence behind student development theory and oral and written communication skills. He further assessed how much entry-level practitioners actually used these various skills and found that ethics was seen as a necessary competency that was both attained at a high level through graduate and professional education and utilized at a high level. However, Janosik et al. (2004) have suggested that despite the essential role of ethics in student affairs practice, there is not enough awareness or understanding of ethical issues and even less attention to ethical issues in the professional literature; in fact, according to these authors, "Ethics is too often left out of our practice-oriented literature" (p. 357).

Ethical Concerns and Issues Facing
Student Affairs Professionals

With limited literature and research on ethics available, student affairs professionals often learn about ethics through on-the-job experiences and training. While many student affairs preparation programs address and infuse ethical issues in their coursework, few stand-alone ethics courses educate graduate students and new professionals and prepare them to tackle ethical challenges. There is a need for more research and practice-oriented literature that examines the ethical challenges that many student affairs professionals face and offers effective ways of coping with those dilemmas. One study, by Janosik et al. (2004), attempted to fill this void by gathering data on the common ethical issues faced by student affairs practitioners. Using an online questionnaire, the researchers asked respondents to list several ethical dilemmas they recently experienced in their current position. Using a qualitative approach, sixteen categories of ethical dilemmas were identified and classified according to Kitchener's (1985) and Fried's (2003) core ethical principles. Ethical dilemmas linked to justice or treating others equally and fairly (32 percent) were most frequently reported by respondents. Beneficence or helping others/doing good (23.6 percent) was the second most frequent response, while fidelity or faithfulness, loyalty, and honesty (22.6 percent) were third. Despite the availability of professional codes of ethics and their ability to address many of the respondents' ethical dilemmas, many people still reported feeling unsure about how to respond to a diversity of ethical challenges. Janosik et al. suggested that "there may be a serious disconnect between what is written about and what the professional experiences in the field" (p. 371). Janosik (2007) asked student affairs practitioners at all levels of experience to identify common concerns about their professional behavior. He identified the top ten key professional concerns as obligation to act, fairness, inconsistency in policy enforcement, respect for privacy, loyalty issues, special treatment, misuse of nonacademic resources, misstatement of facts, inappropriate interpersonal interactions, and respect for personal choice.

Since many ethical challenges grow out of the multitude of daily helping interactions and relationships in which student affairs practitioners engage with students, colleagues, administrators, faculty members, and community leaders, it is especially crucial that student affairs professionals understand the unique dilemmas and circumstances that arise when engaged in helping-, advising-, or counseling-related behaviors. Whether these situations happen on one's own campus or occur on other campuses across the country, being aware of potential ethical dilemmas is the first step to becoming an ethical and effective student affairs professional. Janosik (2005) and others (Fried, 2003; Gehring, 1993, 2001) have emphasized the importance of learning to recognize and anticipate the legal and ethical risks within student affairs practice. Janosik suggested that by scanning the environment for current issues and problems, both on campus and in the larger society, practitioners will be better prepared to respond, rather than just react, to specific problems. It is also important to expand environmental scanning beyond one's immediate environment and look to other educational settings. For example, awareness of the violence that happened on the Columbine High School campus and the need for schools to develop safety plans can provide important information that can be explored and adapted to the college environment. While it has become commonplace for public schools to practice lockdown drills to protect students, faculty, and staff from potential violence and harm, such drills have not been instituted on most college campuses. The large and often disconnected college environment requires a different type of communication and response to adequately deal with potential campus violence. This is just one of many lessons that campuses face in the aftermath of recent events of campus violence, such as those at

Virginia Tech and Northern Illinois University. Specific communication protocols (e.g., communicating with students via e-mail and text messages if an emergency happens) already have been developed and implemented on some college campuses.

In addition to scanning other educational settings for common ethical challenges, it is practical and has heuristic value for student affairs professionals to explore the typical ethical dilemmas and concerns that college counseling professionals face. While the standards and expectations are different for trained counselors, many of the ethical issues are the same. By examining those ethical concerns, student affairs practitioners may be able to develop effective strategies and approaches that can assist them in responding more effectively and ethically to many of these recurring dilemmas on campus.

Several studies have examined the ethical problems that college counselors typically experience. Hayman and Covert (1986) described confidentiality and competence as the most difficult ethical issues to resolve. Tensions about confidentiality and sharing information often result from differences in opinion and campus policy when deciding how much student information can or should be shared with campus or government officials (Gallagher, 1989). Determining the level of competence that is necessary to effectively and ethically address students' emotional concerns is paramount. In addition, Hayman and Covert found that few counselors consulted published professional standards and codes when addressing ethical issues; instead, most reported using common sense, which may not lead to the most ethical choices. Clearly, paying more attention to actual codes and guidelines is essential to ethical practice. Malley, Gallagher, and Brown (1992), in their Delphi study of counseling center directors, identified three significant ethical concerns: confidentiality, dual relationships, and harm to self or others. Many directors reported pressure to reveal confidential information about clients to college administrators. For professional counselors, dual relationships revolve around concerns about setting up therapeutically appropriate boundaries and roles. If professional counselors become too engaged with clients or clients become too dependent on counselors, then it is easy to become confused about the goal and direction of the relationship, which can ultimately harm the client. Similar awareness of boundaries is also important for student affairs professionals.

Finally, dealing with suicidal students is an increasing legal and ethical challenge on college campuses where parents and administrators are demanding accountability. Winek and Jones (1996), through the use of vignettes, identified key ethical issues in college counseling and possible strategies for addressing them. Specifically, they focused on dual relationships, confidentiality, discrimination, and rights to self-determination and autonomy, highlighting the importance of colleagues providing feedback and counsel regarding the ethical decisions of their peers.

Several compelling events during the past few years have brought these crucial ethical issues and dilemmas into the limelight, not only for college counselors, but also for student affairs professionals. Specifically, the complexity of addressing suicidal and violent behavior on campus has led many institutions to struggle with significant ethical issues. Archer and Cooper (1998) and others (Fried, 2003; Young, 2001) have highlighted the ongoing tension between protecting the rights and interests of individual students while also addressing the interests and responsibility of the larger community. The suicide of Elizabeth Shin in 2000 led to a legal battle between her parents and the Massachusetts Institute of Technology, in which the parents sued the institution, counselors, and administrators for wrongful death because they knew of her vulnerable emotional state. Fear of liability has led many institutions to develop policies that require that suicidal students or students with other mental health issues attend mandatory counseling, move off campus, or withdraw from school. Some campuses have required counseling waivers that mandate that information about students seeking mental health counseling be shared with administrators.

These actions have also led to court battles in which the students involved sued for discrimination based on their mental health status, which is specifically protected by the Americans with Disabilities Act (Kinzie, 2006). Campuses are struggling with the legal quandary of invading students' confidentiality regarding their mental health status to protect the larger community in case the students are a risk to themselves or others. On the other hand, if universities do take action and remove or segregate these students, they may also be held liable. Parents and other important stakeholders want campuses to be safe and have difficulty understanding when state and federal laws seem to protect students with mental health issues more than other students. The fallout from the Virginia Tech and Northern Illinois shootings has yet to be fully absorbed by campuses all across the country that are struggling to develop policies that address how to prevent students with significant mental illnesses from becoming a threat on campus. The preliminary and sometimes conflicting legal rulings in recent years have left many campus administrators confused about how to handle these mental health challenges. These complicated issues are relevant particularly for student affairs practitioners, who often either have to create and implement the policies or have to deal with the crises and respond to the students who are in distress. There are no easy answers, and student affairs practitioners may feel pulled by their ethical codes and the demands of their institution on the one hand and by protecting individual students and the larger community on the other (Young).

Gehring (2001) emphasizes that knowledge of the law is essential for all student affairs professionals so that they understand the challenge of ensuring students' rights, not exposing them to unnecessary risks, and protecting the institution from liability. Unfortunately, these legalistic approaches and an emphasis on strict adherence to policies and procedures as a guiding theory (Lowery, 1998) have caused many campuses to minimize the greater ethical responsibilities of student affairs professionals, who are bound to care for the overall well-being of students and to do no harm. According to Winston and Saunders (1998), the goal is to maximize ethical practice while minimizing risk. Dickerson (2006) states that it is the institutions' responsibility to review relevant laws and ethical codes, train staff, and provide adequate information and informed consent to all students. Students, staff, faculty, administrators, parents, and community members need education about these community challenges. The Bazelon Center for Mental Health Law (2007) has created a model policy in its efforts to "help colleges and universities navigate these complex issues and develop a nondiscriminatory approach to a student who is in crisis because of a mental health problem" (p. 2). According to Dickerson, such policy and educational efforts "seek to balance privacy concerns against the health and safety of students and the campus in general" (p. 60). Ultimately, learning how to manage this balancing act will help student affairs professionals handle the complicated ethical demands of being both helper and administrator.

Exploring in more depth the specific ethical concerns most relevant to student affairs professionals who are often helpers is essential to preparing them to act as ethical caretakers and leaders on campus. Fully addressing all the ethical issues facing nonprofessional helpers on college campuses is beyond the scope of this chapter; however, it is possible to detail the most significant ethical expectations and issues that frequently influence student affairs practitioners as helpers. For the purpose of this chapter, the primary ethical issues to be addressed include competence, dual relationships, confidentiality, and suicide and duty to warn. As part of exploring these important issues, the relevant ethical codes and professional standards are highlighted so that professionals can more fully understand the dilemmas involved.

Competence

Like all professionals, student affairs practitioners are expected to exhibit high levels of competence in all aspects of their work. As such, they are responsible for the outcomes and consequences of their actions. According to the ACPA (2006) ethical standards, this includes receiving adequate training for the tasks and responsibilities assigned, pursuing continuing education to enhance or expand existing skills, and representing one's professional competencies, credentials, and limitations in an honest and accurate manner. In meeting the ethical principles espoused by Kitchener (1985), it is essential to provide services that fit within one's expertise; otherwise, one might do harm or act in ways that would not benefit others. Such misrepresentation, intentional or not, is both unethical and dishonest. In terms of being a helper, this means that student affairs practitioners must not identify themselves as personal counselors or therapists (unless specifically trained and/or qualified) or suggest to students that they are able to provide those types of services. Of course, many student affairs professionals, as helpers and educators, are expected to be good listeners and to help students express feelings, identify concerns, and solve both personal and academic problems. However, if at any time a student's concerns become more complicated, problematic, or clinical in nature than the practitioner's ability to address them, the practitioner must make timely and effective referrals to the appropriate individuals or office on campus or in the community. No matter how tempting it might be to want to help students fully resolve their problems, competent professionals always know when they lack the necessary skills and are in over their heads. Learning how to make effective referrals and to ascertain when students need to talk with a professional counselor is an important competency for practitioners. And student affairs professionals must understand enough about mental health issues and problematic behaviors that may result from more serious underlying issues, such as addiction, to be able to make those judgments. Often this self-awareness (knowing when students' problems are too challenging) and basic knowledge (about various mental health issues, like depression or cutting behaviors) are gathered through work and life experiences, supervision, and consultation with counseling professionals.

Dual Relationships

As part of facilitating students' growth and development, student affairs professionals must develop healthy and positive relationships with students. Part of this process means ensuring that they establish proper boundaries. Maintaining positive and constructive boundaries is always the responsibility of the professional, not the student (Winek & Jones, 1996). Based on the ACPA (2006) ethical standards, this means that professionals "avoid dual relationships with students where one individual serves in multiple roles that create conflicting responsibilities, role confusion, and unclear expectations (e.g., counselor/employer, supervisor/best friend, or faculty member/sexual partner) that may involve incompatible roles and conflicting responsibilities" (p. 5). This type of professional distance, while uncomfortable at times, is necessary to protect students, who are always in a less powerful position on a college campus. And when practitioners are acting in the role of helper and students are emotionally vulnerable and disclosing personal information, it is important that the students' privacy and confidentiality be respected. This is not always possible when, as a professional, you have other responsibilities (e.g., disciplinary responsibilities) to fulfill. Professional counselors are bound by their ethical code not to disclose personal information unless that individual or others are at risk; however, as will be discussed later, student affairs practitioners are not under such requirements or expectations. To the contrary, they may feel pressured to disclose relevant information that they gather through the course of their daily interactions with students. These demands create a very delicate balance for practitioners who want to help students and listen to their concerns yet, through the course of those conversations, learn information that may need to be shared, particularly in a living and learning environment. For example, imagine an assistant resident director (ARD) who has a positive relationship with a student in her hall and, through the course of some late-night conversation in which the student discloses her depression and unhappiness with school, learns of some inappropriate or illegal behavior on the part of that student or her roommates and friends. The ARD is expected to address these issues through her disciplinary role. However, such actions, while necessary, will change the dynamics in the helping relationship and possibly cause this student not to trust the ARD and to tell other students not to trust her as well. While it is not always possible to completely avoid dual relationships on college campuses, open and honest communication, along with making every effort to do no harm to students, is critical to building trusting and facilitative relationships with students.

Confidentiality

From an ethical and legal perspective, confidentiality is a complex and multifaceted issue for student affairs professionals. The purpose of establishing confidentiality with students is to create a trusting bond that encourages students to share their thoughts and feelings (Frances, 2000). Without some belief or assurance that what they share will remain private, many students would choose not to disclose. Beyond these broader principles, it is important to realize that student affairs practitioners do not have privileged communication with students in the same way that counselors have with their clients (Winston, 2003). The ethical codes and standards and the legal precedents for professional counselors require very specific behaviors and priorities regarding confidentiality. The expectations are somewhat less clear for student affairs practitioners. While there are certainly legal requirements concerning the Family Educational Rights and Privacy Act of 1974 (FERPA), which protects the right of students' educational records to remain private, developments in recent years have made it challenging at times to determine the legal boundaries, as well as the specific expectations, of a particular campus. Given the lack of clarity, it can be useful to reflect on the original purpose of FERPA (to protect the student), which is connected to the underlying ethical principles of beneficence and doing no harm.

Dickerson (2006) suggested that the right to privacy with FERPA is not without limits. For example, campus administrators may disclose students' educational records without their consent to other school officials who can demonstrate a legitimate educational interest, as well as in response to a health or safety emergency, such as a crisis or when a student engages in self-destructive behavior. FERPA also does not protect information that is gained through personal observation and knowledge. Schools have been able to contact family members and other school officials when a student is in crisis; however, depending on the family circumstances, such actions may not always be beneficial to the student. Many schools choose to interpret this federal restriction quite differently; and as demonstrated with the shootings at Virginia Tech, faculty and staff members are often unclear about what is expected of them, and communication and training may not be what is needed. According to Dickerson, institutions should "engage legal counsel to review pertinent laws and ethical codes, train affected staff and include clear and honest statements about the limits of confidentiality" (p. 59).

While many in the higher education community believe that health and safety should always outweigh privacy rules (Dickerson, 2006; Gehring, 2001; Winston & Saunders, 1998), making such conclusions is not always clear-cut. A perfect example of this complexity is demonstrated when a female resident discloses that she has been raped. Now, a crime has been committed, and student affairs practitioners are required to disclose such statistics to their supervisors and possibly the campus police. However, the student often does not want to press charges and does not want the information to go any further. Such wishes often put the practitioner in one of those ethical binds of deciding which ethical principle to honor. On one hand, the student is in a vulnerable state and needs to be able to trust; however, there is a community at risk because the alleged assailant could potentially sexually assault others. It becomes further complicated when the assailant also lives on campus, potentially in the same residence hall. If practitioners are not clear on the policy and expectations of their immediate supervisors and the residential life office, they may make assurances to the student that they are not able to keep, such as "I will not tell anyone else" or "You will not have to speak to the police." Thorough training and effective supervision that explores possible ethical dilemmas regarding confidentiality needs to be a consistent component of annual training so that practitioners feel prepared to address such challenging and thorny situations.

Suicide/Duty to Warn

Nowhere do the ethical issues on campus get more involved and complicated than when dealing with the issue of suicidal and homicidal ideation and behaviors. Within counseling ethics, counselors are expected to take precautions (e.g., transport to hospital, call parents) to deter and prevent suicidal or homicidal actions whenever possible. In recent years, as studies have indicated, because of the growing prevalence of suicidal thoughts and attempts on college campuses (Benton, Robertson, Tseng, Newton, & Benton, 2003), many nonprofit organizations, federal grants, and individual campuses have made great strides in addressing this issue and developing policies, interventions, and training programs. For example, Web sites—such as

www.jedfoundation.org, www.bazelon.org, and www.ulifeline
.org—provide useful resources and research that explore the
causes and treatments for depression, suicide, and mental illness
among college-age students. In addition, professional journals—
such as the national quarterly *Synthesis: Law and Policy in Higher
Education*, as well as its sister publication, *Synfax Weekly Report*,
both edited by Gary Pavela—share up-to-date research, policies,
and practices of colleges and universities across the country. The
role, responsibilities, and even the possibility of liability of student affairs professionals in addressing campus suicide and violence continue to grow and expand. In the past, administrators
were not held responsible or liable for student suicides; however, conflicting rulings have left many campuses unsure of what
the necessary and appropriate policies and actions are (Kinzie,
2006). Due to recent campus violence, some states have decided
to change their laws to ensure that campus mental health issues
are more actively addressed. Although typical practitioners may
not participate in developing campus crisis policies or risk management procedures, they are likely to be closely involved in
early detection of these thoughts and behaviors.

When addressing the needs and concerns of students who
are exhibiting suicidal, homicidal, violent, or mentally unstable
thoughts and behaviors, the primary ethical issue of doing no
harm mandates that student affairs professionals consult with
mental health providers on campus or in the community in
conjunction with campus and departmental policy and expectations. Clearly, helping students with serious mental health
concerns is beyond the scope and competence of non-clinically-
trained helpers, and practitioners should not hesitate to consult
immediately with their supervisors regarding how to handle the
situation. There are far too many examples of campuses where
limited communication and poor implementation of policy
have put students at heightened risk unnecessarily. And while
it is impossible to create a campus environment with no risks,
student affairs professionals must find ways to act that benefit

and protect others, including individual students, the campus community, and the institution itself (Archer & Cooper, 1998; Winston & Saunders, 1998; Young, 2001). The intricacies and continually changing landscape of campus approaches to suicidal risk do not allow for a complete exploration of such issues in this chapter; however, as mentioned previously, more and more resources are available through the Internet, national conferences, and publications, and those resources can aid campuses and individual practitioners in developing the necessary skills, policies, and practices to create safe and healthy campuses.

Strategies for Addressing Ethical Issues on Campus

To be prepared to effectively address the ethical challenges that occur almost daily, student affairs professionals must learn strategies that enhance their ability to perceive, respond, and make meaning of those events. In particular, practitioners face unique ethical experiences in their role as helpers for which they need to be prepared. Learning to anticipate the dilemmas that might occur takes preparation, which can occur through graduate education and preparation, on-the-job training, supervision, professional development through reading and attending conference programs, and observation of and interaction with other professionals. Janosik (2005) recommended that student affairs practitioners develop an effective scanning and awareness strategy that allows them to anticipate legal and ethical issues on campus. By scanning the broader environment on one's own campus as well as in higher education in general, it is possible to develop a level of sensitivity and observation that makes ethical dilemmas more manageable and less daunting. Canon (1993) emphasized the need to develop this type of scanning ability, or ethical radar, which is the "heightened sensitivity to the situational cues that serve as markers for ethical dilemmas" (p. 329).

In addition to effective environmental scans, personal reflection and exploration are other necessary tools for addressing ethical concerns. According to Gehring (2001), the most meaningful and productive ethical reflection occurs before an actual ethical dilemma happens. Ethical reflection is the critical self-exploration process that enables individuals to make choices before, during, and after ethical dilemmas (Kitchener, 1985). Kitchener viewed the essential components of this reflective process as the facts regarding the situation, a moral understanding of those facts, and well-developed intuition with which one can make judgments and choices.

While there are many reflective models and approaches to ethical decision making (cf. Fried, 2003; Janosik et al., 2004), Young (2001) offered a parsimonious yet useful list: (1) be specific, (2) reflect on your experiences, (3) involve others, (4) understand basic ethical principles, (5) try out alternative solutions, and (6) reflect-in-action. This final reflective effort is interactive and occurs in the moment, thus allowing one to respond and react as events and reactions are unfolding. Nash (1997), in discussing how he teaches ethics to graduate students, emphasized the importance of being aware of one's beliefs, intuitions, and feelings that may influence the ethical decision-making process. According to Talley (1997), this self-awareness decreases the likelihood that personal biases, prejudices, or deleterious assumptions will influence that process.

Many ethics scholars have highlighted the necessity of expanding one's perspective and taking a community approach to ethics (Brown, 1985; Fried, 2003; Sundberg & Fried, 1997; Young, 2001). Brown viewed community as vital to ethical practice in student affairs and a necessary step to creating an ethical environment where issues are openly explored. By creating ethical communities in which dialogue is considered essential to practice, student affairs professionals have the opportunity to model for students ways to respond to ethical dilemmas. Ideally, such conversations help create communities where collaboration and problem solving are the norm. When that type of cooperation and partnership exists across the various functional areas of student affairs, the increased communication and openness create an excellent foundation for managing ethical challenges. By focusing on common ground and identifying possible stakeholders in the resolution of any ethical dilemmas, it is possible to find solutions with which everyone can live (Fried). Finding shared principles and priorities benefits the community and leads to more effective solutions. Nash, Bradley, and Chickering (2008) advocated the value and necessity of higher education institutions creating unique campus cultures where "moral conversations" can occur and controversial topics, such as individual rights versus group safety, can be carefully explored and examined.

From a practical standpoint, Dickerson (2006) suggested that campuses "develop collaborative risk-management teams that will identify risks, evaluate and implement solutions, and train members of the campus community to act in ways that promote health and safety and also avoid or minimize physical and legal risks" (p. 39). Many colleges operate a risk management team whose job it is to react to problematic situations and student behaviors as well as anticipate and prepare for potential difficulties. These teams can lead to increased coordination and more timely decision making. The Bazelon Center for Mental Health Law (2007), in its model policy for supporting students with mental health needs, suggests that campuses create committees that can assist in resolving challenging situations and preventing discrimination toward students with mental health concerns.

Regardless of how it is done, student affairs professionals must accumulate effective and practical tools and strategies to address ethical concerns on campus. "There are many times, perhaps each day, that student affairs professionals, especially when acting in helping roles, face decisions that have professional ethical implications" (Winston & Saunders, 1998, p. 90). Avoiding ethical issues is not a prudent or realistic approach; conflicts between individuals' rights and needs and an institution's demands are inevitable. The growing complexity of who our students are, the increasing expectations for accountability, and the litigious nature of our society mean that the ethical challenges we face as helpers will continue to demand that we be prepared to effectively face these issues.

Preparation and Training for Addressing Ethical Issues on Campus

Despite the importance of ethics in higher education and the expectation that all student affairs professionals have ethical reasoning and decision making as a basic competency to effectively do their work, the student affairs literature rarely discusses how to best prepare new professionals to face those challenges. Many times ethical issues are integrated into preparation program curricula rather than being addressed in a stand-alone course. Nash (1997) provided an example of an ethics seminar used to teach ethical literacy and problem-solving skills. By emphasizing a problem-solving approach, Nash assists his students in the reflection and decision-making process so that they have the tools to address the myriad ethical challenges, anticipated and unanticipated, that will occur throughout their career. He uses ethics briefs and case dilemmas that allow graduate students to ask questions, reflect, discuss, disagree, problem-solve, and fully engage in the complex and multifaceted issues involved in any ethical dilemma.

Janosik (2005) also made some important suggestions to assist student affairs practitioners in their preparation. First, he suggested that they learn from the expertise of other professionals on their campus in a proactive manner. Some peers have more experience and have attended more conferences, so they have insights that other practitioners might find useful. Utilizing periodicals and written resources that are known to be effective and provide useful information is essential; no one ever has enough time to spend on professional reading, so it must be done judiciously. By scanning the environment and reading

the literature, student affairs professionals are able to anticipate and create a manageable list of potential dilemmas that
could occur on campus. It's important not to take this task on
alone; sensitize and involve colleagues in preparation. Using the
Internet and available Listservs (e.g., www.suicide.org) effectively and discriminately can help maximize exposure to vital
information without becoming overwhelmed. It can also be very
useful to follow the activities of local, state, and federal government officials who might affect one's work; being aware of possible legislation that is being developed in reaction to particular
events helps one be more prepared. Many legislatures have been
exploring legislative responses to try to prevent events similar to
those that occurred on the Virginia Tech campus. For example,
several states have been exploring legislation that requires that
students who express suicidal or violent thoughts and behaviors be mandated to receive counseling or removed from campus. Being aware of various educational or advocacy groups that
may be concerned about some of these important issues, such as
the Jed Foundation, can provide vital information and insight.
Finally, developing personal networks of student affairs professionals across the country through conferences and other educational opportunities can assist professionals in their thinking
and preparation. Having the proper insight, knowledge, and
resources helps practitioners in their efforts to respond effectively and proactively to the many ethical challenges that await
them on campus.

Becoming an ethical professional is a never-ending process (Winek & Jones, 1996). There is no defined end point at
which one arrives fully knowing how to effectively and ethically
respond to all the issues and dynamics that can occur on campus. Through "supervision, consultation, and continuous dialogue with other professionals, as well as continuing education
and staying current with the literature" (Winek & Jones, p. 66),
student affairs practitioners can evolve into thoughtful, humane,

and ethical professionals and helpers who fully embrace the ethical principles of the field.

Summary

It is essential that student affairs professionals are aware of the unique and inevitable ethical dilemmas and circumstances that may occur whenever they help students. Having insight about potential ethical concerns, knowledge about professional standards and ethical codes, and strategies to respond to the challenging and sometimes confounding dilemmas that occur as part of student affairs work will help prepare them to address such issues with confidence. This chapter discussed the common ethical concerns facing student affairs professionals and provided information on available resources and strategies to cope with ethical dilemmas. "As the work of student affairs proceeds amidst the ethical challenges within higher education and society, giving greater attention and effort to the field of ethics is both timely and vital to the future of the profession" (Janosik et al., 2004, p. 371).

Chapter Four

Underlying and Relevant Helping Theories

John A. Mueller

For nearly every profession, theories are fundamental to purpose and practice; for that reason they are core to a profession. Theories provide insight and explanation for phenomena and problems encountered in practice, they supply a common language for professionals, they offer guidance in the prescription of appropriate interventions, they help practitioners predict outcomes of those interventions, and they can help frame and guide research to expand a profession's knowledge base (Evans, Forney, & Guido-DiBrito, 1998). Says Krumboltz about the significance of theories in professional practice: "The way we think about problems determines to a large degree what we will do about them" (cited in Parrot, 2003, p. 73).

In applied professions, such as student affairs and counseling, theory is important to understanding and improving the knowledge base and professional practice. The student affairs literature offers much discussion about the value of theory in relation to practice and research (Evans, Forney, et al., 1998; Knefelkamp, Widick, & Parker, 1978; McEwen, 2003; Upcraft, 1993). Similarly, nearly every counseling theory and technique textbook addresses theory as an important facet of the profession's knowledge base and practice (cf. Brammer, 1993; George & Cristiani, 1995; Ivey, D'Andrea, Bradford Ivey, & Simek-Morgan, 2007; Nystul, 2006; Peterson & Nisenholz, 1995; Sharf, 1996).

The purpose of this chapter is to review the counseling theories that may inform student affairs practitioners in their role as helpers. This chapter begins with a discussion of the history of theory in the student affairs profession, establishing theory as a core competency for student affairs practitioners. Following this is an examination of six families of counseling theory in terms of their philosophies and goals, techniques, strengths and liabilities, and relevance in student affairs settings. This chapter concludes with a discussion on the value of having a personal theory of helping, along with suggestions for developing and articulating one.

History of Student Affairs Theory

McEwen (2003) submits, "Theory, some formal, some informal, has no doubt existed in student affairs from the very beginning" (p. 168). While there is evidence of management and organizational theories among the early theories of the profession, McEwen observes that most of the theories were psychological in nature. Moore and Upcraft (1990) offer a historical perspective on the evolution of student development theory in higher education that describes the psychological and sociological influences on student affairs practitioners' understanding of college students. They propose that the principle of in loco parentis was the first student development theory because it dictated the way college professionals viewed and worked with students. By the turn of the twentieth century, psychological theories developed by Freud, Jung, Skinner, and Rogers began to influence the way professionals thought about college students. Yet, argue Moore and Upcraft, these early theories were not specific to the development that occurs during late adolescence and early adulthood. It was the work of Erikson and Piaget that had greater relevance for the profession's current understanding of student development because they, respectively, drew attention to psychosocial (i.e., identity) development and to cognitive development. Another influence on the history of student development theory was the vocational guidance movement of the early twentieth century that emphasized the importance of exploring and finding meaningful work and career plans. By the mid-twentieth century, as higher education became more accessible to broader and more diverse populations, additional theories that examined the many dimensions of that diversity were developed, focusing on race, gender, sexual orientation, and faith, as well as adult learning, multiple intelligences, and learning styles.

Starting in the 1960s, the evolution of a developmental theory in student affairs accelerated and expanded. Emerging from this evolution was an organization of theories into six "families" that have become the theoretical bedrock of the profession (Evans, Forney, et al., 1998; Knefelkamp et al., 1978; McEwen, 2003; Pascarella & Terenzini, 2005). The *psychosocial* theories focus on the content of students' lives—the developmental tasks they encounter, that, to the degree they are resolved, contribute to identity. The *cognitive-structural* theories are concerned with the structure of thinking and how students make meaning of their experiences in increasingly complex ways about matters of morality, faith, and knowledge. The *social identity development* models detail the identity development of college students in terms of their race, gender, and sexual orientation. A departure from the previous families of theories, which focus on change in college students, *typology* models focus on differences in how students perceive and respond to the world around them. The *person-environment* theories focus less on the individual's internal processes and instead emphasize the significant influence of the collegiate environment (from the physical elements to the human aggregate) on student change and development. Related to the environmental theories, but composing a family of their own, are the *college impact* models, which address the dynamics that are unique to a college campus and which influence student involvement and students' decisions to persist in or depart from a particular institution.

Theories as a Core Competence

Because the student affairs field is broad and interdisciplinary, a multitude of theories actually inform the profession. The theories most commonly associated with the profession are student development theories. But it is important to acknowledge that theories about management, leadership, supervision, and organizational development also apply to many functional areas and levels of the profession. Still, the student development theories are most relevant to the discussion of the core counseling theories that this chapter discusses in greater detail because they share a similar philosophy of human growth and development and a common understanding of how students form their identity and perceive and make meaning of their experiences.

Pope, Reynolds, and Mueller (2004) argue that the skill of *theory and translation* is one of the seven core competencies of the student affairs practitioner. This competency involves a deep and comprehensive knowledge of relevant theories that are applicable across the profession. It also involves a thorough understanding of models, mechanisms, and techniques for translating theory into practice, including activities such as individual and group interventions, supervision, and helping and advising. Finally, this competency involves learning to critically examine the assumptions, biases, strengths, and liabilities of these theories in a variety of institutional and cultural contexts.

Although the core competency of theory and translation may be regarded as the "theory competency," the integrated and fluid nature of the Dynamic Model of Student Affairs Competence (Pope et al., 2004, p. 10) suggests that theory is incorporated into each of the remaining core competencies. This is certainly true of the *helping and advising* competency. While Pope et al.'s discussion of this competency does not address how counseling theories fit within the student affairs core competency of helping and advising, familiarity with counseling theories can inform and enhance practitioners' skills in the helping process.

While they may not have the training and knowledge of counselors, therapists, and other mental health professionals, student affairs practitioners should possess adequate knowledge and skills in helping students cope with the problems associated with the college experience. Formal training on and deep knowledge of counseling theories is not essential for helpers; however, familiarity with them can be useful and can inform and enhance practitioners' skills in the helping process. Winston (2003) suggests that while counselors and therapists are better equipped and more focused on serious problems—such as alcohol and drug abuse, depression, eating disorders, and suicidal ideation—student affairs practitioners may be more helpful in assisting students with problems related to the development tasks they face (Chickering & Reisser, 1993), such as transition to college, interpersonal relationships, academic and career decisions, and negotiating the college environment.

Illustrations of Counseling Theory Across Functional Areas

Counseling theory is most certainly applicable across all the primary functional areas within student affairs. Identifying some examples of how various programs and departments can incorporate these theories into their work is important, so that professionals can see these theories and the perspectives and strategies they provide as helpful. These various functional areas can be grouped into the following core areas: (1) counseling-oriented positions like career and personal counseling; (2) leadership development and educational positions (e.g., student activities, Greek affairs, campus life, health and wellness, and residence life); (3) administrative positions like dean of students, judicial affairs, and admissions; and (4) academic affairs positions (e.g., advisement and academic support services).

The use and application of counseling theory seems the most obvious within the counseling area, where much of the work focuses on assisting students with personal, social, and vocational concerns. When helping students with a variety of issues— including relationships, self-esteem, academic and career uncertainty, and overall self-exploration—it is important to have a way to conceptualize the help that you provide. Determining whether you want to address the underlying roots of students' current concerns, to discuss how their thinking and behavior may be exacerbating the problem or helping them cope, or to explore how the environment is contributing in both positive and negative ways is key to providing effective and meaningful support to them. Addressing your underlying assumptions or orientation to the helping process and applying theories is important whether you deliver the services one-on-one or in a group setting.

Within leadership development and educational positions, helping skills and underlying theories are needed for both individual and group interventions. The mind-set and the theories you draw from will vary depending on whether you are dealing with a crisis situation, a group conflict, or a supervisory concern. If a student is in crisis, often the need for immediate relief and quick solutions pulls for a particular type of approach or theoretical perspective. When addressing group dynamic issues, having an understanding of the larger context and environmental influences is as important as knowing the students involved. And if in the process of supervision a supervisor becomes aware that a student leader is not completing required tasks, the approach may need to encompass an understanding of the long-standing personal issues that are interfering with the leader's performance. Without an understanding of helping theories and their accompanying strategies and techniques, addressing these unique situations in the most productive manner is more difficult.

Administrative roles might be the ones that are expected to incorporate counseling theory the least. However, anytime student affairs professionals are in helping roles, they need to have some guiding framework that determines how they perceive the goals of, approach to, and desired outcome of the interaction. This is no different when dealing with the varied tasks of an administrator. Some of the same theories that inform leadership and educational roles certainly apply to administrative positions. When administrators have to deliver difficult news, whether it is a seemingly harsh judicial ruling to a student or news of a student's death to a parent, it is most helpful to have a theoretical grounding to assist in implementing helping skills. Understanding the importance of rapport, genuineness, and positive regard in these types of situations is vital to success. Facilitating the growth of a student worker or new professional requires an understanding of how to empower that person and challenge any self-defeating thoughts that s/he may have that are interfering with her/his development. In fact, the use of counseling theories is an important component of addressing administrative issues.

Finally, addressing how academic affairs' unique interactions with students may benefit from helping theories is important. To respond without theoretical grounding increases the likelihood that practitioners will have a limited understanding of the best way to approach a problem. Being able to help students uncover the personal issues that are interfering with their ability to perform and succeed academically is easier to accomplish when one uses a framework that provides a rationale for focusing on the student's innermost feelings, her/his overarching thoughts and expectations, or the impact of the environment. Counseling theories can certainly provide that framework.

Essential Counseling and Helping Theories

The counseling profession has its own set of theories, just as the student affairs profession does. While student development theories focus on students, their growth and development, and the factors that influence these processes, counseling theories focus on personality and human development, the sources of psychological distress and discomfort, and the goals and techniques used to bring about symptom relief and positive mental health and well-being. Pedersen (1999) describes the primary categories of theories as four "forces" of psychology. These include psychodynamic, behavioral, humanistic, and multicultural. These four forces—as well as two other theoretical approaches, systems/family and eclectic—are discussed in greater detail in this section. The discussion of each of these approaches is framed by the following themes: definition and brief history; philosophy and key concepts; goals and techniques of therapy; strengths and limitations; and finally, relevance of the approach to student affairs' helping roles.

Psychodynamic/Psychoanalytic

The psychodynamic approach to counseling is based on psychoanalytic theory, the earliest of psychological theories. The earliest formulations of psychoanalytic theory are credited to Sigmund Freud, whose work began in the late nineteenth century. Schultz and Schultz (2001) observe that Freud's work was so significant that it has remained influential for more than a century and has been the basis for personality theories developed since that build on Freud's work, respond to it, or oppose it. Other psychoanalytic theorists who followed Freud—including Carl Jung, Alfred Adler, and Karen Horney—adapted Freud's concept of unconscious processes (i.e., mental functioning that is beyond our awareness), as well as his ideas about how the personality is organized (i.e., id, ego, and superego).

The basic philosophy of the psychoanalytic approach emphasizes the unconscious mind, biological impulses, family relationships, as well as past developmental histories—all of which contribute to underlying forces of the human personality. This approach assumes that these forces are often in conflict with one another and are a source of anxiety. As such, this approach proposes that gaining knowledge about, and insight into, past developmental histories can reveal the unconscious roots and motivations of present behavior.

The goals, then, of psychodynamic therapy are to bring unconscious material into consciousness and to strengthen the ego, the conscious level of the mind that is responsible for reconciling our most basic instincts and drives with the demands and expectations of our immediate environment (e.g., parents and family) as well as the larger society. Okun (2002) details a number of ways these goals may be realized, including questioning and interpreting content, dream analysis, free association, and analysis of resistance (e.g., defense mechanisms). In sum, the principal means of helping people and changing behavior in the psychodynamic approach is talk therapy by which one can work through and resolve past or recent developmental issues.

Despite its long-standing and highly influential role in counseling theory, the psychodynamic approach is not without its limitations. First, the use of this approach requires extensive study and supervised practice, typically by those who have undergone psychoanalysis themselves. Second, it requires a great amount of time (typically years) and highly verbal clients to be effective, making it largely inaccessible to most individuals (Ivey, Ivey, & Simek-Morgan, 1993). Third, the approach has a pessimistic and deterministic view of human nature, with concepts that are based on the study of unhealthy people, classified as neurotics. Finally, the approach rests on premises and concepts that are difficult to observe, measure, and test (e.g., the unconscious).

Still, the psychodynamic approach, and the psychoanalytic theory on which it rests, has had an enormous influence on psychologists, counselors, and helpers of all kinds. Our tendency to understand human behavior as a function of past developmental experiences, inner forces, and ego defenses largely results from psychoanalytic theory's emphasis on these factors.

Relevance to student affairs helping roles. While no student affairs practitioner or helper would be expected to employ this approach, aspects of the psychodynamic approach may inform and be relevant to student affairs practitioners in helping roles. First, this approach can remind helpers of the potential impact of unconscious factors that lie beneath surface problems. This can encourage helpers to, as one practitioner put it, "listen to the music, not just the words" when working with students. Making students more aware of unconscious forces, in a non-threatening and nonauthoritative way, can be useful when they are not aware of some of their feelings, behaviors, and contradicting thoughts. Second, basic concepts from psychoanalytic theory, such as anxiety and defense mechanisms, provide a framework for understanding the many and various ways (from adaptive to nonadaptive) that students may cope with their past and current issues (Hall, 1983).

An example of a student affairs professional who incorporates this approach in helping a student might be one who is meeting with a distressed student on the verge of being dismissed from the institution because he is having difficulty meeting deadlines for courses and other administrative tasks, like submitting financial aid forms. Through their discussions, the practitioner may become aware that the student's behaviors are really a form of self-sabotage, a function of an underlying anxiety and fear about not being able to perform well in college. Procrastination and carelessness, in the student's unconscious mind, are better excuses for being dismissed than his own perceived inability. The helper can bring this to the student's attention, and together they can focus on the actual problem: the student's fears about academic competence.

Cognitive-Behavioral

Cognitive-behavioral therapy (CBT) has its origins in the mid-twentieth century and can be traced to the work of John B. Watson in the 1920s and B. F. Skinner in the 1950s. Both psychologists argued that to help people, we must be able to objectively observe, measure, evaluate, and respond to overt cognitions, emotions, and behaviors. Since feelings, thoughts, needs, drives, unconscious memories, and other internal forces and processes do not lend themselves well to scientific scrutiny and understanding, they are not helpful in assisting individuals with life's problems and challenges. Between the 1950s and 1980s, such theorists as Albert Ellis, Albert Bandura, and David Meichenbaum broadened the behavioral approach to the cognitive-behavioral approach by focusing on how cognitive processes—such as learned responses, beliefs, expectancies, and appraisals—can influence emotions and behaviors.

The goals of CBT reflect the underlying philosophical assumption of this approach, which is, simply put, to cure "unreason by reason" (George & Cristiani, 1995, p. 115). In other words, CBT focuses on replacing irrational or unproductive thoughts, ideas, and attitudes with rational and productive ideas and attitudes. Another goal of this approach is to learn and to develop new and more socially desired behaviors designed to enhance coping and functioning in one's environment (Ivey et al., 2007; Peterson & Nisenholz, 1995). Accomplishing these goals can minimize or eliminate emotional disturbances and maladaptive behaviors.

Strategies to address these faulty ways of thinking include confronting the irrational thoughts, demonstrating new ways of thinking about life events and circumstances, teaching coping skills and self-control behaviors, engaging the client in guided imagery, facilitating systematic desensitization for anxiety, and role playing to change behaviors. Another common technique is to assign homework to raise clients' awareness of their thoughts outside the counseling setting.

Cognitive-behavioral theories, because of their objective nature and their focus on the symptom (behavior) of problems, are viewed quite positively by some. Their effectiveness is easier to measure and evaluate than some other theories (i.e., psychodynamic and humanistic) and, thus, are well supported by research. Also, the focus on specific strategies for specific symptoms can lead to quicker, more efficient, and cheaper treatments. Finally, the many techniques and strategies of these approaches have wide applicability in a number of clinical and educational settings.

Critics of the approach argue, on the other hand, that this approach reduces the complexity of human personality to simple units of behavior or thought. Related to this is the deterministic nature of these theories, suggesting that humans merely respond to reinforcements in the environment, with little free will, creativity, or ability to reach their individual and innate potential. The CBT approach to counseling also tends to be viewed as mechanical (i.e., application of specific techniques) and overly directed by the counselor (i.e., little emphasis on the client's inner ability and potential). Finally, Okun (2002) points out that an assumption of the cognitive-behavioral approach is that it is not the social forces themselves that impact a person's feelings and behaviors but how the person thinks about those social forces. This, Okun argues, may result in people who experience oppression because of their race, gender, or sexual orientation to feel as though they are to blame for their feelings and resultant behaviors.

Relevance to student affairs helping roles. Student affairs practitioners might find this approach very useful to their work as helpers. First, this approach emphasizes the specific and overt behaviors that practitioners often attend to with students. This approach has great appeal because of its orientation toward action. Second, this approach emphasizes the influential role of the environment, which is, again, the realm of the student affairs practitioner (Strange & Banning, 2001). Practitioners are often aware of and responsive to environmental conditions that may influence student behaviors. Finally, as noted earlier, this approach provides an array of techniques and strategies that can be easily learned and employed in a number of settings and situations. It is not uncommon for practitioners to do training on

contracting with a student or assessing and altering reinforcements in the environment, teaching various coping and life
skills (e.g., time management, conflict resolution, career exploration), and applying the principle of cognitive dissonance (Evans,
Forney, et al., 1998) to encourage students to think more com-
plexly about difficult situations and issues (e.g., lack of assertiveness or intolerance of differences).

An example of this approach in practice might be the student affairs professional who is working with a student in his
senior year who is disheartened by his job search and has suddenly stopped applying to jobs. The student reports that his first
two interviews resulted in rejection letters. During the conversation, the student states that he will never get a job because
"these rejections obviously mean I am not capable or competi-
tive." The professional addresses the faulty reasoning that is
leading to the student's feelings and behaviors. Together they
discuss the realities of the job search and how his first two experiences with rejection need not dictate his prospects for finding a
job. Other applications could involve practitioners working with
students who engage in unproductive or undesirable behaviors,
such as procrastination, constant Internet surfing, toxic relationships, or nail-biting. The practitioner may discuss what events
and circumstances trigger, and even reinforce, these behaviors.
Once the reinforcements are identified, the student can attempt
to reduce or eliminate them and develop new behaviors with
new reinforcements and rewards.

Humanistic

The term *humanistic psychology* was first used in the 1930s, by
Gordon Allport, and flourished in the 1960s and 1970s with
the work of Carl Rogers and Abraham Maslow. It was developed in response to the two prevailing forces in American psychology, psychoanalysis and behaviorism, which were argued
to be too limited and too pessimistic in their views of human

nature. Humanistic psychology focuses on the positive aspects of humans—including their strengths, creativity, free will, virtues, and potential—exploring "what people are like at their best, not just at their worst" (Schultz & Schultz, 2001, p. 281). Also located within this theoretical family is Gestalt theory, which focuses on self-awareness and accepting responsibility for one's experiences and behaviors.

There are a number of related theoretical terms (i.e., phenomenological, person-centered, experiential, affective, and existentialism) that are sometimes used interchangeably with humanism and that share its underlying philosophy: that human beings have a natural desire to grow and the ability to reach their fullest potential. Problems (i.e., psychological pain) occur when individuals are not able to invest their full energies and capabilities to resolve the conflicts and overcome the obstacles that life may present (Peterson & Nisenholz, 1995). This philosophy is best represented by several concepts. First, humanistic theories focus on the present, the here and now, rather than the past or even the future. What is most important, then, is the individual's unique and actual experience and how s/he perceives and feels. Second, these theories assume that people possess the ability to make meaning of their experiences and are free to make choices. As a result, they are ultimately responsible for the choices they make. Third, these theories stress the self-concept, or how individuals view themselves. When their self-concept is congruent with their experiences and when their behaviors are consistent with their self-concept, the result is psychological well-being and wholeness. Finally, these theories emphasize emotions and the impact emotions can have on thoughts and behaviors. As such, they place great importance on the awareness of feelings and the process of working with feelings.

The goals of humanistic counseling include helping individuals explore and gain an awareness of and comfort with their feelings, understanding the full range of their choices and the responsibility that comes with the choices they make, and helping them accept and integrate their experiences with their self-concept. The mechanism for change in this approach relies heavily on focusing on the individual and on the authentic relationship between the client and the counselor. Also emphasized are the present (as opposed to the past), understanding (as opposed to interpretation), and issues and themes (as opposed to specific and immediate problems).

Despite its appeal to many practitioners and counselors, the humanistic approach is not without its critics. One criticism is that many of the concepts contained in this set of theories (e.g., self-concept, self-actualization, meaning of experiences) are vague and highly subjective, making them difficult to evaluate or verify scientifically. Another criticism is this approach's tendency, with respect to treatment, to minimize or even disregard the client's past history as a source of problems. In addition, the passive techniques employed (e.g., reflecting) in this approach may not be suitable for individuals who need structure or direction (e.g., someone in crisis). Finally, Okun (2002) argues that the emphasis on individual responsibility and self-determination may disregard cultural differences and the realities of oppression, limiting the applicability of these concepts and the established techniques to marginalized groups. Still, regardless of these criticisms, the work of humanistic theorists has had a remarkable impact on the counseling profession. Ivey et al. (2007) note that the humanistic approach to counseling (particularly the focus on the client-counselor relationship) permeates all other counseling practice regardless of theoretical orientation or the practitioner's level of professional preparation.

Relevance to student affairs helping roles. The already noted goals, techniques, and strengths of the humanistic approach to counseling are very appealing to student affairs practitioners in their helping roles. The underlying philosophy of the humanistic approach is consistent with the profession's emphasis on the potential for growth, student responsibility, and the importance of creating and maintaining mutually respectful and trusting practitioner-student relationships. Many of the specific skills that are characteristic of this approach lend themselves well to the preparation and training of student affairs professionals and paraprofessionals and are useful across a wide range of personal and interpersonal problems. These skills include empathetic and accurate listening, open-ended questions, attending skills, nonverbal behaviors, and reflecting on content and feelings. Effectively implementing these skills can help students feel understood, respected, and accepted—all of which allow them to safely explore their feelings.

An example of this theoretical approach in action is the practitioner who is approached by a student who, after ending a long-term relationship with someone, is starting to date again. She tells the student affairs practitioner that in her dating history she has only dated one person at a time and asks whether it is all right to have multiple dating partners. While the practitioner has a personal perspective and beliefs about the issue, she keeps them to herself and allows the student to explore her own needs and wants as well as her value system and self-concept. Through their conversations, the student makes a decision about her future dating behavior that feels right and comfortable for her.

Systems/Family

Most counseling approaches focus on the problems of the individual. The systems/family approach emphasizes an individual's interactions within the family or other social units (such as schools, neighborhoods, or workplaces) and the degree to which these interactions contribute to, maintain, and define that individual's psychological problems or issues. System/family theories move the focus from the intrapersonal to the interpersonal. The roots of this approach can be found in the work of John Bell and Gregory Bateson in the 1950s and 1960s.

The main philosophical assumption in this approach is that an individual's mental health cannot be understood and addressed independent of her/his primary family context (and other relevant social systems). Okun (1997) details three important concepts of this approach: (1) the individual is a system of interacting components, such as affective, cognitive, and physiological; (2) the individual is also a member of a family, as well as a broader social context, such as the school, the workplace, faith communities, and political institutions; and (3) an individual's psychological distress may be a function of difficulties within a social system as much as it might be from internal problems. When examining the social system in particular, Ivey et al. (2007) point out that the relationships, the rules (norms), and the roles are specific concepts that must also be considered.

The goals of therapy in this approach are as much (if not more so) to bring about awareness and change in the social system (e.g., the family) as in the individual. While symptom reduction in the individual is important, what is paramount is the healthy psychological functioning of the family unit. Ivey et al. (2007) observe that this approach has been particularly effective in treating issues such as anxiety, conduct disorders, eating disorders, and drug abuse. Systems/family theories commonly use techniques from other theories—such as psychodynamic, humanistic, or cognitive-behavioral approaches—with all members of the family at one time, with certain members, or with the parents only.

As with the other theoretical orientations, these theories have their benefits and their limitations. Among the benefits is the perspective offered by this approach: that some psychological issues do not exist in a vacuum and should therefore not be treated as such. Because humans are social beings and are active in a variety of social networks, attention to those contexts in treating mental health issues is an important and helpful consideration for counselors. There is strong evidence in the literature that supports the significance and effectiveness of this approach. The systems/family approach has been successfully applied in a variety of social units, including group homes, social groups, businesses, and college residence hall communities. This approach also emphasizes the whole and the parts. It provides a framework for understanding individual functioning and development—as well as an individual's affective, cognitive, and behavioral domains—embedded in larger contexts such as family, school, and the workplace. This adds richness and depth to understanding and responding to psychological concerns.

On the other hand, some critics believe that this richness and depth can lead to complexity and intensity that can become overwhelming for the counselor, and thus, effective use of this approach requires significant training and supervision (Okun, 2002). Ivey et al. (2007) also note that counselors must reconceptualize and expand their notions of family beyond Western, Euro-American, patriarchal constructions of a "normal" family to include a single parent, same-sex parents, or grandparents acting as primary caretakers. Limited or biased notions about how a "healthy" family is constructed can make applying family therapy unsuccessful and potentially harmful.

Relevance to student affairs helping roles. Student affairs practitioners, although rarely dealing with families when helping students, can make good use of many of this approach's principles. First, as Okun (2002) notes, this approach makes clear the importance of environmental variables (e.g., family) in the creation and/or maintenance of problems. As an example, Okun suggests that the first-year college student who experiences homesickness in the form of depression or anxiety when returning to campus after a weekend at home may actually be dealing with guilt and anxiety related to leaving at home two parents who are in a very unstable marital relationship. The focus of helping would be more effective with this student if it acknowledged family dynamics and dysfunctions rather than just the student's problems (Okun). Second, more recent literature on characteristics of today's college students (Coomes & DeBard, 2004) highlights the importance of families in students' lives. Oftentimes, family closeness is regarded as a source of support for students; however, it also can be a source of stress for the student and may need to be addressed when helping students face the pressures of college. Finally, since college students often participate in a variety of social groups and social settings, practitioners may find that extending the principles of systems theory or family therapy to groups—such as fraternities or sororities, residence hall floors, RA staff teams, athletic teams, and choral groups—may help not only individuals in psychological distress but also the development and health of these larger social circles.

As an example of this approach, consider the student who comes to a practitioner about her frustration with her fellow orientation leaders, explaining that the staff gossips a lot. She comments that it has reached a point where she has chosen to distance herself from the group, focusing only on the tasks of the job and not on the social aspect of being on the team. The practitioner and the student may discuss healthy ways of dealing with the intragroup conflict by choosing healthier behaviors for the student, such as not engaging in gossip, confronting others who come to her to gossip, or initiating a dialogue among her fellow orientation leaders to openly discuss the issue and develop strategies to improve communication and relationships, which will benefit the whole group.

Multicultural/Feminist

The multicultural/feminist approach to counseling and helping does not embrace any particular theoretical model previously discussed and may, in fact, effectively integrate components of all of them in practice. What distinguishes this social justice approach is that it questions the relevance of these aforementioned approaches to women and to other marginalized groups

(Okun, 2002) and advocates that they be applied in culturally meaningful and sensitive ways (Ivey et al., 2007). The multicultural/feminist approach is regarded as the fourth theoretical force that emerged in the mental health profession in the latter half of the twentieth century.

Accounting for culture in counseling and human interaction is fundamental to the philosophy of the multicultural/feminist approach, which assumes that the causes and maintenance of psychological distress and mental illness must be understood and treated within a sociocultural context. In addition to having different ways of defining conditions of mental health, various groups and cultures may have meaningful and equally effective ways of addressing mental health issues or problems that differ from those based in Western, European, and male perspectives and traditions (Okun, 2002).

The primary goals of therapy, then, in this approach are as follows: (1) to help clients to see how their problems may be rooted in or are a reflection of societal issues about race, gender, class, and so on; (2) to empower and "strengthen clients' sense of efficacy and broaden their options and opportunities" (Okun, 2002, p. 152); and (3) to enhance clients' identity related to race, gender, sexual orientation, and so on and to help them understand the implications of their identity in terms of the interactions they have with those who do and don't share that identity. Okun (2002) and Ivey et al. (2007) also note that the pursuit of these goals is enhanced when the counselor is sensitive to how the client views the world and relationships, as well as cultural norms about language, space, time, and expression of emotions. Finally, Okun submits that counselors must be self-aware in terms of their biases, attitudes, and the influence of their own social identities.

To accomplish the goals just outlined, the counselor may employ and integrate strategies from the psychodynamic, cognitive-behavioral, and/or humanistic approaches. Ivey et al. (2007) provide examples of what this might look like. For instance, the cognitive-behavioral approach provides the counselor with strategies aimed at helping the client learn new behaviors, such as assertiveness or self-management, or understanding and eliminating irrational beliefs that are a product of internalized oppression. Counselors may use the humanistic approach in their efforts to help clients understand themselves, their reality, and their responsibility for the decisions they make in forming healthy and genuine connections with others. Ivey et al. suggest other techniques that extend from the multicultural/feminist approach. For example, counselors may collaborate with individuals and resources in the client's typical or traditional helping networks. This network may include the client's immediate and/or extended family, spiritual advisers, neighbors, and traditional healers, such as Native American medicine men.

With respect to the strengths and weaknesses of this approach, Ivey et al. (2007) sum it up well in their observation that this approach provides as much challenge as opportunity. Among the challenges are the time, effort, commitment, and personal investment this approach requires to develop the awareness, knowledge, and skills that underscore it. The requisite knowledge alone is quite demanding: knowledge of traditional approaches to counseling; the sociopolitical environment and its relation to oppression; and the histories, needs, strengths, values, resources, and developmental processes of a wide range of multicultural groups. Also, given that this approach is relatively new, the research base on various techniques and their effectiveness is still small (but growing). Finally, Corey (2001) believes that a possible limitation of this approach is the potential for counselors to impose a set of values on their clients, rather than let them decide which values to live by. However, this criticism is probably valid for all theoretical approaches. Still, as Ivey et al. note, the multicultural/feminist approach is highly practical in that it compels counselors to face and account for the reality of differences and power in our society. It also adds a new dimension by acknowledging and incorporating a sociocultural context to our conceptualization of mental health and well-being, expanding the domains beyond the intrapersonal and the interpersonal. Finally, the principles and interventions of this approach can be incorporated into and enhance other therapy approaches.

Relevance to student affairs helping roles. The multicultural/feminist perspective has done much to inform and influence the work of student affairs practitioners in their many varied roles, including the helping role. This is especially evident in the multicultural competencies that Reynolds and Pope (2003) have outlined in the student affairs helping context, which include increasing one's awareness of biases and attitudes; understanding cultural concepts and differences in cultural groups; developing culturally sensitive responses; understanding the dynamics that exist when working with someone who is culturally different from oneself; deconstructing assumptions and values that underlie the counseling process; and developing advocacy skills that reshape the institutional environment and support the work that happens in the one-on-one helping relationship.

An example of this approach in a student affairs helping situation might be the practitioner who is helping an African American first-year female student who has come to college from a largely white neighborhood and is finding her transition to a highly diverse, highly selective state college more difficult than she anticipated. She has experienced a number of situations with other black students, and white students, who have questioned her self-perceptions about her race, even referring to her as an Oreo. As the student recalls these situations, she describes an assortment of feelings—from guilt, to confusion, to anger. At one point, in anger, she tells the helper, "If being seen as white means that I'm smart, hard working, and trustworthy, then I'd rather people see me as white." The helper in this role, aware that this student may be encountering her racial identity for the first time, allows her to sort through and explore these feelings. The helper may also encourage the student to talk about what being black means and what being white means. Together the two may strategize ways the student can explore her racial heritage and history. There are a number of strategies from other counseling approaches that might be appropriate here and could empower the student to understand her experiences, feelings, and behaviors in the context of race and racism.

Eclectic/Transactional

Eclectic is defined as "drawn from many sources" (Parrott, 2003, p. 406). In the counseling profession, practitioners who identify as eclectic are very familiar with and trained in all the theoretical families presented thus far and know when, where, and how to use them to meet the various needs of their clients. The term is commonly misunderstood and misused by people less acquainted with it as a counseling orientation. Indeed, eclecticism does not mean the absence of a theoretical orientation. Nor does it mean random and incoherent use of a grab bag of counseling principles and techniques. To be eclectic in one's orientation means to intentionally synthesize the assumptions, principles, and techniques from many viewpoints and to systematically and consistently apply them in therapy based on solid empirical support (Brammer, 1993; Peterson & Nisenholz, 1995). The genesis of this theoretical orientation—also referred to as integrative, multimodal, transtheoretical, or transactional—dates as far back as the 1930s but gained momentum in the 1960s, when it became as respectable to draw from multiple approaches as it was to work within a single theoretical framework.

The underlying philosophy of this approach is to use the theoretical premises and techniques that are most appropriate for a given problem or to fit the approach to the client, not vice versa (per Cavanaugh, as cited in Parrott, 2003). Although his approach emphasizes the technique more than the theoretical underpinning, Lazarus's (1986) multimodal therapy perhaps best exemplifies this approach's key concepts. According to Lazarus, a client's personality is organized in seven interrelated dimensions, all of which need to be attended to in therapy: behavior (observable actions); affect (emotions); sensation (perception through the five senses); imagery (creating mental pictures); cognition (thoughts, ideas, attitudes); interpersonal relationships (nature of one's interactions with others); and drugs (nutrition, drugs, exercise) (Okun, 2002). The acronym BASIC ID is a useful tool to remember these dimensions or modalities.

The goal of therapy, then, is to develop a treatment plan with the client that addresses as many of these modalities as possible. Techniques derived from various theoretical approaches are then applied as appropriate. For example, when attending to strong feelings (the affective modality), techniques from the humanistic approach might be most appropriate. Likewise, when attending to indecision (the cognitive modality), techniques from the cognitive-behavioral would be suitable.

Not surprisingly, the eclectic approach is not without its critics and advocates. Critics of the approach argue that it lacks a coherent and theoretical foundation. This, in turn, may lead a counselor to employ a mixed bag of techniques with no sound rationale, which may be not only ineffective but also unethical (Brown & Srebalus, 2003). Others, however, contend that this integrative approach—when comprehensive, consistent, and systematic in its application—can be highly responsive to individual clients and their unique concerns. Okun (2002) is favorable in her review of the multimodal approach, suggesting that it is easy to learn and use in a variety of settings.

Relevance to student affairs helping roles. For student affairs practitioners, the eclectic approach holds some appeal, since it does not dictate adherence to a particular theory to be used with every student in every circumstance. Also, the eclectic approach may resonate with practitioners because of its emphasis on holistic assessment and interventions (this is particularly true of the BASIC ID multimodal approach). Practitioners are often trained to focus on the affective, behavioral, cognitive, and physical domains. Finally, this approach is reminiscent of process models used to apply student development theory, such as Practice to Theory to Practice (Knefelkamp, Golec, & Wells, 1985) and Grounded Formal Theory (Rogers & Widick, 1980), that urge a review and incorporation of multiple theories in developing individual and campus interventions.

In student affairs practice, the eclectic approach can be very useful in understanding a student's issue and deciding on an appropriate intervention. Take, for example, the heavily involved campus leader who struggles with the decision to accept an invitation from the dean of students to serve on a search committee for a new student activities director. In her discussion with the helper, the stressed and overwhelmed student describes the many demands already placed on her. She fears that saying no to this latest invitation will make her appear unwilling or unable to help out and that her refusal will result in no student representation on this important search committee. The helper may employ a more humanistic (i.e., client-centered) approach with the student, allowing her to explore her feelings about how she sees herself and how she perceives that others see her when she says no. Together the helper and the student discuss how the student can become more comfortable with setting limits. The helper may also approach the situation from a more cognitive-behavioral approach and initiate a discussion about the student's assumption that her refusal to participate means that the committee will not (or cannot) have any form of student representation. Through the discussion, the student may realize that the dean will likely understand her need to decline the offer and will simply approach another student to serve on the committee. Of course, the helper may use aspects of both approaches and facilitate an open discussion about the student's feelings about herself as someone who is allowed to say no as well as the logic she uses to conclude that if she doesn't serve on the committee, it will have no student representation.

This multifaceted approach may lead to an even more fruitful discussion and outcome.

Core Theoretical Helping Assumptions

Evident in each of the described theoretical perspectives is the interaction between the counselor (or helper) and the client (or student). Depending on the theoretical approach, the nature of the relationship and the nature of the interaction, in terms of goals and techniques, will differ. Regardless, each perspective is based on a relationship, and the quality and character of that relationship is worth further consideration.

Corey (2001) suggests that a major contribution of Rogers's client-centered approach to counseling is its emphasis on building a trusting relationship between the client and the helper and that this counseling feature applies to all other therapeutic approaches. Openness on the part of the counselor and the client is central to building this type of relationship (Okun, 2002) and is the foundation for conditions of therapeutic change. Rogers (1967), based on his clinical experience, identified six conditions that were not only sufficient but also necessary for change to occur. The conditions have been synthesized and summarized by a number of scholars (cf. Brammer, 1993; George & Cristiani, 1995; Okun; Sharf, 1996) and are described here:

- *Contact:* The client and the counselor must have contact that has the potential and capability for each to make a difference in the experience of the other. George and Cristiani (1995) suggest that this sets the stage for a "two-way interaction rather than a process where the counselor does something *to* or *for* the client" (p. 62).

- *Incongruence (client):* A core concept in Rogers's theory of personality is that anxiety, stress, fear, and other forms of distress result from an incongruence between the client's self-concept and her/his experience. This state of incongruence (or psychological vulnerability) must be present for the client to engage in counseling. In fact, the more aware the client is of this, the more motivated s/he will be for change.

- *Congruence (counselor):* In a way, the client's incongruence between the self and the experience are a necessary condition, as is the counselor's congruence between the self and the experience. In other words, counselors must be aware of their inner feelings, thoughts, and attitudes in their interactions with clients and must be able to experience them, access them, and express them (verbally and nonverbally) in a way that is genuine, appropriate, and consistent. That is to say, the most effective helpers are those who are able to be fully real and genuine.

- *Unconditional positive regard:* Genuine acceptance of the client's experiences, feelings, behaviors, and attitudes is an important condition for the client to develop positive self-regard, or a sense of worth and ability to grow. This includes accepting all aspects of the client's feelings, actions, and thoughts—the painful and the peculiar as well as the positive. This can be challenging at times and, in some instances, becomes more of a goal than an actuality. Also, unconditional positive regard does not mean the counselor always agrees with the client; rather, it means that the counselor strives not to evaluate or judge the client's positive or negative qualities or to impose her/his own values on the client.

- *Empathy:* Empathy is the primary means to understanding the client. It comes from the German word *einfuhlung,* which means "feeling into." To be empathic, the counselor, as much as is possible, enters the client's internal frame of reference—to try to understand the client as if s/he were the client her/himself.

- *Client perception:* As important as it is for the counselor to convey empathy and positive regard, it is equally important for the client to perceive that and to feel valued and under-stood. When the client experiences and perceives genuine-ness, acceptance, and empathy, therapeutic change is most likely to occur.

Having unconditional positive regard and empathy for the client is meaningless and useless if the counselor does not convey this to the client. Sharf (1996) notes that of these six conditions, Rogers emphasized genuineness, acceptance, and empathy, with the greatest emphasis on genuineness. Rogers believed that if the counselor was genuine in the relationship, that alone could foster growth—even if the unconditional positive regard or empathy was not present. Brammer (1993) observes that there is some controversy over whether Rogers's conditions are necessary and sufficient. For example, while many agree that positive regard is important, fewer believe that it must be unconditional to be helpful. Still, there is wide agree-ment that the conditions that Rogers outlines are desirable and can be incorporated in a variety of therapies.

Norcross (2002) and Prochaska and Norcross (2003) have a slightly different perspective on the essential and sufficient con-ditions of the therapeutic relationship. They assert that, based on clinical and empirical evidence, there is nearly unanimous agreement on the importance of the client-counselor relation-ship across all therapies. In other words, the client-counselor relationship is not solely a feature of the humanistic approach; it is facilitative (and necessary) in the cognitive-behavioral and the psychodynamic approaches as well. Furthermore, they assert that, again based on research evidence, some clients will gain most from a more directive relationship and others from a more nondi-rective relationship (i.e., characteristic of the six conditions just explored). Norcross recommends that therapeutic relationships that contain less warmth and are more directive are most suitable for compliant and less resistant clients as well as clients whose problems are more intrapersonal (e.g., anxiety or negative feelings about self). Conversely, clients who are resistant to or ambivalent about change or who are experiencing interpersonal problems and are focused on relationships may benefit more from a nondirective approach with more warmth. Norcross suggests that therapists can develop a range of therapeutic styles (more warmth vs. less warmth and nondirective vs. directive) and that those with a larger repertoire should, when deciding on an approach, first assess client motivation, resistance, desire, and past experience with varying styles. Prochaska and Norcross suggest that "different folks do indeed do better with different strokes" (p. 551).

Developing a Personal Theory of Helping

As a resident assistant, this author learned an important lesson in a training session on helping skills with students: it is important for the helper to learn and understand a variety of theories and established techniques, but it is also important to recognize that applying these theories and techniques is ultimately an extension of the helper's personality and her/his way of being in the world. This lesson speaks to the importance of developing a personal theory of helping. After having reviewed multiple counseling theories, their similarities and differences as well as the limitations and contributions of their respective concepts and techniques, the helper can decide which concepts are most applicable to a student's concerns and which techniques are most appropriate. It is also the helper's task to develop a personal theory that can be a lens for understanding and describing how students develop and how they change. This portion of the chapter considers the value of developing a personal theory and offers suggestions for creating a personal theory.

Value of Having a Personal Theory

Peterson and Nisenholz (1995) suggest that becoming an effective counselor or helper is not unlike becoming a talented singer, artist, or athlete. The requisite knowledge and core skills of each of these roles must be learned and mastered, but eventually the individual singer's, artist's, or athlete's own style will emerge. The student affairs helper will, likewise, learn, model, practice, and eventually master the knowledge and skills needed to be effective in that role. In the process of doing this, s/he will also develop a personal theory of human nature, growth, and change. To illustrate this point, consider a reference made by Ivey et al. (2007) to a graduate student who, while reading a textbook on counseling theory, reworked the book in her own way: "The book I am rewriting in my head is mine; my own general theory that is similar in some ways to the book, but in other ways very different" (p. 480).

Okun (2002) proposes that we all have a personal theory about human behavior, whether or not we are aware of it or can articulate it. Not only do we possess a personal theory, but that theory affects our actions and behaviors, particularly in interpersonal relationships (such as counseling). While our daily interpersonal interactions affect our personal theory, so too do our family backgrounds, culture and social identities (gender, race, sexual orientation, etc.), socioeconomic status, belief system, education, work environments, and many other important variables.

It is important to recognize, develop, articulate, and express our personal theories for a variety of reasons. First, a personal theory can serve as a reference point for assessing the relative value and contributions of key concepts from a variety of existing formal theoretical perspectives (Okun, 2002; Peterson & Nisenholz, 1995). For some, awareness of a personal theory can become the rationale for adopting a particular theoretical perspective (Peterson & Nisenholz). Second, a personal theory can become a lens for understanding and describing how students develop, how they change, and what influences that change. This knowledge can lead to a set of effective practices and techniques that are consistent with one's personal theory.

This can help professionals develop integrity in their work and to practice what they believe and value (Okun). Finally, George and Cristiani (1995) point out that counselors without a cohesive set of assumptions and a systematic point of view (i.e., a personal theory) may resort to merely applying techniques to help clients or may be inefficient in their interventions; in either case, the counselor may be doing more harm than good.

Creating a Personal Theory

Developing a consistent, cohesive, and articulate personal theory is a very challenging and ongoing task (George & Cristiani, 1995). A variety of sources offer suggestions on accomplishing this task (Brammer, 1993; George & Cristiani; Okun, 2002; Peterson & Nisenholz, 1995), and their suggestions are summarized here:

- *Knowledge about existing theories:* Counselors or helpers must become highly familiar with the concepts and established techniques of the major theoretical perspectives. This knowledge should include the strengths and liabilities of each approach. Increased knowledge about existing theories can inform one's own personal theory as one embraces elements of formal theories that are consistent with one's own views and questions or rejects elements that are not consistent.

- *Knowledge about self:* All counselors, having experienced life and relationships, have formulated a set of beliefs, values, motivations, needs, and goals that begin to define their sense of self. These must be brought into greater awareness (Okun, 2002). One method for doing this, not unlike an approach Rogers employed (cited in Brammer, 1993), is to develop a "personal myth"—that is, a personal story about one's life experiences, significant events, and the influence of family and culture. Reading others' autobiographies can serve as an inspiration and a model for writing one's own personal story.

- *Nature of helping:* Since counseling is about helping others lead healthier, authentic, and more productive lives, a personal theory of counseling must include statements about how one views the helping process. Some questions that might guide this include the following: What does it mean to be helpful to another person? How am I helpful to others? What is my view of an effective, well-functioning person? What is a healthy personality? Who decides what is deviant or unacceptable? What is my responsibility to others?

- *Nature of change:* Counseling is a process that involves openness to change and facilitating that change in others. In developing a personal theory about counseling, examining questions about change is important: Can people change? How do they change? Is change externally driven or internally motivated? What prevents people from changing? How do we learn?

- *Nature of humanity:* If one's personal theory is the mighty oak, then one's view of human nature is the acorn. Even though a helper may not be acutely aware of or able to articulate a personal theory, s/he is still operating on assumptions about human nature. Enos (1998, p. 3) proposes a set of opposing images of human nature that can serve as a starting point for discovering one's view of human nature: (1) Do we consciously direct our own actions, or do other forces govern them? (2) Are we influenced more by heredity (nature) or our environment (nurture)? (3) Are our personalities fixed by early events, or can adulthood experiences affect them? (4) Is the personality of each human unique, or are there broad personality patterns that fit large numbers of people? (5) Are humans motivated to maintain psychological balance, or do they have an urge to grow and develop? (6) Are we basically good or basically evil?

Attending to these strategies and questions can be demanding and difficult and requires a great deal of time and energy. Brammer (1993) acknowledges that some of the questions about human nature, change, and helping have been debated for centuries with no clear or unanimously agreed-on answers. Still, addressing the steps just outlined and engaging in some of the activities suggested can reveal new insights, complexities, and realities that can inform a comprehensive personal theory about counseling.

Summary

Student affairs practitioners play a variety of roles on campus—among them, managers, trainers, supervisors, and helpers. In all these roles, practitioners interact with people and, in those interactions, use a set of beliefs (or theories) about what constitutes mature and well-functioning people, why people behave the way they do, and how people change (George & Cristiani, 1995). To varying degrees, practitioners rely on their personal and informal theories to navigate the complexities of student development and to help students negotiate the challenges of the college experience and life in general. Practitioners, regardless of their educational background and training, may also find that exposure to formal theories of personality, development, and counseling can further inform and enhance their informal and personal theories and their eventual practice. This chapter discussed the significant role of theory in student affairs practice, from its historical roots to its recognition today as a core competency. In addition, this chapter described how theory is foundational to the student affairs core competency of helping and advising students. To that end, several families of counseling theory were described in terms of their respective philosophies, goals, therapeutic techniques, strengths and limitations, and relevance for student affairs practitioners as helpers. Finally, this chapter provided suggestions for considering formal theories as a basis for developing a personal approach to helping students. This chapter maintained from the beginning that theory plays a very important role in professional practice and that formal theories are foundational to developing a well-informed, practical, and ethical personal theory that aids practitioners in effectively helping college students with the challenging, uncomfortable, and stressful life circumstances they may face.

Part Two

Essential Helping Skills

In Part 2 of this book, essential helping skills that all student affairs practitioners need—no matter what their specific job responsibilities—are fully explored. Each chapter offers illustrations of how the helping competence is needed across the various functional areas within student affairs. Specific helping competencies and strategies for each skill cluster, such as group work or crisis intervention, are examined. Benefits and challenges in those cluster areas are identified, and the major preparation and training issues to be considered receive the attention they deserve. Importantly, full exploration of how to incorporate multicultural competence within the helping role is also addressed in each skill area. Finally, the closing chapter highlights the main points of the book and looks to the future and how student affairs professionals can integrate their helping role more effectively and intentionally into daily work.

Chapter Five

Becoming a Multiculturally Competent Helper

The complex cultural dynamics of higher education require student affairs professionals to be better prepared to address multicultural issues and work effectively with culturally diverse populations and their issues (Pope & Reynolds, 1997). Cultural issues are central to most of the important conversations on our campuses, such as admissions policies, core curricula, campus violence, and how diverse student groups relate to one another. These complicated and sometimes controversial issues are shaping every aspect of campus life. The makeup of our student body is changing continually by becoming more racially diverse, older, more international, and more openly lesbian, gay, bisexual, and transgender (LGBT). The policies we develop are influenced increasingly by multicultural issues, such as whether to designate a unisex bathroom on campus for transgender students. Debates about the cultural relevance of the curriculum have been raging for over thirty years. These examples are why "multicultural issues, questions, tensions, and debates have become a hallmark of campus life today" (Reynolds & Pope, 2003, p. 365).

Many student affairs scholars have suggested that a commitment to multiculturalism, including multicultural competence, is a responsibility of all student affairs professionals (Blimling, 2001a; Cheatham, 1991; Fried, 1995; McEwen & Roper, 1994; Pope, Reynolds, & Cheatham, 1997; Talbot, 2003). Long gone are the days when it was feasible for a few multicultural experts, such as a director of multicultural affairs or affirmative action, to adequately address all the multicultural issues on campus (Pope, Reynolds, & Mueller, 2004). Instead, all student affairs practitioners need to create programs, policies, curricula, and environments that nurture and support multicultural education and diverse populations (Talbot, 2003).

Multicultural competence, while a central component of the counseling literature for over twenty years, was introduced to the student affairs literature and lexicon by Pope and Reynolds (1997) and later expanded by Pope et al. (2004). The Dynamic Model of Student Affairs Competence by Pope et al. identified multicultural competence as one of the seven core competencies within student affairs. This model suggests that all student affairs professionals need a level of multicultural awareness, knowledge, and skills to enable them to work more effectively and competently with diverse students and colleagues. It is not expected that all practitioners will become multicultural experts (any more than they are all required to be experts on technology or assessment); however, a basic level of competency is essential so that all students' needs and concerns are addressed.

The purpose of this chapter is to identify the specific multicultural awareness, knowledge, and skills that student affairs practitioners need to apply their helping skills to meet the needs of all students. Best practices and approaches for working across cultures are explored, as are the challenges facing student affairs practitioners and helpers in becoming multiculturally competent. Finally, strategies for developing multicultural helping competence are identified.

Multicultural Competence

Given the shared histories and common professional goals of both the counseling psychology field and the student affairs profession, adapting the multicultural competence model from counseling psychology is a reasonable and prudent approach in student affairs. Multicultural competence is one of the core theoretical constructs within the field of counseling (Sue, Bingham, Porche-Burke, & Vasquez, 1999; Sue et al., 1998; Sue, Ivey, & Pedersen, 1996). Introducing multicultural competence as an essential perspective for the counseling profession began almost thirty years ago with the delineation of the tripartite model of multicultural competence: awareness, knowledge, and skills (Sue et al., 1982). This tripartite model has become the foundation for multicultural training, practice, and research. There have been ongoing revisions and expansions of the original multicultural competence guidelines (Sue, 2001; Sue, Arredondo, & McDavis, 1992; Sue et al., 1998). The counseling profession has been exploring, cultivating, and enriching its understanding of multicultural competence through empirical research, training, and implementation of multicultural counseling standards and guidelines (cf. Abreu, Chung, & Atkinson, 2000; American Psychological Association, 2000, 2003; Chang & Sue, 2005; Choudhuri, 2005; Manese, Wu, & Nepomuceno, 2001; Sue, 2001; Tori & Ducker, 2004).

Research on multicultural competence has been growing in both the counseling (cf. Chao, 2006; Constantine & Gainor, 2001; Constantine & Sue, 2007; Fuertes et al., 2006; Inman, 2006) and student affairs literature (cf. Martin, 2005; Miklitsch, 2006; Mueller & Pope, 2001, 2003; Weigand, 2005). Multicultural competence instrument development has been a central aspect of that research in counseling and student affairs (D'Andrea, Daniels, & Heck, 1991; LaFromboise, Coleman, & Hernandez, 1991; Ponterotto et al., 1996; Ponterotto, Rieger, Barrett, & Sparks, 1994; Pope & Mueller, 2000; Sodowsky, Taffe, Gutkin, & Wise, 1994). These instruments are used to assess individual multicultural competence and evaluate the effectiveness of some educational and training interventions. These instruments allow for more in-depth exploration of multicultural competence and the various factors influencing it. And while the multicultural competence research in student affairs is more limited, it has been growing in importance.

Establishing a common definition and understanding of multicultural competence is essential to developing training and educational interventions. Pope et al. (2004) describe multicultural competence as the awareness, knowledge, and skills needed to work with others who are both culturally different and similar in meaningful, relevant, and productive ways. When exploring multicultural competence, it is most common to focus on cultural difference. However, it is also important to understand that even when there are major cultural similarities, there is multicultural work to be done. Whites exploring racial issues with other whites or men addressing gender issues with other men can also be considered multicultural work. Over time our understanding of multicultural issues has grown in depth and complexity. Initially, multicultural training, in both counseling and student affairs, primarily focused on helping whites become more sensitive to issues and concerns of people of color. Since then, exploring multiculturalism has expanded to include other issues, such as sexual orientation and social class, and multicultural training now attends to the unique multicultural training needs of practitioners of color and other underrepresented groups.

Expanding our comprehension of multicultural competence is essential in applying it to helping behaviors in a higher education context. Grasping the specific awareness, knowledge, and skills necessary to being multiculturally competent allows us to assess our level of competence, design effective training interventions, and provide multicultural supervision in a relevant manner. A broad understanding of multicultural awareness, knowledge, and skills in a higher education context provides a useful starting place.

Multicultural awareness consists of the beliefs, values, attitudes, and assumptions needed to work with students, staff, and faculty who may be culturally different from the student affairs professional (Pope et al., 2004). Being aware of oneself and the impact that beliefs, attitudes, and assumptions have on relationships is an important first step to preventing cultural encapsulation and building multicultural competence. Active self-evaluation helps individuals uncover any inaccurate, inappropriate, or biased views, assumptions, or stereotypes. Sue and Sue (2003) suggested that all individuals hold worldviews that affect their perceptions of themselves, others, and the surrounding world. That worldview is shaped by many factors, such as racial and cultural identity, life experiences and opportunity, childhood zeitgeist, gender socialization, family influences, and spiritual and religious beliefs. Understanding worldview and evaluating awareness and comfort with multicultural issues is necessary to accurately evaluate one's multicultural strengths and weaknesses.

Gathering specific knowledge and information about various cultural groups is the foundation of multicultural knowledge. Most student affairs professionals have multicultural knowledge gaps because preparation program curricula give limited attention to multicultural issues (McEwen & Roper, 1994). Understanding the cultural history of various cultural groups, especially as that history relates to their participation in higher education, is essential. This information can increase empathy and create insight into the unique cultural issues and concerns affecting a specific group. For example, knowing the history of education of Native Americans in this country is necessary to fully grasp the difficulties of their full integration into higher education (Fox, Lowe, & McClellan, 2005). In the nineteenth and twentieth centuries, boarding schools, supported by religious and governmental organizations and institutions, required that Native Americans cut their hair, adopt Christian names, and give up their language and religion (Deloria, Foehner, & Scinta, 1999). This forced assimilation created intergenerational trauma that still influences Native Americans' comfort and trust in educational institutions today (Duran, 2006). Learning about the present-day experiences and realities of the various cultural groups with whom we are likely to work is equally important.

In addition to content knowledge about various cultural groups, student affairs professionals need to comprehend the impact of oppression and how it functions in the sociopolitical system, including higher education. According to Jenkins (1999), "Oppression may be inflicted in response to any dimension of diversity, and is insidious, demoralizing, and systematic" (p. 219). The deleterious effects include distorted perceptions of self and others, delayed development, stress and trauma, self-hatred, and strained relationships with others. Understanding the complex and multidimensional impact of oppression on individuals, groups, and institutions is necessary to work with members of oppressed groups in meaningful ways. It is important to be aware of the institutional barriers within higher education that affect the experiences and potential for success for groups that have been historically underserved and underrepresented. For example, there is growing evidence that the stressful experience of racism may have a significant effect on the ability of students of color to succeed in a collegiate environment (Baldwin, Chambliss, & Towler, 2003; Harper & Hurtado, 2007; Neville, Heppner, & Wang, 1997; Utsey, Chae, Brown, & Kelly, 2002; Utsey, Ponterotto, Reynolds, & Cancelli, 2000). The cumulative effect of the stress and strain of daily racism has a negative impact on motivation, self-efficacy, self-esteem, concentration, and thoughts about specific racism encounters, and it puts students of color at increased risk for mental and physical illnesses, such as depression, anxiety, hypertension, and headaches (Brown & Robinson Kurpius, 1997; Clark, 2004; Johnson & Arbona, 2006; Landrine & Klonoff, 1996; Lopez, 2005; Utsey et al., 2000). Comprehending the effect of oppression on college students is part of culturally sensitive and efficacious practice.

Finally, being knowledgeable about salient cultural constructs, such as acculturation and cultural identity (e.g., racial identity or gender identity), helps student affairs professionals comprehend the diverse experiences, identities, attitudes, and behaviors within various cultural groups as well as how campus services, programs, and interventions may affect them. Increasing knowledge about the experiences, values, and realities of different cultural groups is an important step toward multicultural competence. However, it is not uncommon for people to make generalizations about individuals based on their membership in a particular cultural group. In those situations, cultural knowledge, when applied to all members of a cultural group, becomes akin to stereotypes and does not acknowledge the unique individual experiences and identities that constitute group differences. In fact, Carter (1995) and others have suggested that racial group membership (whether one is black, Asian, white, etc.) is not as important as what that membership means to individuals; in other words, those people's racial identity has a more powerful effect on who they are and how they relate to others than their racial background. Awareness of group differences helps practitioners individualize and personalize their interventions so that those interventions are more relevant and meaningful. Without this awareness, practitioners can make dangerous assumptions. When a student affairs professional works with an Asian student, the practitioner might make certain attributions about that student based on her/his racial group membership. However, imagine that this Asian student was transracially adopted and raised in a predominantly white community in the Midwest where she had very little interaction with other Asians. Then such assumptions would invalidate the student's experiences and reality and possibly make it difficult to form a positive relationship.

The final aspect of the multicultural competence tripartite model, multicultural skills, is composed of the behaviors that allow us to use multicultural awareness and knowledge to design and implement culturally relevant and meaningful interventions. First and foremost, being multiculturally skilled means effectively communicating across cultures and being aware of how culture influences the content and process (verbal and nonverbal) of communication. Expanding one's repertoire of skills and interventions beyond those typically taught in graduate preparation programs means including alternative theories, approaches, and activities that might be more effective, relevant, and culturally sensitive with a diverse student body. Developing the comfort and ability to recover from the cultural errors inherent in cross-cultural communication is an example of another valuable multicultural skill. Implementing individual- and institutional-level interventions that encourage deeper and more structural multicultural change demonstrates an important depth of multicultural skill (Pope et al., 2004). And lastly, the ability to deconstruct the embedded cultural assumptions in the theories and practices of student affairs work is one of the most important, and often overlooked, skills needed to effectively work with all students. Such deconstruction requires actively exploring the core beliefs underlying theories, such as the assumption that individuation from one's family is necessary for healthy development. Being aware of these assumptions allows one to provide more accessible and relevant services rather than relying on generic student development theories or standard helping skills based on the belief that such theories and practices are universal (Reynolds, 1995c).

Multicultural Awareness, Knowledge, and Skills Needed to Be a Helper

Multicultural competence in a helping context involves the attitudes, knowledge, and skills necessary to work with and help others who are culturally different from oneself and address their concerns, issues, and problems, individually or in a group (Pope et al., 2004). Multicultural scholars believe that, without incorporating multicultural awareness, knowledge, and skills into helping interactions, many individuals' important values, worldviews, and realities are ignored, minimized, or viewed as irrelevant (cf. D'Andrea et al., 2001; Reynolds, 1995c; Ridley, 2005; Sue & Sue, 2003). Incorporating the unique experiences and perspectives of individuals from diverse cultural, religious, racial, social class, and sexual orientation backgrounds into helping theories and practices allows student affairs professionals to develop insight, empathy, and openness to others. The risks of not addressing these cultural realities when helping others are great. When student affairs professionals do not fully understand the internal conflict that many Native American students feel when they enter a predominantly white campus or the importance of faith to many African American students, those practitioners are not adequately prepared to provide support to help such students be successful. When student affairs practitioners assume that all students are heterosexual or identify as male or female, they are likely to alienate, hurt, or disempower LGBT students and increase the chance that those students will not reach out for support. And when student affairs professionals do not fully grasp the everyday knowledge that a first-generation college student may lack about the college experience, they are less able to anticipate those students' needs and effectively assist their transition to the college environment. Therefore, it is vital that student affairs practitioners increase their multicultural helping competence to provide the most affirming, effective, and ethical services.

Multicultural scholars have suggested the need for specific multicultural counseling awareness, knowledge, and skills. Through exploring the complex definitions and components of multicultural competence, especially in a helping context, student affairs professionals are better prepared to apply their multicultural awareness, knowledge, and skills to real-life situations and challenges. Although specific characteristics, domains, and components have been proposed for multicultural counseling, "there have been few efforts to integrate these multicultural helping skills into a student affairs context" (Pope et al., 2004, p. 85). Reynolds (1995c) provided the initial elucidation of multicultural helping competence for student affairs professionals, which was later expanded by Reynolds and Pope (2003) and Pope et al. The initial framework evolved by adding advocacy skills and multicultural organization development tools as necessary helping skills to combat oppression and other barriers to multiculturalism on campus. According to Pope et al., because these barriers negatively affect students, student affairs professionals have an ethical responsibility to assist college environments in becoming more multicultural in their values and practices.

This concrete list of multicultural helping competencies for student affairs professionals and educators provided by Reynolds and Pope (2003) included the following: (1) develop appreciation, knowledge, and understanding of cultural groups, especially those that have been underserved and underrepresented in higher education; (2) increase content knowledge about important cultural constructs, such as racial identity, acculturation, worldview, and LGBT identity; (3) augment awareness of one's own biases, stereotypes, and cultural assumptions, and learn how to honestly evaluate one's own multicultural skills and comfort level; (4) learn how to use that multicultural knowledge and awareness to develop more culturally sensitive and responsive interventions; (5) enhance awareness of any interpersonal dynamics that may occur within a multicultural dyad; (6) explore and then deconstruct the underlying cultural assumptions embedded in the helping process and the values and assumptions of higher education; and (7) use advocacy skills to help create a more multiculturally sensitive and affirming campus. Jenkins (1999) provided an illustration of the value of concrete competencies when she emphasized the centrality of the helping relationship when intervening with students of color. She highlighted that openness, flexibility, and mutuality are especially important in these relationships because many relationships in the past may have been noncollaborative, judgmental, and lacking in reciprocity.

The various frameworks suggested by multicultural scholars range in their degree of specificity and breadth. Sue (2001) offered the Multidimensional Model of Cultural Competence in which he emphasized specific ways to create multicultural change in individuals, institutions, and society. He suggested that "individuals are not multiculturally competent unless they invest in changing institutional structures, professional core values and practices, and societal assumptions and systems" (Pope et al., 2004). Within the field of counseling psychology, social justice and social advocacy began as an offshoot of multicultural competence and has become its own entity that includes an expanding literature base (cf. Hage, 2005; Toporek, Gerstein, Fouad, Roysircar, & Israel, 2006; Vera & Speight, 2003) and organized groups within professional associations like the American Psychological Association (APA) and the American Counseling Association (ACA). Both major counseling professional associations, APA and ACA, have developed and published specific multicultural competency and advocacy guidelines that address the unique awareness, knowledge, and skills needed to be an effective counselor with diverse populations (ACA, 1992; APA, 2000, 2003, 2007; Sue et al., 1992). Within student affairs there have been discussions about social justice and the importance of being social justice allies for many years (Broido, 2000; Reason, Broido, Davis, & Evans, 2005; Washington & Evans, 1991).

While there has been no sanctioned list of multicultural helping competencies or guidelines within the student affairs profession, Pope and Reynolds (1997) offered a list of specific characteristics of multiculturally competent student affairs practitioners. Pope and Mueller (2000) ultimately used this inventory of concrete awareness, knowledge, and skills in developing the Multicultural Competence in Student Affairs Scale. These types of lists and guidelines can be useful to practitioners because they specify some of the multicultural attitudes, knowledge, and skills that may be needed in helping encounters. According to Pope et al. (2004), "Creating an effective repertoire of culturally sensitive helping, advising, and counseling skills is a necessary component of becoming a multiculturally competent professional" (p. 97).

Illustrations of Multiculturally Competent Helping Behaviors Across Functional Areas

Using the functional areas within student affairs divisions previously identified in this book (counseling-oriented positions, leadership development and educational positions, administrative positions, and academic affairs positions) and providing examples of multiculturally competent behaviors within those domains as illustrations or exemplars may assist professionals in expanding their repertoire and range of multicultural awareness, knowledge, and skills.

Within the counseling functional areas (e.g., counseling and career centers), much of the multicultural competence needed focuses on both the content and the process of the interaction. The process of counseling or helping involves core microcounseling skills, like listening, paraphrasing, and nonverbal communication. Some individuals from various cultural groups communicate in culturally specific ways. In some cultures direct eye contact is a sign of disrespect, while in other cultures individuals who look away and do not make eye contact are assumed to be dishonest. The comfort zone of physical space and touch can also vary across cultures. In terms of the content of communication, views on silence and how much private emotions should be shared can also differ among different cultural groups. Having content knowledge about some of these potential cultural differences is important to developing competence. Being aware of the attitudes and assumptions that may create barriers in the helping relationship is very important. Of course, the identity development or acculturation level of individuals, rather than their group membership per se, tempers these group differences. Increasing sensitivity to the nuances of cross-cultural communication and its effect on human interaction and the helping relationship is a vital step in the process of becoming multiculturally competent.

The multicultural competence necessary within leadership- and educational-oriented positions also focuses on the centrality of cross-cultural communication. Applying multicultural competence to teaching, mentoring, supervising, advising, and conflict resolution are just a few of the areas in this domain that involve some unique characteristics and skills. Facilitating cross-cultural communication or resolving cultural conflicts within and between student organizations requires specific multicultural competence. Allowing for diverse expressions of leadership, learning how to create a trusting bond with a supervisee or mentee, and realizing that different individuals require unique educational/training environments to grow and thrive are essential to effectively working across cultures.

Within administrative positions, where some of the work requires interacting with parents and community members, it is necessary to be aware of how people from individualistic versus collectivistic cultures communicate, view conflict, and interact with authority. To be successful, individuals must be able to build a certain level of cultural credibility that allows them to be viewed as trustworthy in another cultural context. Understanding how culture influences expressions of emotion and conflict can assist one in effectively managing a cultural conflict or judicial situation in a manner that is fair to all involved.

Finally, academic affairs positions require some of the same multicultural awareness, knowledge, and skills needed within the other three domains. The importance of education has a different impact on members of different cultural groups; however, racism or other forms of discrimination or bias such students may have faced often affects their motivation and their ability to succeed. Not being exposed to a wide range of career role models or not being told that they could succeed are some of the burdens that students may bring with them into an academic context, and a multiculturally competent professional needs to know how to address these issues.

Challenges and Benefits to Being a Multiculturally Competent Helper

There are many challenges and benefits to becoming a multiculturally competent helper on a college campus. One of the central challenges or obstacles is the lack of a unified definition of multiculturalism (Talbot, 2003). Some individuals view cultural competence only in terms of race, while others choose a more inclusive definition that includes social class, gender, sexual orientation, religion, age, and disabilities. Without a mutual understanding of the definition of multiculturalism, it is difficult for student affairs practitioners to develop common goals and expectations about what constitutes multicultural competence.

Another major obstacle to becoming a multiculturally competent helper is cultural encapsulation, which was first introduced by Wrenn (1962). Cultural encapsulation is when individuals are so involved and potentially invested in their own reality and worldview that they are not aware of their own cultural biases or assumptions and the many alternative cultural realities surrounding them. Pedersen (2002) identified the following important characteristics of cultural encapsulation: (1) defining reality based on one set of cultural assumptions, (2) being insensitive to alternative worldviews and assuming that one's worldview is correct, (3) believing one's cultural reality even when there is conflicting evidence, and (4) using these encapsulated assumptions to evaluate the normalcy and value of others' attitudes, behaviors, and reality. Deconstructing the cultural assumptions embedded in the counseling or helping process, as well as the larger student affairs profession, is essential to developing multicultural competence (Reynolds, 1995b).

A final and significant barrier to the development of multicultural competence is individual and institutional resistance to change. Sabnani, Ponterotto, and Borodovsky (1991) and others (Chao, 2006; Constantine & Gainor, 2001; Ridley, 2005; Sodowsky, Kuo-Jackson, Richardson, & Corey, 1998) have identified how racial identity, color-blind attitudes, emotional intelligence, racial defense mechanisms, social desirability, and other factors influence how open individuals are to expanding their cultural assumptions about themselves, others, and the world around them. Understanding these mechanisms and their impact on the helping process is crucial to working with individuals who are culturally different from oneself.

In addition to individual barriers to change, there are also institutional barriers to change. Institutional resistance to multiculturalism has long been documented in all types of settings (Carter, 2001; Pope & Thomas, 2000; Reynolds, 2001; Talbot, 2003). Pope (1995), Reynolds (1997), and others (cf. D'Andrea et al., 2001; Sue, 2001) have emphasized the need for multicultural interventions at the institutional level. Without these systemic and systematic efforts aimed at institutions' underlying assumptions, structures, practices, and policies, the culturally encapsulated status quo will be maintained.

Most multicultural scholars describe the journey toward multicultural competence as a lifelong process (Pope et al.,

2004; Talbot, 2003), and while some might perceive that as a challenge, it can also be viewed as a benefit. Striving for multicultural competence can often place one in a constant process of self-discovery, creating opportunities for relationships and experiences that would otherwise not be part of one's life (Heppner, 2006; Reynolds, 2001). Building meaningful connections with individuals who are culturally different creates learning and self-awareness experiences that are stimulating, challenging, and inspirational. And once the desire for growth and multicultural development becomes personally meaningful and relevant, the benefits and value of this internal paradigm shift are boundless.

Strategies for Developing Multicultural Competence

Many multicultural scholars have been critical of higher education's effort in creating more multicultural campuses (Barr & Strong, 1988; Cheatham, 1991; Fried, 1995; Manning & Coleman-Boatwright, 1991; McEwen & Roper, 1994; Pope et al., 1997; Pope et al., 2004; Talbot, 2003; Talbot & Kocarek, 1997). These criticisms focus on the shortcomings of the higher education institutions themselves, as well as the graduate preparation programs that train student affairs and higher education professionals. Increasing the profession's overall multicultural competence will require an extensive and coordinated effort on the part of graduate preparation faculty, senior-level administrators and leaders within higher education, and elected leaders and staff members of professional associations.

Some scholars and practitioners within the student affairs profession have suggested specific strategies, tools, and techniques to enhance and develop practitioners' multicultural competence that can be used by individuals as well as by educators, supervisors, and administrators who want to enhance others' multicultural competence (e.g., McEwen & Roper,

1994; Pope et al., 2004; Talbot, 2003). The journey toward multiculturalism is a lifelong developmental process that requires a balance of challenge and support from our personal, educational, and work environment. Although multicultural competence cannot be developed without the commitment and effort of the individual student affairs practitioner, this work needs to be supported and sanctioned by a similar commitment at the professional level by professional associations like the American College Personnel Association and the National Association of Student Personnel Administrators, graduate preparation programs, and the individual campus student affairs divisions and departments that sponsor educational, training, and professional education efforts.

Graduate Preparation and Training

Research has indicated that the multicultural training efforts within graduate preparation programs are uneven and often inadequate (Talbot, 1992). While most graduate training programs offer diversity courses, those courses are not always required (Flowers, 2003). Talbot (1996) found that often only a few courses, such as student development theory and student services, even narrowly focus on multicultural issues. Depending on the faculty's diversity and research interests, some programs may have no faculty to take the lead in addressing multicultural issues. Other programs attempt to address and infuse multicultural issues but may have difficulty doing so across all courses. This includes any counseling courses that students are required to take. There also may be unbalanced efforts in terms of which cultural groups are explored; some preparation programs do an excellent job of integrating issues of race but rarely explore sexual orientation, religion, or social class. Many programs are unsure how to develop multicultural competence on a comprehensive basis (Ponterotto, Alexander, & Grieger, 1995). Reynolds (1997) and

Ponterotto et al. suggested using a multicultural organization development model to infuse multicultural components within the curriculum.

Talbot and Kocarek (1997) highlighted faculty competency as being essential to the creation of multiculturally sensitive graduate preparation programs. Unless all members of the community—including students, faculty members, and staff—have a personal investment in multicultural change and are willing to contribute, it is difficult to create a multiculturally affirming campus (Talbot, 2003). In her study of graduate student perceptions, Talbot (1992) found that graduate students observed faculty members to see whether their actions matched their verbal support of diversity—in other words, how active their commitment was. According to Pope et al. (2004), "Preparation faculty can play a significant role in fostering the multicultural competencies of graduate students by articulating expectations for multicultural knowledge and skill attainment and by creating opportunities for them to explore multicultural issues throughout the curriculum" (p. 175).

McEwen and Roper (1994) and Talbot and Kocarek (1997) emphasized the need for preparation programs to provide opportunities within the curriculum for students to engage in multicultural exploration that furthers their awareness, knowledge, and skills. Such opportunities may include course assignments, practicum experiences, and in-class training exercises that expose students to opportunities to expand their knowledge, enhance their self-awareness, and develop new skills. Reynolds (1995a) highlighted the importance of approaching multicultural training from a multidimensional perspective that incorporates cognitive and affective learning, experiential or hands-on activities, and skill development. Extending multicultural learning opportunities beyond the classroom and into internships, assistantships, and other field-based experiences is an ideal way to link theory and practice (Gayles & Kelly, 2007).

Professional Education and Development

Ongoing professional education is an essential component to multicultural change efforts within the student affairs profession. Mueller and Pope (2003) suggested that multicultural training needs to focus on all student affairs practitioners and not just graduate students and entry-level professionals. Multicultural training has been shown to have an impact on professionals' multicultural competence and sensitivity (Choi-Pearson, Castillo, & Maples, 2004; Miklitsch, 2006; Mueller & Pope; Weigand, 2005). However, not all professionals participate in development activities; Choi-Pearson et al. found that white professionals did not attend as many multicultural training experiences as did professionals of color. Creating incentives for student affairs professionals to participate in multiculturally oriented professional development, such as increasing funds for attending multicultural conferences, is an essential aspect of a multicultural strategic plan (Grieger, 1996). And administrators and campus leaders need to sanction and support multicultural training (Carpenter & Stimpson, 2007; Pope et al., 2004).

Carpenter and Stimpson (2007) emphasized the need for professional development to be application oriented, explaining, "encouraging professionals to apply what they learned is a natural and appropriate extension of professional development" (p. 274). Using multicultural training tools, such as case studies and cultural exercises, is an ideal way for student affairs departments and divisions to engage their staff members in meaningful and useful exploration and application of multicultural competence (Pope et al., 2004; Talbot, 2003). Professional development activities are essential not only for personal and professional growth but because they ultimately improve student affairs professionals' competence and enhance the opportunities for developing multiculturalism on campus (Choi-Pearson et al., 2004).

Summary

A multiculturally competent helper in a student affairs context has the necessary awareness, knowledge, and skills to effectively work with individuals from all cultural groups. These multicultural helping skills allow practitioners to understand how culture influences all aspects of the helping interaction. Across the various domains of student affairs work, from counseling-oriented positions to more administrative positions, different multicultural awareness, knowledge, and skills are required to work in a culturally sensitive, meaningful, and relevant manner. These competencies are best developed through training and work experiences. This chapter delineated some of the specific multicultural helping competencies that student affairs practitioners need; it shared some of the barriers and challenges to developing multicultural competence and suggested some specific graduate preparation and professional education strategies to ensure that the student affairs profession is adequately prepared to work with students, faculty, and staff members from all cultural groups (Chao, 2006; Constantine & Gainor, 2001; Ridley, 2005; Sodowsky et al., 1998).

Chapter Six

Microcounseling Skills

Marcia Roe Clark

Student affairs administrators are among the most prominent helpers on many college and university campuses. Entry-level student affairs professionals are employed in positions with high levels of student contact, providing direct services to students in the form of facilitating, advising, problem solving, mentoring, supervising, and training (Burkard, Cole, Ott, & Stoflet, 2005). In their roles as admissions counselors, residence hall directors, student organization and first-year experience advisers, intramural and recreation coordinators, financial aid and academic advisers, and career services counselors and health/wellness educators, new professionals cultivate relationships with students that can span a semester, a year, or a student's entire college career.

As a consequence of prolonged and regular contact with students, student affairs professionals may find themselves in the position to recognize and respond to a variety of student needs, concerns, and issues. The scenarios are nearly limitless. In some instances, students initiate their interaction with a chosen helper or practitioner. A varsity athlete may approach his team's academic adviser with a concern about a teammate's unhealthy eating behaviors. A first-year student may seek out her residence hall director to discuss a problem with a course or a professor. At other times, student affairs professionals must take the first steps to initiate a conversation with students when they are concerned about the students' well-being. An admissions counselor may notice a decline in a work-study student's demeanor and performance in the office and approach the student to express concern. A judicial officer may recognize that college transition issues underlie a student's behavioral problems and address those issues during the disciplinary process. A student organization president who appears distressed during a substance awareness workshop may welcome an observant wellness educator's discreet invitation to talk privately. As Winston (2003) noted, student affairs professionals "cannot predict or choose when they will be called upon to be helpers; opportunities and challenges are presented daily" (p. 501). And while administrators in most student affairs departments (with the exception of counseling services) are neither equipped nor expected to engage with students in prolonged counseling relationships, all student affairs professionals need basic helping skills and knowledge to serve students effectively, both individually and in groups (Pope, Reynolds, & Mueller, 2004; Winston).

Fortunately, student affairs professionals can learn and develop the specific skills necessary for effective helping. One potential obstacle, however, is the belief that certain helping competencies are the result of personal characteristics rather than learned abilities. Burkard et al.'s (2005) study of experienced student affairs professionals illustrates this dynamic. Reflecting a consensus of a hundred-plus mid- and senior-level administrators, the researchers identified human relations skills and personal qualities as the two most important competency areas for entry-level professionals, noting that these skills span across functional areas as diverse as admissions, residence life, athletics, and academic services. Human relations skills include competencies such as collaboration, active listening, and multicultural competency. In contrast, confrontation, oral communication, and interpersonal relations were among the competencies categorized as personal qualities, or "unique individual characteristics" (Burkard et al., p. 293). Goal setting was identified as a third area of administrative and management competence. These entry-level competencies are notable in particular because they also represent important elements of effective helping interactions. Categorizing some as qualities and others as skills, however, suggests a distinction between innate and acquired abilities that does not fit with prevailing counseling perspectives on helping and helper training. In fact, and as this chapter will illustrate, all the helping competencies just noted (and many others) are skills that can be studied, practiced, and strengthened.

This chapter identifies general helping approaches that are appropriate for the types of interactions, relationships, and contexts typically faced by student affairs administrators. Three phases of the student affairs helping process will be introduced, followed by an examination of six skill clusters that characterize effective helping. The chapter closes with a discussion of temptations and fears observed among student affairs helpers in training. The content throughout the chapter emphasizes a nonclinical perspective that is informed by counseling and student affairs literature and is further shaped by the author's observations and insights as both an experienced administrator and a trainer of new helpers preparing for their careers in student affairs.

Three Phases of Helping in Student Affairs

The helping facet of student affairs work draws heavily from the counseling and communication fields, among other disciplines. In exploring the helping relationship, experts have suggested that the helping interaction consists of client needs and helper actions (Egan, 1975). Among the varying perspectives on the helping process (e.g., Brammer & MacDonald, 1999; Carkhuff, 2000; Carkhuff & Anthony, 1979; Dainow & Bailey, 1988; Eddy, 1981; Egan, 2002; Hill & O'Brien, 1999; Okun, 2002; Parsons, 2004), there is widespread agreement that helping unfolds in a series of phases or stages. Within the context of student affairs helping in general and new helper training in particular, it is useful to conceptualize the helping process in three phases: establishing rapport with the student and exploring the dilemma, gaining insight into the dilemma and focusing, and taking action. This perspective on helping represents a synthesis of counseling literature viewed through a student affairs lens.

Three phases of helping

- Establishing rapport with the student and exploring the dilemma
- Gaining insight into the dilemma and focusing
- Taking action

Phase 1: Establishing Rapport with the Student and Exploring the Dilemma

In the first phase of helping, the helper's primary goals are to establish effective communication with the student and understand the student's experience. This begins with providing a climate of warmth and respect so the student feels safe to explore her/his "beliefs, values, attitudes, feelings and behaviors" (Okun, 2002, p. 52). Professional counselors typically begin creating a safe environment when a client initiates a helping interaction. In student affairs, however, the process can and probably should occur even before a helping interaction begins. Student affairs helpers often communicate their openness to students and helping through their surroundings (e.g., office decor that mirrors a variety of student interests and perspectives) and how they interact with students daily (e.g., greeting students by name, inquiring about their classes and activities, demonstrating knowledge of current student issues on campus). This foundation enhances student affairs helping in two important ways. First, students struggling with personal problems may identify and initiate helping interactions more readily with student affairs administrators who have already created safe, supportive environments. Second, these early relationships enable student affairs helpers to recognize when students are in need and respond accordingly. Establishing this type of rapport is unique to student affairs and allows for both helper-initiated and student-initiated helping interactions that can be central to students' well-being.

Once the helping interaction begins, the helper continues building rapport and trust by cultivating and maintaining a "working alliance" (Okun, 2002, p. 4) with the student. Rapport is essential to the helping relationship and provides the foundation for the remaining helping phases (Okun). Without rapport, the helper can be viewed as a distant and authoritative person, which decreases the likelihood that the student will seek help. For example, a work-study student in the recreation center may share a strong rapport and feel safer discussing her confusion about her major choice with her recreation supervisor than with her faculty adviser.

Through rapport and collaboration, the helper's task is to guide students to tell their stories by expressing their thoughts and feelings about their current situation or concern. To accomplish this, helpers rely primarily on two clusters of helping skills: listening, and reflecting and summarizing.

Phase 2: Gaining Insight into the Dilemma and Focusing

In the second phase of helping, the helper strives to discover the true core of the student's dilemma and to make connections that can help the student reframe or interpret the dilemma in a new way. Evans, Hearn, Uhlemann, and Ivey (1998) referred to this as "restorying," or helping students "find new meanings in their stories and, perhaps, even write new narratives and interpretations of what happened" (p. 1). Egan (2002) called it identifying and breaking through the "blind spots that prevent [students] from seeing themselves, their problem situations, and their unexplored opportunities as they really are" (p. 27). This can include identifying ways that students contribute to or maintain their current, undesired situations because of an inability to "see, understand, realize or appreciate how they are doing themselves in" (Egan, p. 177). The overarching purpose is to guide the student toward a deeper understanding of her/his cognitive, affective, and behavioral responses to the dilemma. According to Evans, Hearn, et al., "This broader understanding enables students to make different choices, engage in new, more functional behaviors, and obtain an increased sense of responsibility and control" (p. 186). To prompt this insight and focus, helpers add two more skill clusters to their repertoire: questioning and clarifying, and interpreting and confronting.

Continuing with the previous example, careful listening and reflecting during phase 1 has revealed that the work-study student is an accounting major who has always struggled with the mathematics demands of her accounting classes but recently discovered a new interest in history and wants to change her major. Because academic exploration is encouraged at the college, the possibility that the student has found a discipline better suited to her interests and abilities could be viewed as a positive educational development that would add certainty to her life. But the student is clearly anxious about the situation and confused about what to do. So the supervisor invites her to continue describing her experience and learns that the student's parents are recent immigrants to the United States who own a small convenience store near the college. They have strong opinions about the value of accounting as an academic major and a lucrative career for their daughter; they are unaware of the difficulties she experiences in her accounting classes. In addition, the student has begun a new romantic relationship with another work-study student at the recreation center who is majoring in history. With this deeper understanding of the student's story, the supervisor is prepared to help the student think about her dilemma in new ways. The supervisor may guide the student to interpret her dilemma differently by suggesting that the core of her story is not uncertainty about the major she wishes to pursue but anxiety about approaching her parents with her decision about changing her major and uncertainty about how they might respond to her. Or the supervisor may note the coincidental timing of the student's romance and her newfound interest in history and invite the student to consider the ways that her relationship may be connected to her academic decision. Gaining deeper self-understanding and developing a meaningful, accurate restory provide the focus necessary for the final phase of helping.

Phase 3: Taking Action

Students typically initiate helping conversations with student affairs professionals because they want something in their lives or experiences to be different from what it is currently—in other words, they want to resolve their dilemmas (Parsons, 2004). In most instances, this implies that students will identify and engage in actions that will lead to positive changes for them. According to Brammer and MacDonald (1999), action includes observable behaviors as well as covert or internal behaviors, such as "how people think about themselves, how they feel about other people, or how they view their world" (p. 125). The helper's tasks in the third phase of helping are to assist students in setting effective goals and developing a feasible plan for achieving those goals. In some instances, appropriate helper action includes referring the student to other professionals who are better equipped to continue the helping process that the student affairs professional has begun. Developing goals and action plans and making referrals represent the final two clusters of skills used in effective helping.

With enhanced self-understanding, the work-study student in the example is now ready to identify the problem within her restory that she wants to address. Deep exploration into the student's initial uncertainty about changing majors has

revealed additional underlying issues that may be blocking her
from taking action: her inadequate mathematics skills and sub-
sequent poor course performance are damaging her academic
self-confidence and eroding her original interest in accounting;
her hectic schedule offers her very little free time for her new
romance, and she fears that the relationship will die; she worries
that studying history will not prepare her for a job after college;
and finally, changing her major would be perceived within her
family's culture as a powerful demonstration of disrespect toward
her parents and their wishes, and she fears the consequences of
such an action. In a spirit of continued empathic understanding and collaboration, the supervisor guides the student in identifying her most prominent concern and developing a plan for
positive action.

Whether the helping interaction is one meeting or an
ongoing relationship cultivated over time, these three phases
of helping represent a critical sequence for achieving effective
helping outcomes within the student affairs context. These
phases may vary in length, depending on the nature of the helping interaction, but effective helping requires that all three
phases occur. For example, stalling in phase 2 without progress-
ing to a remedy in the form of goals and actions is typically
inadequate for creating positive changes in students' experiences
(Egan, 2002). In a similar sense, the phase 3 helping task of taking action is ineffective without first establishing rapport and
gaining insight (Okun, 2002). In the example helping scenario,
self-understanding or insight alone is not likely to improve the
work-study student's academic performance or schedule, nor will
it relieve her underlying worries about her relationships or her
future. Conversely, moving her toward action prematurely without a deep or shared understanding of her dilemma may result in
a plan that targets the wrong goal, overlooks or neglects important influences, and runs a high risk of failure. For instance, a
plan for changing majors that includes visiting the career center
to research career opportunities for history graduates but ignores

important family concerns is likely to be too challenging for this student to implement successfully.

Illustrations of Helping Behaviors Across Functional Areas

Student affairs practitioners use helping skills and all phases of the helping process in every functional area of student affairs and at every level of the organization. The skills that are typically used across functional areas are determined less by the specific area and more by the helper's individual skills and preferences. In keeping with the schema used elsewhere in the book, this chapter identifies the functional areas within student affairs and highlights examples of the types of skills that practitioners may engage in: (1) counseling-oriented positions like career and personal counseling; (2) leadership development and educational positions (e.g., student activities, Greek affairs, campus life, health and wellness, and residence life); (3) administrative positions like dean of students, judicial affairs, and admissions; and (4) academic affairs positions (e.g., advisement and academic support services). A brief exploration of the range of helping skills and how they may be uniquely applied in a helping relationship across the functional areas can raise awareness of the diverse demands facing student affairs professionals.

Within the counseling functional area, student affairs professionals are most likely to engage in ongoing helping relationships. While some students may see a personal or career counselor for one session, many students pursue counseling in an ongoing fashion. With more time, counselors may be able to fully develop a rapport and encourage the students to tell their story. Depending on one's theoretical orientation (as explored in Chapter 4), the helping phases that are emphasized will vary— for example, how much a particular counselor focuses on insight versus action. However, if counselors want students to return for assistance, they must create the right blend of insight and action. If they spend too much time on insight, many students may become impatient because their day-to-day experiences and feelings may not change. And if counselors move too quickly to action, without helping students more fully understand their dilemmas, then true awareness and change may not happen. In terms of helping skills used, career and personal counselors undoubtedly will have the opportunity to use all six skills to varying degrees, depending on the client's concerns and needs.

Within leadership development and educational positions, helping occurs in a variety of contexts and occasions, and the wide range of possible individual and group interventions requires all the helping phases and skills. Unlike counselors, who often engage in helping in their personal offices, student affairs professionals who work in leadership development and educational positions are often on the move. They actively work with students in a variety of settings—sometimes before or after meetings, in a hallway, or during meetings. Building rapport and exploring students' concerns takes on a different meaning in that type of context. It is also likely that some of the rapport building may occur in the context of staff and leadership training where you get the chance to know the various student leaders and they can check you out as well. Practitioners who work with students in such diverse settings need to be intentional in their efforts to set aside one-on-one time to provide support, guidance, and supervision. It is important to realize that many students will not come looking for support when they are in need, so it is the professionals' responsibility to attend, listen, question, and clarify to determine which students are in need. In terms of operating as supervisors and mentors, practitioners who work with student leaders and workers need to actively engage in setting goals and action plans to support the students' efforts as executive board members, sorority presidents, resident assistants, and related roles. In addition, working with students in crisis and conflict is a common occurrence in these positions, so professionals need to have their strongest helping skills available. It is likely that those who work in leadership development and educational positions use all six helping skills in their work with students.

In administrative positions, where student affairs practitioners act as mediators, disciplinarians, and decision makers, their contact with students can be much more arbitrary and contrived. Building rapport in those circumstances can be difficult and may not be as valued by the practitioner as getting the job done. In addition, administrators are likely to work with a variety of individuals—including faculty members, parents, community members, and staff members—where the purpose of the interaction is quite different from what occurs with students; often they are addressing a problem or concern. Given these circumstances, it is not unusual for individuals to approach administrators without expecting to be "helped" in the traditional use of the term. It is up to the administrator to actively and intentionally work at building rapport and exploring the dilemma or story that students, faculty members, or parents bring with them. Being an active listener who clarifies what s/he is hearing makes it easier to find common ground and work together, whatever the purpose of the intervention.

Finally, within academic affairs positions, student affairs professionals work in similar fashion to counselors in that many times their work is individually oriented. Those individual interactions often differ from counseling in that most students come to address concerns and solve problems that are academic in nature. But sometimes significant personal issues underlie those academic concerns. And determining whether there is more beneath the surface requires effectively implementing all the core skills. When deeper personal and emotional issues are uncovered, most practitioners in academic-oriented positions will refer such students for more personal counseling. It is important not to underestimate how personal academic concerns are and how they can be truly rooted in deep feelings and personal dynamics that are not immediately apparent to the practitioner or even the student. Through effectively listening, clarifying, and interpreting, a practitioner can assess and understand what a student is really trying to say. Other types of interactions commonly faced include group interactions with students; whether it is group advising during orientation or skills training for tutors, such settings require the full range of helping skills.

Helping Skills

As the helping conversation unfolds through the three phases, helpers rely on a wide range of skills. Counseling texts are excellent resources for exploring and learning microcounseling skills in greater depth (suggested skill-building references for student affairs professionals include Brammer & MacDonald, 1999; D'Augelli, D'Augelli, & Danish, 1981; Egan, 2002; Evans, Hearn, et al., 1998; Hill & O'Brien, 1999; Okun, 2002; Parsons, 2004). For the purposes of student affairs helping, however, it is reasonable and useful to synthesize these skills into six clusters: listening, reflecting and summarizing, questioning and clarifying, interpreting and confronting, developing goals and action plans, and making referrals. As suggested previously, the helper's skill repertoire expands throughout each phase of the helping interaction. The clusters presented here are intended to introduce skills that are central to student affairs helping. They do not reflect the complete array of microcounseling skills; however, they are offered as a guide to the helping terrain in student affairs and a framework for organizing and engaging in ongoing, intensive skill building and training.

Helping skills clusters

- Establishing rapport with the student and exploring the dilemma
  - Listening
  - Reflecting and summarizing

- Gaining insight into the dilemma and focusing
  - Questioning and clarifying
  - Interpreting and confronting
- Taking action
  - Determining goals and action plans
  - Making referrals

Skill Cluster 1: Listening

In many respects, student affairs professionals often are natural helpers—after all, the ability to connect with people in both professional and personal relationships can be one of the skills that draws some of them to student affairs careers in the first place. That is why it can come as a surprise to beginning helpers to discover that they may need to develop this fundamental helping skill—listening—further. What appears to be a fairly straightforward, natural ability is in fact a complex and nuanced skill. Taking time to relearn how to listen or to learn how to listen in new ways may feel awkward at first, but it is time well spent.

First and foremost, effective listening requires approaching the helping interaction with a proper frame of mind (often referred to as "attending"). It is important for student affairs professionals to develop appropriate helping attitudes and demeanors during their training as helpers. Also, because helping interactions in student affairs often occur at unexpected times and places, it is equally important for administrators to be intentional about adopting an appropriate frame of mind and readying themselves for effective helping at the beginning of each new encounter. That may mean slowing down and making an intentional decision to focus on the student rather than the long to-do list at the office.

An important key to success in any helping relationship is empathy, which Okun (2002) defined as "both understanding another person's emotions and feelings from that person's frame of reference and conveying that understanding" (p. 13). Through careful attention to both verbal and nonverbal messages, the helper strives to understand the student's dilemma—behaviors, thoughts, and feelings—as the student experiences it. One condition of effective listening, therefore, is the helper's willingness and ability to adopt the student's frame of reference as completely as possible. This skill is especially important when students have different life experiences or a different cultural background. Being open to their reality and how it may be different is an essential aspect of empathy.

In addition to empathy, effective listeners embrace and express an attitude of unconditional positive regard, which means accepting students as worthwhile and valuable people regardless of their backgrounds, their statements, or their actions (Okun, 2002). Unconditional positive regard fosters a climate of helping that allows students to express themselves honestly, without fear of judgment or loss of respect. A second condition of effective listening, therefore, is helpers' willingness and ability to temporarily suspend their personal assumptions, judgments, and values. While it is easy to recognize how negative perceptions or judgments can influence a helper's ability to be effective, a seasoned student affairs helper also recognizes that strong positive emotions and assumptions about a student can be hindrances as well.

Effective helpers pay close attention to students, attending to both the verbal and nonverbal messages they receive, as well as the ones that they send. They communicate a supportive perspective to students through their actions and their words. Egan (2002) offers the acronym SOLER as a quick checklist for listening behaviors: "*straight*, face-to-face body orientation, with *openness* in body posture and a slight, forward *lean*, while maintaining *eye* contact, and all done in a *relaxed* manner" (Parsons, 2004, p. 51). Helpers use verbal techniques to enhance their listening as well. Verbal prompts, such as "yes" and "mm-hmm," convey a helper's attention and interest in the student's message and encourage the student to continue communicating. When a student hesitates after saying very little, the effective listener understands that the most appropriate response early in the helping process may be simply to invite the student to continue talking, saying "Tell me what you mean" or "Tell me more about that." At the same time, a helper who listens and attends well does not become flustered by pauses during the conversation. Indeed, silence is an important element of listening and attending and one of the most effective skills for new helpers to cultivate (Brammer & MacDonald, 1999; Parsons). Silence demonstrates to the student that the helper is completely focused on the conversation and allows both the helper and the student to reflect for a moment on what the student just said. In general, many of the communication patterns identified in the SOLER approach are very culture specific. Some behaviors—such as direct eye contact, physical space, or use of silence—can be interpreted quite differently across various cultures, and accommodating those differences gracefully can convey the helper's sensitivity and respect for a student's culturally based communication patterns (Pederson & Ivey, 1993).

One of student affairs helpers' greatest challenges to listening is embracing the slow pace necessary to allow students to tell their stories and helpers to begin to understand the students' experiences (Parsons, 2004). Many things can interfere. Unchecked enthusiasm about the topic of conversation can prompt a helper to interrupt the student to share a similar personal experience. Discomfort can lead a helper to fidget or adopt a closed posture, often unwittingly. Fatigue or hunger can intrude and shift a helper's focus from listening to struggling to remain alert or ignore a growling stomach. Multitasking of any sort also powerfully undermines the helping interaction. Thinking about other responsibilities or tasks during a helping conversation will likely diffuse the helper's attention. Reading

e-mail, jotting notes to oneself, and conducting similar activities simultaneously during helping communicate that the helper
is not fully engaged with the student or the helping interaction.
Distracted or distracting helpers are ineffective helpers. With
experience, helpers can become skilled at "turning down the
volume" around them—both internally and externally—and
minimizing the influences outside the immediate helping conversation; they can learn to be fully in that moment.

Skill Cluster 2: Reflecting and Summarizing

A central purpose of any helping interaction is to gain and convey a clear, empathic understanding of the issue that is causing
concern for the student. This can be a challenge for beginning
and seasoned helpers alike. Students who initiate a helping conversation for a stated reason in fact may be experiencing a need to
discuss aspects of the situation that are not immediately evident,
or a reason that is altogether different from the conversation's
starting point (Winston, 2003). Effective helpers begin a helping
interaction by exploring the student's thoughts and feelings about
the situation or dilemma, as the student is currently experiencing
it. Reflecting is a general technique of rearticulating the student's
verbal and nonverbal communication with the goal of achieving an accurate, shared understanding of the student's experience (Brammer & MacDonald, 1999; Okun, 2002). Two forms of
reflecting common in helping interactions are reflections of content (sometimes called "restatements") and reflections of feeling.
Helpers use reflections of content to paraphrase the thoughts or
behaviors that the student is expressing: "You believe that your
relationship has been damaged" or "You do not understand how
to organize the project." Reflections of feeling focus on the emotions that the student is experiencing regarding the dilemma and
expressing both verbally and nonverbally during the helping
conversation. When reflecting feelings, helpers typically rely on

variations of this format: "You feel _____ because _____."
For example: "You feel unhappy because your roommates are
getting ready to graduate and move away" or "You're feeling
proud because you won the student government election." This
approach allows students either to feel fully heard or to provide
an opportunity to clarify their feelings with the helper. Reflecting
feelings in this manner may seem awkward at first, but it becomes
easier over time as new helpers develop their personal technique
and make the skill their own.

Meier and Davis (2005) noted four primary feelings that can
emerge in a helping interaction: anger, sadness, fear, and happiness. Unfortunately, it is easy to rely on a fairly limited vocabulary to reflect students' emotions, including words like *frustrated*,
upset, and *bored*. New helpers can resist this tendency and
enhance their effectiveness by making a detailed list of emotion
words, focusing particularly on generating multiple synonyms for
the terms that arise most frequently in their students' conversations. For instance, descriptive adjectives that a helper might
use to explore and better understand a student's use of the term
frustrated include the following: disappointed, thwarted, dissat-
isfied, discouraged, baffled, unhappy, insecure, defeated, ineffec-
tual, disheartened, embittered, resentful, irked, stymied, beaten,
crushed, and saddened. Having a broad repertoire of terms
allows helpers to explore and identify a student's dilemma in a
more specific manner and gain a more accurate understanding
of a student's emotional experience (Carkhuff, 2000).

As the helping conversation unfolds, the student may begin
to ramble, jump from topic to topic, or become repetitive. At
these points, summarizing the student's thoughts or feelings can
help establish order and add some direction to the conversation. To do this, the helper identifies a thought or idea that has
emerged as a possible core dynamic and distills the student's
communication into one or two sentences that attempt to capture and convey the core message. Consider the following

scenario: a student who is about to complete graduate school made a decision several weeks ago not to look for a job because of health reasons (physical and mental) and now is questioning that choice. After listening to the student's lengthy narrative, the helper offers the following summarization: "You've really thought about your situation and your decision a lot, and your family is supportive; it is your peers' opinions that you are concerned about right now." This summarization proved to be very effective in this real helping situation: the student agreed with the helper's response and then continued by adding the new, unknown factor of future employers' perspectives as another potential cause for concern. The goal is to work toward accurate summarizations that capture and convey an authentic understanding of students' thoughts, feelings, and experiences. Similarly, an effective summarization can guide the student away from distractions and dead-end topics and toward valid, valuable points that the helper and student can continue to explore together.

Skill Cluster 3: Questioning and Clarifying

As the helping conversation progresses into phase 2, a helper may find it necessary to begin asking questions to gain deeper insight into the student's reasoning for certain actions or feelings about specific circumstances or to guide the student to focus. For example: "What were your thoughts as you were making that decision?" or "How do you feel about your parents' decision to move?" or "Out of everything you've said, what is your top priority right now?" In other instances, students may say something that is difficult to understand or could be interpreted in various ways, and the helper will need to ask a question to clarify the meaning that the student intends to convey: "What do you mean by 'senioritis'?" or "What is stress for you—what does it look like?" For example, in any college generation and/or culture, there are certain colloquialisms prevalent in students' daily communication. Students may use terms that seem straightforward—such as *stressed, overwhelmed,* or *freaked out*—on many different occasions and in vastly different ways. Students may also use their own jargon with meanings that are not readily apparent to helpers. As a helper, it is important to understand the student's meaning accurately; therefore, it is the helper's responsibility to clarify any potential confusion or misunderstanding.

To illustrate the helping approach, consider the following statement from a student who is discussing a concern about her parents: "My parents are so annoying; I don't think I want to go home for Thanksgiving." There are many potential meanings behind a statement such as this. For example, the student may fear that his parents will discover a secret that he has been keeping from them, such as the academic difficulty that he has encountered this semester or the large credit card debt that he accumulated recently. The student may feel neglected at home because his parents are newlyweds and openly affectionate or are experiencing marital difficulties and openly hostile. Or the student may feel angry because his parents have instructed him to find a carpool ride home for break instead of driving him themselves. Unless the helper has already engaged in extensive conversations and possesses a clear understanding of the student's home life, the most appropriate response to his statement is likely to be a clarifying question: "When you say that your parents are annoying, what do you mean exactly?" or "What is it about your parents that you find annoying?"

When questioning becomes necessary in helping, there are important techniques to remember that make this skill most effective. First, in most helping interactions, open-ended questions are more productive than closed-ended questions. Open-ended questions in helping often begin with *how* or *what*. For example: "What are your thoughts about the situation right now?" and "How are you feeling about that relationship at this point?" These types of questions are useful in helping conversations because they elicit longer responses and more detailed information from students. Closed-ended questions, in contrast, are those that can be answered with a single word (usually *yes* or *no*) and will begin with such phrases as "do you," "can you," "will you," or "should you," to name just a few. Although some students may respond to a closed-ended question with a paragraph instead of a single word, that will not always be the case. To minimize that possibility, effective helpers use open-ended questions whenever possible.

The second technique in questioning is to avoid asking a question beginning with *why* (Brammer & MacDonald, 1999; Meier & Davis, 2005; Okun, 2002). Curiously, people often find it difficult to answer why they act or feel or think the way they do. Therefore, the most common response to a *why* question is likely to be "I don't know," which then requires the helper to ask follow-up questions. To resolve this dilemma, effective helpers rephrase *why* questions into *what* or *how* questions (Brammer & MacDonald). For example, "Why did you cheat on your exam?" becomes "What were your reasons for cheating on your exam?" or "What were you thinking/feeling while you were cheating?" or "How did you make the decision to cheat on your exam?"

Third, when questioning or clarifying, a very effective approach is to offer a restatement or reflection first and then follow with the question (Parsons, 2004). For example: "It appears that you want your mom's help, and yet she adds some stress on top of everything else. What are some examples of her behaviors that cause you to feel stress?" or "In listening to you, I'm getting a sense that there are lots of feelings associated with this situation for you—some of the feelings I am hearing are anger, resentment, abandonment, loneliness, helplessness, maybe even a little self-pity—and I'm wondering, which ones are the strongest for you right now?" Asking questions in this manner demonstrates that a helper has heard what the student said. This technique is also an effective way to make a helper aware of how frequently s/he is using questions in the helping conversation and thereby prevent the conversation from becoming an interrogation.

Beginning helpers are often surprised to discover that questions are used relatively sparingly during effective helping. They often rely on questions too early in the process, which blocks the natural progression of the helping relationship and the student's story. Experienced helpers understand that questions can feel confrontational and controlling to a student (Brammer & MacDonald, 1999; Meier & Davis, 2005; Okun, 2002), even when that is not the helper's intent. Oftentimes, the information that the helper is seeking with a question can be obtained through the use of an effective restatement of content or reflection of feelings. Why? Because students may not require the direction or focus of a question but simply an invitation to continue with their story.

Skill Cluster 4: Interpreting and Confronting

As noted earlier, the purpose of phase 2 in student affairs helping is for both helper and student to gain a clearer understanding of the student's dilemma and its place within the larger context of the student's life experience. Interpretations are helper statements that provide ways of thinking about the dilemma that the student may not have considered before. They are hunches or hypotheses about the student's dilemma that emerge from the helper's empathic understanding of the student's experience (Egan, 2002; Evans, Hearn, et al., 1998). Helpers offer their interpretations of "the messages behind the messages or the stories behind the stories" (Egan, p. 204) to suggest alternative meanings and explanations that they believe may add value to the student's evolving understanding of her/his dilemma (Evans, Hearn, et al.). Effective interpretations help students "make connections between disparate statements and events, identify patterns of behavior and recurring themes in the discussion, relate present occurrences to past events, and develop a new orientation to their feelings and behaviors, including their impact on others" (Evans, Hearn, et al., p. 185). For example, a career counselor may suggest the following interpretation to a graduating senior who is procrastinating in her job search: "You've experienced a lot of rejection lately that you didn't anticipate and couldn't control, mainly from your parents and your former partner. I wonder if you are resisting searching for a job now because it means exposing yourself to possibly even more rejection."

Students—and sometimes helpers—can get caught up in viewing and discussing a dilemma or concern in very narrow terms. Parsons (2004), citing the work of Arnold Lazarus, described a tool that is useful for analyzing a student's dilemma in general and aids the helper in attending to the range of possible components of the student's experience. BASIC ID (Parsons), which was explored earlier in Chapter 4 on theories, is an acronym for the following elements:

- *Behavior:* The student's actions, including habits and ongoing or prolonged behaviors
- *Affect:* The student's emotions
- *Sensation:* The student's bodily, or biological, feelings
- *Imagery:* The student's self-perceptions, including accurate and inaccurate views, actual and fantasy images, and desired and feared self-concepts (e.g., these can be experienced and/ or expressed in dreams and nightmares)
- *Cognitive:* The student's thoughts and beliefs
- *Interpersonal relationships:* People who are influencing the student's experience or contributing to the dilemma in some way—whether or not the student recognizes their influence
- *Drugs/biology:* The student's consumption (which includes alcohol/drugs, medications, and even food/diet) and elements of the student's biological state, such as being underweight/overweight or experiencing insomnia/fatigue (p. 93)

This framework can assist the helper in considering the presence and potential influence of each element and making connections among important aspects of the student's experiences. An activities coordinator may offer the following observation to a distraught and temperamental club president: "As I listen to you, it occurs to me that you are sacrificing almost all of your personal needs in order to be liked and respected by the club members—including your class attendance, your grades, your relationships with your family and professors, your sleep, your exercise routine, your meals—even your happiness!"

Counselors may rely on a wide range of psychological theories, such as cognitive-behavioral and existential-humanistic, to inform their interpretations (Ivey, Ivey, & Simek-Morgan, 1993; Parsons, 2004). While student affairs helpers do not analyze students in a clinical sense, there is a wealth of student affairs theories, concepts, and models that offer insight and guidance in helping interactions with students. Student development and college impact theories are appropriate tools for student affairs helpers to use to identify and interpret potential reasons for students' feelings. Psychosocial (e.g., general identity, career development, adult development), cognitive-structural (e.g., cognitive reasoning, moral reasoning, faith development), social identity (e.g., racial, sexual, gender, multiple identities), typological (e.g., personality, learning), and student success (e.g., socialization, student departure) perspectives (McEwen, 2003) can inform a helper's interpretation of a student's experiences. Excellent, comprehensive overviews of these theories are offered by Komives and Woodard (2003) and Evans, Forney, and Guido-DiBrito (1998).

Discovering a possible interpretation is only half of the helper's task, however. The second, equally important challenge is introducing the interpretation to the helping interaction in an effective manner. Experienced helpers recognize that their interpretations may suggest a new point of view that the student may find threatening. It is essential, therefore, to offer any interpretation tentatively. For example: "So when you feel like you're not doing well in a course, you kind of give up on yourself—is that what you're saying?"

An effective interpretation can elicit a variety of responses. Usually, it will prompt the student to take pause, both intellectually and literally, as s/he considers the helper's suggestion and tries out the new perspective. Responses such as "I never thought of it that way . . ." or a similar "aha" reaction signal that the helper's observation has resonated with the student. It is important to give the student time to reflect and process the new idea by being silent and observing the student's behaviors.

Students will not always embrace or confirm the interpretation that a helper has offered, which is no cause for worry. When a helper suggests an interpretation that may be incorrect, it is important to allow the student to offer a correction. The helper must *remember* what the student says and modify the interpretation so that it is more accurate. It is vital to remain flexible in interpreting and avoid leading students into interpretations that they don't support.

A helper who has established trust and rapport and gained a deep understanding of the student's experience may also begin to notice discrepancies or inconsistencies in the student's story. Egan (2002) termed these discrepancies "blind spots" because they reflect mind-sets and behaviors that students are "unaware of or choose to ignore in one way or another" (p. 179). Helping students identify and confront their blind spots is critical to helping them move toward more effective patterns of thinking and behaving (Egan). Confrontations (also called "challenges") in student affairs helping may address inconsistencies between student statements: "You say that you don't mind your roommate's threat, but everything else that you have told me leads me to believe that you mind it quite a bit." Effective helpers notice discrepancies between a student's verbal and nonverbal communication and bring that inconsistency to the student's attention: "I am noticing two things right now: you are telling me that the situation isn't affecting you, and at the same time, you appear to be very tense." Helpers may also need to confront conflicts between a student's behaviors and stated viewpoints, beliefs, or values: "I'm trying to understand what would make you want to choose behaviors that you know are going to hurt you or threaten your academic success." Blind spots can obscure students' strengths as well as their limitations and require confrontations to get students "in touch with unexploited opportunities and unused or underused resources" (Egan, p. 194): "You are worried about your writing assignments and confused by the professor's comments, and at the same time, you are hesitant to accept the professor's offer to meet and review your work" or "You demonstrate resourcefulness and time management skills in your internship that you do not appear to apply to your academic assignments."

Effective confrontations, like effective interpretations, are offered tentatively and respectfully within a strong, established helping relationship. Through confrontation, helpers offer honest feedback and invite students to explore their blind spots in a manner that is nonaggressive, noncombative, nonjudgmental, and affirming (Evans, Hearn, et al., 1998; Heron, 2001). When in doubt about confronting, experienced helpers rely on a valuable counseling rule with a familiar student affairs theme: "Confront as much as you have supported" (Meier & Davis, 2005, p. 13).

Skill Cluster 5: Developing Goals and Action Plans

Student affairs professionals are typically experienced at identifying good goals and knowing how to attain them. This strength is critical for complete and effective helping (Egan, 2002). To be effective, however, helpers must remain focused on collaborating *with* the student and not allow themselves to slip into problem solving *for* the student: "Problems belong to clients; it therefore follows that solutions must belong to them as well" (Dainow & Bailey, 1988, p. 78).

Once the helping process has generated a clear understanding of the student's dilemma, the helper's next task is to aid her/him in identifying and specifying goals that can alleviate her/

his dilemma. Parsons (2004) suggests using future-oriented questions to help students conceptualize goals and directions. For example, questions such as "What would your life look like if the dilemma did not exist?" or "In an ideal world, how would you handle this situation?" move the student from thinking about the current dilemma to imagining a more desirable situation in the future. This provides a good foundation for identifying future goals. Helpers often use goal-setting guidelines to assist students in formulating and articulating their goals. Goal-setting guidelines create goals that are personal and positive, challenging, stated as clear and concrete outcomes, specific in direction, achievable and sustainable, measurable, attainable within a reasonable time frame, and of value to the student (Dainow & Bailey, 1988; Egan, 2002; Parsons, 2004). Parsons further suggests that effective goals imply that the student has fully considered the impact that the goal may have on her/his life. Egan referred to this as "identifying competing agendas," such as when achieving one goal means compromising fulfillment of another valued goal (p. 299). For example, achieving the goal of socially integrating into college may compete with a student's desire to remain connected to her high school friends and neighborhood relationships. In effective helping, however, committing oneself to specific goals means accepting the possible consequences and outcomes of one's actions. For example, the student who commits to the goal of earning better grades understands and accepts that achieving this goal may interfere with his current level of involvement in extracurricular activities.

Without a plan of action, however, even the most powerful goals may become meaningless. Effective helpers use a variety of techniques to assist the student in the process of identifying an appropriate path to achieving a goal. Developing an action plan begins with first helping the student generate an array of possible paths or courses of action through brainstorming (Egan, 2002; Parsons, 2004). Helpers facilitate brainstorming by encouraging students to suspend their judgment and generate as many ideas as possible and piggyback or build on earlier suggestions. Once an exhaustive list has been compiled, the next challenge is to evaluate the multiple options to identify viable possibilities and eventually choose a direction. Conducting a cost-benefit analysis of several choices can help the student pinpoint the action plan most connected to the desired goal, identify important resources, and own the solution (Egan; Parsons).

A second means for determining a feasible course of action is through force-field analysis (Parsons, 2004). The process centers on identifying the forces in a student's experience that may facilitate *and* restrain her/his progress toward a desired goal and evaluating the strength of those influences. Students may experience powerful forces (physical, psychological, or social) coming from inside themselves as well as from their environment (including the helper). In student affairs helping, an analysis of facilitating and restraining forces can help a student create workable, valid goals from a lengthy list of possibilities. In turn, a force-field analysis of a desired goal provides a valuable blueprint for action. To move from goal to action, students consider each facilitating force identified in the analysis and identify specific strategies or actions that will enhance the positive influence of that force. The student repeats the same process for each restraining force, identifying specific strategies or action steps that will weaken or eliminate the negative influence of each restraining force. By the end of the process, the student has created a detailed plan of action for achieving the desired goal. Developing an action plan in this manner helps a student break down a challenging primary goal into a manageable series of subgoals and action steps.

Arriving at goal setting and action planning in the helping process can feel like a welcome return to familiar turf for student affairs helpers. Inexperienced helpers may be tempted to offer advice about the student's goals or actions at this point, especially when confronted with a student's direct request to do so. Giving advice poses several threats to effective helping, however, and generally should be avoided. To begin, advice signals that the helper has shifted from listening to "fixing" the student (Meier & Davis, 2005). It presumes that the helper is more capable of developing goals and actions than the student, which can introduce an unhealthy element of dependence into the relationship (Brammer & MacDonald, 1999). Advice can sound like demands to students and add burdens of obligation and judgment to the helping interaction (Okun, 2002). Lastly, advice often backfires! Students who seek it rarely follow it; those who follow it find it easy to blame the helper when the advice fails to get the desired results (Brammer & MacDonald).

It is essential for helpers to maintain the same spirit of collaboration during goal setting and action planning that they worked hard to cultivate throughout the helping interaction. In addition to introducing and facilitating the techniques just described, effective helpers will continue to rely on the core skills of listening, summarizing, clarifying, and interpreting to facilitate students' progress toward self-understanding and positive action.

Skill Cluster 6: Making Referrals

Some helping interactions reach a point where the helper's levels of skill, knowledge, and/or responsibility are not appropriate or adequate to address the student's dilemma, and the student would be better served by continuing the process with a different helper. When this happens, an effective helper identifies an appropriate alternative resource for the student and initiates a referral. In most cases, the severity of the problem and the helper's expertise in the problem area will dictate when to refer (Parsons, 2004). To make effective referrals, therefore, student affairs helpers must be able to accurately understand and acknowledge the limits of their own expertise and recognize when a helping interaction requires different or greater assistance than they are able or willing to provide. Referral opportunities are typically plentiful and varied. For instance, appropriate referrals for a student who wants to withdraw from a course or take a leave of absence for a semester may include a course professor, an academic adviser, and the registrar. For a student with an eating disorder or substance addiction, appropriate referrals include a mental health counselor, a medical doctor, or a nurse practitioner. A student with excessive credit card debt may benefit from referrals to a financial aid counselor and a career counselor (for assistance finding a part-time job). Effective referrals for a student who is feeling homesick and lonely may include a student activities coordinator, a residence hall director, and an international student services coordinator.

Accurately assessing a student's dilemma is central to making a successful referral. Winston's (2003) framework for conceptualizing students' concerns offers a useful tool for identifying a range of possible student dilemmas, evaluating their severity, and determining the appropriate helping resources. At one end of the spectrum are adjustment/situational and developmental concerns, which represent experiences and dilemmas that could be defined as typical and normal for healthy students and are therefore the most appropriate matches for student affairs helpers. Okun (2002) called these students the "worried well" (p. 4). Examples of developmental concerns include problems that are consistent with developmental theory or are appropriate at certain points during college; problems concerning environmental situations, relationships, skill or knowledge deficiencies, and students' satisfaction or comfort levels; and problems that students are able and willing to address and solve through taking action.

At the other end of the conceptual spectrum are the remedial concerns; many of these dilemmas are outside the expertise of most student affairs helpers. Students who are experiencing one or more of the following types of remedial dilemmas need prompt and effective referrals to appropriate helping/counseling resources: problems inconsistent with developmental theory or normal college expectations; dysfunctional behaviors that interfere with the student's ability to perform daily tasks; problems that are psychological, chronic, or rooted in past experiences, including intentions to harm oneself or others.

Winston (2003) identified a final category of student concerns that exists between the two extremes noted already, which may reflect a combination of developmental and remedial concerns. Defined as unclear concerns, these dilemmas may be appropriate matches for student affairs helpers initially. However, as the helping interaction progresses and the nature of the student's dilemma becomes clearer, helpers will need to determine whether the student requires a developmental approach or a referral to a remedial helping approach. Unclear concerns may be identified through students' behaviors demonstrated during the helping interaction, including an inability to identify the source of their concern, to analyze their behaviors realistically, or to focus in general; emotions or nonverbal behaviors that are not consistent with the stated problem; an inability or unwillingness to take action; and blaming others for the problem. For example, a sophomore athlete on academic probation is presenting an unclear concern when she tells the coach that she is worried about her grades this semester and angry at her professors because they "don't teach" and they don't grade fairly. In fact, she may be academically underprepared and struggling and is afraid to admit it but instead is quick to blame others.

Helpers must offer referrals with the same care as interpretations and confrontations, bearing in mind that students may feel threatened by the suggestion that their dilemma requires expert or professional attention. To be effective, helpers must present the referral in the spirit of respect and collaboration, which may include taking the first steps to arrange the initial contact between the student and the referral, either by telephone or in person. It is critical, therefore, for student affairs helpers to become familiar with the resources available to students, beginning with those offered on their own campuses. Effective helpers maintain files of accurate information regarding the locations, phone numbers, staff, and specific services offered by various offices. Taking the initiative to visit offices and meet members of the professional and support staff paves the way for future referral interactions. Being able to connect a student with a specific staff member can make the difference between a referral that succeeds and one that never comes to fruition.

Challenges for New Helpers: Temptations and Fears

Student affairs professionals who are new to helping have often already developed some helping skills. For example, they may be comfortable and adept with techniques such as questioning and developing goals. Effective helping, however, involves not only acquiring helping skills but also knowing how and when to use them. One of the first challenges in learning to be an effective helper, therefore, is to resist the temptation to rely heavily on the skills that feel most comfortable. There are a number of temptations that can challenge new helpers; the four discussed here occur frequently among student affairs helpers in training.

Temptation 1: Excessive Questioning and Fact-Finding

At the beginning of a new helping conversation, it is easy to become distracted with discovering the facts and minutiae of the situation that is creating a concern for the student, which can cause a helper to overwhelm the student with questions. Although it can seem counterintuitive and uncomfortable at first, it is not necessary for a helper to have a crystal-clear picture of all the details to be effective. On the contrary, excessive fact-finding can interfere with a helper's ability to focus on the student and prevent the helping process from ever truly beginning. Student affairs helpers are neither police officers nor judges; they are not required to re-create the dilemma nor determine beyond the shadow of a doubt whether a student's perceptions of a situation are valid or justified. Instead, during the first phase of helping, it is important to remember that the student's perception of reality is the only salient reality, and the helper's primary task is to identify and understand the thoughts and emotions that the student is experiencing in response to the situation.

Excessive questioning also includes the habit of asking two or more questions during one helper response. Helpers may ask multiple questions while they are still gathering their thoughts. Multiple questions also may reflect the helper's indecision. Anxiety can lead to excessive questioning, as the helper struggles to identify a possible focus for the helping interaction. Multiple questions pose barriers to effective helping because they may confuse the student and hinder the helper's ability to guide the helping conversation. Instead, a student confronted with multiple questions is left to guess which one the helper wants answered. To avoid multiple questions, new helpers must train themselves to take time, pause, and collect their thoughts.

Temptation 2: Emphasizing Third Parties

Helping conversations often stem from a student's concern about an interpersonal relationship. Students may approach a helper with the hope of gaining a deeper understanding about the thoughts and/or emotions of people who are not present in the conversation (i.e., third parties), such as roommates, friends, partners, or parents. Helping conversations that focus on the thoughts or feelings of someone who is not present are typically unproductive, however, and draw attention away from the helper's efforts to understand the student who *is* present. Experienced helpers understand that they cannot help or change any person who is absent from the helping conversation, nor can they fully understand that person's thoughts, feelings, or actions. Instead, the goal in effective helping is to remain focused on understanding the student who is participating in the helping interaction. This is true even when students would prefer to try to analyze or diagnose individuals other than themselves. When confronted with this situation, effective helpers focus attention on exploring the knowledge that *is* available (i.e., the student's own experiences) and facilitating a deeper understanding of the student's own thoughts, feelings, and actions in response to the third person.

Temptation 3: Premature Self-Disclosure

Beginning helpers often perceive self-disclosure as an effective way to establish rapport with a student. This is a very natural tendency—sharing personal experiences is the foundation for most healthy friendships to begin and grow. Experienced helpers understand, however, that developing a helping relationship with students is distinctly different from developing a friendship with peers (D'Augelli et al., 1981). Offering stories about the helper's own experiences too early in the helping process may have the undesired effect of drawing the focus away from the student and toward the helper (Okun, 2002). This can stall the helping interaction. Instead, beginning helpers are best advised to limit their self-disclosures to phases 2 or 3 of the helping interaction, and then only for the purposes of insight, interpretation, and enhancing the student's self-understanding.

Temptation 4: Premature Problem Solving

It is likely that one of the strongest skills among beginning helpers in student affairs is the ability to set good goals and get things accomplished. Indeed, experienced administrators rank problem solving highly among common responsibilities of entry-level student affairs professionals (Burkard et al., 2005). During the helping interaction, however, new helpers who feel pressure to "fix" a student's problem can quickly move to goal setting or action before adequately exploring students' emotions or thoughts. The desire to make students feel better can prompt a helper to overwhelm them with advice and overly optimistic interpretations (Parsons, 2004). This interferes with a helper's ability to recognize students' true dilemmas and may cause the student to feel neglected in the helping process. Although student affairs helpers do not conduct ongoing therapy with students, they do have the responsibility to provide care and support to students by listening to their concerns and difficulties and to assist them by accurately identifying the type of help that they need and how to attain it.

In addition to these common temptations, helpers in training often experience certain fears that may inhibit their helping.

Fear 1: Saying the "Right" Thing or Making "Mistakes"

New helpers may feel significant pressure to say the "right" thing—such as the right question, the right insight, the right piece of advice. There are a variety of techniques that can assist helpers in overcoming this fear. First, helpers can relieve themselves of this pressure by remembering that they are collaborators with students in the helping process: the student has sought the helper's assistance in understanding something that is a concern, and together they will determine the nature of the dilemma and how to address it. Second, open-ended questions that invite the student to identify and share accurate thoughts and feelings can be effective devices for helpers who feel pressure to ask the right questions. Closed-ended questions, in contrast, increase pressure by shifting the onus onto the helper to identify accurate thoughts or feelings for the student to either confirm or deny. And finally, when a helper is struggling to think of what to say next, the best response may be simply to pause: "Let me think about that for a minute." Meier and Davis (2005) put it succinctly: "When you don't know what to say, say nothing" (p. 11).

A related concern is the fear of making mistakes during the helping conversation. It is important to remember that almost any "mistake" that helpers make during a helping conversation can be remedied immediately. For example, a helper who realizes that he has missed exploring an important element of the student's experience can remedy the situation by redirecting the conversation: "Let's go back to an earlier point." A helper who finds herself asking too many questions can simply pause and say, "Wait, let me rephrase that," and reword her next question into a restatement or reflection. As one helper in training noted: "If you say something that doesn't work, it doesn't ruin the entire helping conversation—you only have to try another technique."

Fear 2: Silence

New helpers often report feeling uncomfortable with silence. Pauses of a few seconds or more during the helping conversation seem to last an eternity. Inexperienced helpers who are uncomfortable with any gaps in the helping conversation often resort to asking questions to fill the silence. But silence often signals and facilitates important progress in a helping conversation (Brammer & MacDonald, 1999; Parsons, 2004). As noted earlier, allowing silence to occur demonstrates to the student that the helper is completely focused on the conversation and lets the helper reflect for a moment on what the student has just said. In later helping phases, silence permits students to reflect on the helping interaction and possibly gain new insights on their own. Tape-recording practice helping conversations enables new helpers to listen to the flow of their conversations and begin to perceive the silences more accurately. It is also important to reiterate that silence has different meanings and is dealt with differently across cultures and that not all graduate students and professionals will have difficulty with this skill.

Fear 3: Exploring Feelings

Some new helpers feel uncomfortable or tentative about exploring a student's feelings because they fear they're intruding into the student's private life. This is often a mistaken caution, however. Schlossberg and Rendon (cited in Evans, Forney, et al., 1998) have long identified the importance of mattering and validation in fostering students' success in college. An effective way for helpers to validate students is to demonstrate that they are receptive and willing to listen to the topics that concern students most. Emotions, in turn, often provide powerful clues about the true nature of a student's concern and are central to the helping process. Evans, Hearn, et al. (1998) further suggested that "discussing feelings is often an important prerequisite to solving problems" (p. 64). Therefore, regardless of the helper's or student's level of comfort exploring and expressing emotions, Meier and Davis (2005) advise, "When in doubt, focus on feelings" (p. 17).

Fear 4: Practicing

It is impossible to develop helping skills simply by reading about them. Instead, a new helper must become actively involved in learning microskills to gain competency (Meier & Davis, 2005; Okun, 2002). Only practice can make the unfamiliar familiar. Ironically, the idea of participating in practice helping conversations, even with classmates, can cause anxiety among beginning helpers. Practicing with a small group of trusted classmates who are willing to offer honest feedback is a powerful learning experience for student helpers, however. An even better way to monitor progress and truly assess one's own strengths and weaknesses as a helper is to engage in practice helping conversations that are tape-recorded and can be reviewed afterward. While many student helpers in training never feel completely comfortable listening to the sound of their own recorded voices, they discover insights into their own helping styles and abilities that are impossible to recognize in the moment.

Summary

Student affairs professionals are members of a large community of campus personnel dedicated to helping students succeed and thrive during their college years. They approach the challenges of that responsibility armed with energy, enthusiasm, and the good intentions of providing the best help possible. Truly effective helping, however, demands all that and much more. Effective helping is not accidental, but rather the intentional result of a skilled and structured interaction intended to foster rapport, self-understanding, and positive action. Effective helping requires honest self-reflection and self-assessment. Most important of all, effective helping—similar to effective leading—can be learned. Through presentations of helping processes, skills, and challenges, this chapter explored the complexities of the helping conversation as a unique interaction within student affairs work. It is offered as a starting point for reflection and continued development for both beginning and seasoned helpers.

Chapter Seven

Conflict and Crisis Management

As helpers, student affairs professionals are often on the front lines of any crisis or conflict that involves students. According to Duncan (1993), "It's almost impossible to work for any period of time in student affairs without facing a campus crisis" (p. 340). As a matter of routine, campuses experience many challenges and tragedies, such as the death or suicide of a student, domestic violence and stalking, hate crimes, rape, bomb threats, and other disturbing events (Epstein, 2004). Many campuses also find themselves facing large-scale crises or critical incidents that significantly affect the entire campus community, such as fires, environmental disasters like tornados, major health epidemics, or large-scale acts of violence. Rollo and Zdziarski (2007) offered a brief synopsis of some major campus crisis events of the past twenty years. In addition, dealing with campus conflict has become a major responsibility of student affairs practitioners. Rollo and Zdziarski suggested that such work grows out of the student affairs profession's ethic of care that helps practitioners "put a human face" on their institution (p. 5). According to Creamer (1993), many student affairs administrators spend as much as 40 percent of their time managing conflicts among individuals, units, and groups; they are often "called upon to relieve conflicts among people across the entire spectrum of the organization" (p. 314). Being able to respond effectively to these diverse and demanding crises and conflicts is fast becoming a basic competence for student affairs professionals.

The "increasingly complex and vexing problems" within colleges and universities requires student affairs professionals to become better prepared to recognize and react to these concerns in meaningful and constructive ways (Pruett & Brown, 1990, p. 3). The first step is to be aware of the potential for crises and conflicts on campus; unfortunately, higher education is not immune to the chaos, unrest, violence, hatred and discrimination, seemingly random environmental events, and interpersonal discord and incivility that exist in the larger society. "Given the number of potential crises that may be faced by student services, administrative, and emergency service personnel in higher education, emergency preparedness is a necessity" (Dunkel, Griffin, & Probert, 1998, p. 147).

The purpose of this chapter is to explore the different ways that crises and conflicts occur on college campuses and the role of student affairs professionals in addressing these issues. Being prepared with the necessary awareness, knowledge, and skills to resolve conflicts and address the various crises that can occur on a college campus is essential for every practitioner. Specific strategies for responding to campus crises and conflicts are explored, and illustrations are used throughout the chapter to explore what to do and what not to do to address these issues effectively. Finally, preparation and training concerns for addressing crises and conflicts are examined.

Although crisis intervention and conflict resolution and management are two distinct areas of helping with their own literature and scholarship, they require some similar awareness, knowledge, and skills. For example, awareness of your own comfort with chaos, knowledge of the impact that crises and conflict have on students' personal and academic success, and the ability to handle intense emotions (yours and others') are some of the competencies student affairs professionals need to respond to and manage both crises and conflicts on campus in effective ways. Further exploration of what defines crises and conflicts and what impact they have on the individuals who experience them is important before exploring the specific awareness, knowledge, and skills needed and possible strategies for addressing these events on campus.

When discussing campus crises, it is useful to understand that crises can encompass a wide range of intrapersonal, interpersonal, and societal events. It can be one individual's own emotional and psychological struggle, an interpersonal conflict, or a large-scale critical incident that has a significant effect on the community. A suicidal student or one in the throes of an emotional breakup may approach a student affairs professional in crisis. A student on the verge of failing out of the university may be in distress because he has never told his parents that he is in academic jeopardy. A young woman sexually assaulted in the laundry room of a residence hall is likely traumatized, as are the members of her community. A tornado or campus fire that leaves behind both physical and emotional devastation is another example of a campus crisis to which student affairs practitioners will need to respond. College is full of many events and experiences that can trigger a crisis; many of these are managed effectively by students with the help of roommates, friends, parents, resident advisers, and other campus personnel. However, sometimes the initial crisis is never fully resolved or escalates, which can lead to diminished functioning and coping (Pruett, 1990).

Not every major life event creates a crisis (Pruett & Brown, 1990). Often what constitutes a crisis is not the event itself but rather an individual or community's view of or response to the event. The same event can be experienced by multiple individuals, traumatizing some but not others; it is the intense emotional experience that often creates the crisis more than the situation itself (Okun, 1997). According to Okun, "A crisis is a state that exists when a person is thrown completely off balance emotionally by an unexpected and potentially harmful event or difficult life transition" (p. 229). Pruett and Brown viewed a crisis as a barrier to important life goals that is not easily overcome by the usual problem-solving approaches. When past ways of solving problems and coping no longer seem to work, it may lead to frustration, confusion, or disorganization (Okun). During a crisis individuals may feel out of control of their lives (Okun) and may view the experience as a threat, loss, or significant challenge (Pruett & Brown). This reaction may result from previous life events or experiences or how one has responded to minor crises during childhood and adolescence. A person's sociocultural background and experiences may also influence the meaning s/he gives to a potential crisis and the impact it has (Okun). These "stressful events impact survivors in their bodies, their personal psychology, and in how they interact with the world" (Halpern & Tramontin, 2007, p. 81).

Some campus events are more universally viewed as a crisis, such as a weather-related or environmental disaster. According to Halpern and Tramontin (2007), there are both human-caused and natural disasters. The natural disasters include events like floods, hurricanes, tornados, wildfires, earthquakes, extreme heat or cold, and blizzards. Human-caused disasters include residential fires, transportation disasters like plane crashes, infectious diseases, large-scale violence, toxic waste, terrorism, and hoaxes. According to Rollo and Zdziarski (2007), there are several characteristics that constitute a campus crisis: (1) perception of the event or outcome, (2) element of surprise, (3) limited response time, (4) interruption of operations, and (5) threat to safety and well-being. This definition is a foundation that can assist campuses in their planning process: "A crisis is an event, which is often sudden or unexpected, that disrupts the normal operations of the institution or its educational mission, and threatens the well-being of personnel, property, financial resources, and/or reputation of the institution" (Zdziarski, 2006, p. 5). These types of crises or critical incidents often have a stressful impact that is significant enough to overwhelm the usually effective coping skills and equilibrium of any individual or group. These experiences are often outside the range of ordinary human experience and typically have a traumatic effect on groups of people and organizations

(Okun, 1997). This shared experience usually has a lasting impact on groups, roles, and the relationships between people. The definition used is essential because "how an institution or organizational unit defines crisis has a significant impact on the crisis management system it develops" (Rollo & Zdziarski, p. 30).

Halpern and Tramontin (2007) suggested that the scope, intensity, and duration of the event likely determine, or at least influence, the reaction and reality of the survivors. Typically, the larger the crisis or disaster, the stronger the reaction will be. The larger the scale of an incident, the more it will affect an individual's support system and her/his daily life. Big events may lead to evacuation, relocation, and ultimately, more uncertainty, which can be very stressful (Halpern & Tramontin). Scope, intensity, and duration also affect more individualized crises, like domestic violence, sexual abuse, or the loss of a parent or partner. "The meaning given to a life event determines whether it becomes a hazard and triggers a crisis" (Pruett & Brown, 1990, p. 5). In addition, certain characteristics—such as resilience, hardiness, and other positive strengths—determine how one views or is able to cope with a crisis or disaster.

Okun (1997) identified six types of individualized emotional crises: (1) dispositional—lack of information and difficulty making a decision; (2) anticipatory life transitions—normal developmental time periods, like going to college or becoming a parent; (3) traumatic stress—external stressful situations that are often overwhelming, like rape, assault, sudden death of a loved one; (4) maturational/developmental crisis—developmentally expected challenges, such as responding to authority, dependency, or a midlife crisis; (5) psychopathological—caused by a preexisting pathology that makes it difficult to respond effectively to a crisis; and (6) psychiatric emergencies—impaired functioning due to a psychiatric crisis when one is a danger to her/himself or others or incapable of self-care. Any one of these situational or developmental events can occur on a college campus and will likely require different responses and interventions.

Similar to campus crises or critical incidents, campus conflicts range in severity and intensity. They can be minor and somewhat uncomplicated conflicts, such as those that might occur between two roommates or within a classroom, or become complicated with major consequences and risks, such as major conflict and crisis between two student organizations (Creamer, 1993). Gibson (1995) suggested that the pressures of student life can lead to conflict: "Students' exposure to academic stress, frequent challenges to their beliefs, fatigue, shared living quarters, and other trying facets of campus culture make interpersonal and group conflict an inevitable part of student life" (p. 27). These conflicts can be intrapersonal, intragroup, or intergroup and involve academic, interpersonal, economic, ethical, or cultural dynamics and pressures.

Conflicts are a normal and natural part of human interaction; however, they can have either a constructive or a destructive effect on the individuals involved and the surrounding climate. According to Baron (1990), this effect is determined by the type of conflict and how it is handled. If handled effectively, conflicts can lead to improved communication and critical thinking, increased cooperation and collaboration, broader vision, and other positive outcomes (Creamer, 1993). Conflict can be a natural, healthy process that encourages self-examination and personal growth. Warters (2000) suggested that "many good theories, innovative new practices, and well-prepared, critically thinking students have emerged from the crucible of campus conflict" (p. 1). However, Creamer suggested that unresolved or ineffectively handled conflicts can lead to disruption, territorialism, breakdowns in communication, lack of empathy, narrow-mindedness, and even worse, violence. On a more personal and academic level, Gibson (1995) suggested that without effective conflict management, college students' retention and academic success is in jeopardy; ultimately, this leads to "increasing hardship on the individuals, the departments, and the institutions" of higher education (Holton, 1995a).

The intersection of developmental issues, intellectual rigor, and interpersonal dynamics causes higher education to be "a fertile environment for conflict" (Creamer, 1993, p. 314). Some scholars have suggested that increasing pluralism among students (in terms of ideas and identity) makes intergroup conflict more likely (Archer & Cooper, 1998; Warters, 2000). Conflicts can occur between students and faculty members, between students, between parents and administration, and between student organizations, for example. In fact, some practitioners believe that conflict on campuses has become more prevalent in recent years (Holton, 1995c). While some believe that higher education should be above the petty conflicts that occur in the corporate world or other traditional organizations, in reality, campus conflict is not something that can or should be avoided (Findlen, 2000).

Illustrations of Crises and Conflicts Across Student Affairs Functional Areas

Examining the different types of situations and contexts in which student affairs practitioners work with conflict and crisis can increase one's awareness and readiness. This book previously identified various functional areas within student affairs as a way to conceptualize the types of roles and responsibilities that practitioners may face: (1) counseling-oriented positions like career and personal counseling; (2) leadership development and educational positions (e.g., student activities, Greek affairs, campus life, health and wellness, and residence life); (3) administrative positions like dean of students, judicial affairs, and admissions; and (4) academic affairs positions (e.g., advisement and academic support services). The rest of this chapter identifies various examples to increase awareness of how crises and conflicts may manifest themselves.

Within the counseling functional area, student affairs professionals are very likely to interact with students who come to them asking for assistance with personal problems, which may include crises and interpersonal conflicts. This may occur when students make an appointment at the counseling center because they are not sure how else to solve their problems or they have been in counseling in the past and found it helpful. Or sometimes students will approach other helpers on campus, such as a career counselor, and begin by talking about their academic or career concerns because it feels safer than addressing their personal or emotional concerns. Students may initiate these conversations and ask for assistance or advice. Other students do not feel comfortable asking for help, but their behavior may indicate that they are troubled by something. If a student leader's behavior or appearance changes drastically (e.g., he quits showering and taking care of his appearance) or he seems withdrawn or emotional, practitioners need to ask him whether everything is all right. If a positive working relationship is established, such discussions should not be difficult; it can be a natural result of the ethic of care suggested by Rollo and Zdziarski (2007). Sometimes students may approach a practitioner for the first time, and it is obvious that they are in distress. Under such circumstances, student affairs professionals must focus their full attention on the problem at hand. In addition, when there are campuswide critical incidents or crises, practitioners with well-established helping skills may be asked to volunteer their time and energy to assist community members. They may even be asked to serve as part of critical-incident or emergency-preparedness campus teams. In terms of campus conflict on the individual or broader scale, counseling-oriented professionals may be asked to assist in resolving conflicts because of their unique skill set. Assisting an individual student with a roommate conflict or consulting about a conflict between the student newspaper and a student organization are just two examples.

As part of leadership development and educational positions, many student affairs professionals often assist students who are struggling with interpersonal conflict and possibly personal crises. A significant aspect of these positions involves working with peer helpers (e.g., resident advisers, health educators) or student leaders, and it is not uncommon to form positive, strong relationships with these active and dedicated students. Such relationships make student affairs professionals likely confidants, and they may find themselves invited into the personal lives of the students with whom they work. A student leader may happen to drop into the office of a student affairs practitioner and begin to talk about some very private family problems or concerns. In addition, training, staff meetings, and organizational/government meetings offer opportunities to observe how students interact with each other. Undoubtedly, these observations allow student affairs professionals to witness interpersonal and group conflict, such as when two student leaders on the executive board of a student organization openly fight at board meetings, or when two campus organizations hold an interactive campus program and major conflict erupts. The challenge in these situations is deciding when to observe and allow the students to handle the conflict and when to intervene. Ignoring or avoiding the conflict is definitely not the message practitioners want to send; however, it is also important to allow the student leaders the opportunity to learn and grow from interpersonal challenges.

In many administrative positions, student affairs professionals often address student crises or conflicts as they are happening, as in certain campuswide critical incidents, or after the fact, as in judicial or disciplinary cases. Many practitioners who work in predominantly administrative positions are often responsible for addressing students' behavioral issues and the effect of such issues on the community. While these administrators may not always directly mediate the actual conflict that can occur between students and student organizations, they are often responsible for ensuring that such mediation occurs. In addition, when there are significant crises on campus, it is not usual for primary administrators—such as the director of residence life, dean of students, or vice president of student affairs—to have some major responsibility for coordinating the response. Events like a drug overdose in the residence hall or a fight in the student union are often addressed, if not resolved, with the direct intervention of student affairs practitioners. Such interventions can include dealing directly with the students, staff, faculty, parents, and community members affected by these crises. This involvement requires specific helping skills that assist practitioners in their helping and crisis management efforts.

Finally, individuals in academic affairs positions are likely to come into contact with crises or conflict situations as a result of their helping interactions with students. As they develop meaningful and effective bonds with students, they may be able to build enough trust so that when the students are upset or in need, they will initiate discussing their current crisis or conflict. If a student wants to change her/his major against her/his parents' wishes, it may cause a major conflict with the parents that causes the student to experience a major crisis. Or a student may be having an ongoing conflict with a professor that is affecting her/his academic performance. In these situations administrators need to have well-established interpersonal and helping skills that allow them to intervene effectively and, when necessary, refer students to the appropriate staff members on campus.

Specific Crisis and Conflict Management Competencies for Student Affairs Professionals

There are many important crisis and conflict competencies that assist student affairs professionals in confronting the challenges of working on college campuses. Many of these competencies—awareness, knowledge, and skills—are similar to what is needed to work effectively with mental health issues. However, there are also some unique competencies needed to address the specific and singular realities of crisis and conflict work.

In terms of the awareness needed to work effectively with crises and conflict situations, there is none more important than accepting that crises and conflicts are a natural part of life.

Accepting them as a common response to life's challenges allows practitioners to be open-minded and accepting of where students are. Many college students experience developmental upheavals that cause them to struggle with values conflicts, autonomy and rebellion, interpersonal competence, acceptance of difference, and identity confusion and transformation. Is it any wonder that they experience challenging intrapersonal crises as well as interpersonal conflicts? It is important that practitioners be aware of their own reactions to students' perceptions and assumptions about what constitutes a crisis and conflict. Being nonjudgmental is essential to building trust and helping others. A student may ask for help in dealing with a major crisis, and when the student affairs professional finds out that it is "just" a relationship breakup, s/he may have difficulty taking the problem seriously, which means that the student will not get the needed help. For practitioners, awareness includes being cognizant of their own reactions and emotions that might possibly interfere with effective helping. Sometimes being around the intense emotions that crises and conflicts may cause is difficult because of individuals' previous experiences, particular beliefs, or assumptions about emotionality. Being aware of these reactions and being able to channel them is essential to being an effective and ethical helper (Duncan, 1993). In addition to emotionality, being comfortable with actual conflict is important. Because we are all raised with different messages about how we should express our emotions and how we should argue and deal with conflict, we need to know ourselves well enough to know our own comfort and discomfort zones. It is also important for practitioners to be comfortable with the ambiguity and unpredictability that sometimes comes when dealing with conflict and crises. Whether it is an individual crisis or large-scale critical incident, when individuals are under stress they do not always act in predictable ways. Without such self-awareness, student affairs practitioners may not be able to be supportive and help students resolve their crises and conflicts. In these situations it is vital that practitioners be trustworthy and dependable because "how student affairs professionals deal with crises will have a lasting influence on the lives of the students who are touched" (Duncan, p. 347).

The importance of developing a knowledge base about crises and conflicts cannot be overemphasized. Crisis work and conflict/mediation work is not like general helping. There is literature that discusses the stages that individuals go through when dealing with a crisis or critical incident, and those stages influence which strategies are most effective in addressing the concerns. Without this knowledge and understanding, student affairs professionals will not be able to provide the support and assistance needed to be helpful with this population. Gathering information through reading, attending professional conferences, and talking with knowledgeable colleagues helps prepare practitioners to be effective responders to both crises and conflicts. Some of the best literature for addressing these concerns comes from outside the student affairs and higher education literature and does not address unique applications for college campuses; however, the basic knowledge gathered from these sources can build an excellent foundation on which effective interventions can be based. Being well read and professionally educated allows one to discern among conflicting ideas, theories, and practices. For example, without some knowledge about the literature on large-scale crisis intervention and critical-incident debriefing, one would not understand the current controversy about which methods are useful and which methods may be harmful to individuals in distress (e.g., Epstein, 2004). Or, without an understanding of how individuals may grieve differently, it is difficult to determine accurately the students on a residence hall floor who need support in dealing with the death of someone who lived in the building. It is not always the emotional and upset person who needs support; many individuals mask their grief and may even act out inappropriately. Student affairs professionals do not have to become experts in crisis work; that is not typically their primary training or job responsibility.

However, it important to be educated enough to be able to ask effective questions and knowledgeable enough to discern when to consult with experts.

Cultivating the unique helping skills necessary to respond effectively to crises and conflicts on the individual, interpersonal, and campuswide levels is crucial. It is likely that such skill development will come primarily through on-the-job training, professional education through conferences, online Listservs, teleconferences, and supervision. Being able to establish rapport quickly with an unfamiliar student in crisis or learning how to conduct a brief lethality check before referring students to the counseling center to ensure their safety are just two examples of some important skills that student affairs professionals likely need as part of their work with students. Likewise, practitioners need to develop the skills to facilitate a meaningful mediation or conflict resolution between individual students or organizations. Learning how to ensure that all individuals involved in a conflict feel heard and are able to respect the rules for finding common ground represent two essential abilities needed to intervene in conflict. There is no substitution for practice, experience, and learning from one's mistakes when it comes to developing helping skills; however, there may be times when the stakes seem too high to learn as you go. When students are in extreme distress or practitioners are worried that the conflict could evolve into violence, it is appropriate and necessary to involve others. In those situations there is no substitution for supervision and consultation with professionals who possess expertise in these areas.

It is important that the influence of culture on crisis and conflict situations be acknowledged because culture is relevant to the individuals involved in such events and how they make meaning of the experience. Cultural differences in how various racial/ethnic groups handle conflict have been well established. For example, if there is a conflict between two male students, one African American and one white, the students' racial background can affect how they interpret that conflict and how it

plays out (Kochman, 1981). The typical view in the domi-
nant white culture is that a fight begins when the first punch
is thrown; however, black culture often views earlier stages of
the confrontation, such as verbal threats and physical confrontation in use of space, as the beginning of a fight. If such a racial
divide in perception exists and goes unaddressed and unac-
knowledged, the true underlying conflict, and how both parties
feel about it, will not be resolved.

Another way in which culture can influence a campuswide
crisis or conflict is when the event affects a member of a particular underrepresented or underserved group. If there is a homophobic event on campus, how the campus addresses it effectively
does not always determine the reaction of the cultural groups
involved. If members of these groups on campus already feel
misunderstood, ignored, or mistreated, the event itself can
highlight those feelings and further the students' isolation and
heighten their frustration. The campus climate or the identity
developmental level of the individuals involved can influence a
negative reaction. It is important in any campus crisis or conflict
that student affairs professionals assess the degree to which cultural realities are influencing what is happening. Understanding
the cultural realities and influences surrounding communication style, the meaning of conflict, identity development, and
campus climate experience is an important part of multicultural
competence that is essential to effectively addressing crisis and
conflict on campus.

Strategies and Tools for Addressing Crises and Conflicts on Campus

Entire books and journal articles already exist that discuss the
necessary strategies and most effective approaches to addressing
conflicts and crises (cf. Epstein, 2004; Holton, 1995a; Pruett &
Brown, 1990; Warters, 2000; Zdziarski, Dunkel, Rollo, & Associates, 2007), and fully exploring this literature is beyond the

scope of this chapter. It is possible to identify some of the most central tenets and approaches for crisis and conflict management to further understanding of what addressing the various crises, critical incidents, and conflicts that can occur on a college campus entails.

Crisis Work

The first and possibly most important strategy or tool for dealing with campus crises is assessment or detection. The earlier that we are aware that a crisis is occurring for an individual student, an organization, or the campus as a whole, the easier it is to intervene in a positive, constructive, and proactive manner. If we wait to see whether the crisis blows over or if we are not aware of a problem until it has become a full-blown crisis, then our ability to respond in meaningful ways is diminished. The key to early detection is being engaged with our students and our surroundings on a constant basis, rather than only when there is a problem. Sometimes practitioners are consumed with their daily administrative tasks and demands, which keep them tied to their desks or offices. And yet, when student affairs professionals walk around campus, attend student meetings, and initiate informal conversations with students, they have a better sense of what is happening on campus. In addition, scanning the larger educational and societal environment is important because at times what is happening in the larger world influences what happens on campus.

Strengthening one's ability to address crises on both a small and large scale is a necessity for student affairs professionals. However, it is important to remember that preventing crises and disasters is paramount (Pruett & Brown, 1990). Halpern and Tramontin (2007) identified three stages to prevention that are especially relevant to mental health disasters: (1) primary prevention happens before a critical incident occurs and includes activities that reduce the catastrophic effect, such as stress inoculation or emergency-preparedness drills; (2) secondary prevention, encompassing early or acute interventions, occurs during the actual crisis and often targets at-risk groups; and (3) tertiary prevention occurs after the impact of the event and addresses the needs of those most obviously affected by the crisis. Primary prevention is the level of intervention that is often neglected; however, it seems that since September 11, 2001, more campuses are engaged in emergency preparedness. Dunkel et al. (1998) emphasized the need for systematic and comprehensive planning for dealing with traumatic and crisis events. Primary prevention should be a major component of such a plan. Secondary prevention means identifying individuals whom an event is likely to affect. For example, when there is a rape or sexual assault on campus, it is important to quickly reach out to female community members—whether they are students, faculty, or staff—to provide support and remind them how to be safe in that environment. While tertiary interventions occur after the fact, they are still considered prevention because they prevent the situation from getting worse. This involves any follow-up interventions as well as any programs targeted toward strengthening preexisting support services. According to Pruett and Brown, minimizing the debilitating effects of a crisis increases the likelihood that individuals can grow from the experience. Ideally, preventing crises and tragedies from occurring is the goal; however, when that is not possible, the secondary approach might be building coping skills to help individuals survive the crisis (Pruett & Brown). After the crisis has occurred, it can be helpful to have a postvention phase that evaluates the responses and interventions (Pruett, 1990). Grieger and Greene (1998) offered one example in their description of a psychological autopsy that was used following a suicide or suicide attempt. According to Crafts (1985), it is not possible to spend too much time evaluating and planning for future crises: "Preparation and planning will help to prevent an individual tragedy from becoming an institutional disaster" (p. 30).

Different types of clues indicate that there is a crisis. There are behavioral clues (how an individual acts alone or as part of a group). Any significant change in a student's behavior is worth noting and exploring. Certainly, signs that a student may be depressed (e.g., the student is withdrawn, lethargic, isolated, or experiencing mood changes) should be addressed immediately. However, any behavioral change—for example, if a student quits studying or attending class—may warrant a conversation to further explore what is happening. In terms of student groups, sometimes an incident occurs on campus that affects them, and they increase their activity and meet more often. By being aware and anticipating potential problems or conflicts, a student affairs professional can become engaged in the moment rather than just receiving complaints and concerns from students. In addition to behavioral clues, there may be verbal clues. Listening to what a student is saying, and sometimes not saying, can be very enlightening. Finally, situational or environmental clues provide additional information about what is happening with students. Students in a romantic relationship who appear to be very unstable or friends on a residence floor who have a significant falling out that leaves a resident isolated or alone are examples of situational changes that merit exploration.

Halpern and Tramontin (2007) emphasized the need for psychological first aid once an actual crisis has occurred. The four goals of psychological first aid are (1) to relieve physical and emotional suffering, (2) to improve immediate or short-term functioning/coping, (3) to assist with ongoing recovery, and (4) to provide connections to essential resources. Pruett and Brown (1990) identified additional steps or stages to the crisis response. The first step involves some detective work to gather relevant and sensitive information. When individuals are in crisis, they may not be the best source for information. If they are very emotional, their attention is likely elsewhere, and they may not be able to easily access their thoughts and recollections. If this is the case, talking with other interested parties who may have important insight or information to share may be more ideal. Additional steps include "establish rapport, identify the precipitating event, understand previous coping and why it failed, and identify new coping skills and resources that may be available" (Pruett & Brown, p. 7). Emphasizing coping resources is a foundational approach to crisis work. Identifying previously successful coping and problem-solving patterns and times when the individuals involved have been resilient and resourceful will allow most of them to reconnect with their positive and effective patterns from the past (Okun, 1997).

These same steps are useful for both individual crises and larger-scale critical incidents. The primary difference is that with critical incidents or disasters, a campus may need to focus more attention on basic human, physical, medical, and safety needs. These needs are often more immediate and concrete, such as food or shelter. The more traumatic the event, the more likely there are to be significant emotional needs. Larger-scale crises call for increased and enhanced communication, as well as an established emergency plan, to guide efforts (Dunkel et al., 1998). In addition, it is important to actively and intentionally attend to the personal or individual needs of those affected during larger-scales crises (Halpern & Tramontin, 2007). Early identification of the individuals whom the incident most strongly affected is essential (Duncan, 1993). There is significant debate within the disaster literature and critical-incident profession about how to best address the emotional needs of the survivors of any major critical incident. Historically, venting one's emotions and recollections of traumatic events was viewed as an essential, positive, and healthy approach; however, more recently, there has been significant critique of such methods and concern that debriefing could actually cause harm (Epstein, 2004).

Halpern and Tramontin (2007) and others have suggested important characteristics and skills that are needed for helpers working in crisis situations. They suggested that helpers need to

remain calm; show warmth, caring, and empathy; provide validation; be genuine and open to the emotions and pain of others; and empower others. Being direct and active is important
because crisis work often occurs in a brief time period; it is not
uncommon for problem solving to occur at an earlier phase of
the helping process. Okun (1997) suggested that helpers need to
be able to use common sense, responsive listening and communication skills, and physical gestures (such as hand-holding) to
demonstrate caring, and that they need to communicate comfort, support, and respect. Despite the sometimes scary nature of
helping students who are emotional and in crisis, in many ways
crisis work is not that different from typical helping skills. It is
essential that helpers project the message that "you can cope
and I will be here if you need me" (Pruett & Brown, 1990, p. 9).

When dealing with the inherent intensity of crises, regardless of their scale, it is important that student affairs professionals take care of themselves (Duncan, 1993). Being worried and
dealing with others who are upset and emotional can take a toll.
Getting enough sleep, talking with others, finding outside distractions or releases, staying centered, and maintaining a sense of
humor and perspective are just a few examples of self-care behaviors that are necessary for effective crisis response. If practitioners
are unable to take care of themselves properly, it is unlikely that
they will be able to take care of others (Duncan; Okun, 1997).

Conflict

Similar to crisis management, there are multiple approaches and
models to conceptualize and respond to conflicts on campus.
Holton (1995a) identified three phases to conflict management:
(1) identify the conflict, (2) identify solutions, and (3) implement the solutions. During the first phase, it is important to
determine who is involved, what the actual conflict is, when and
where it happened, what attempts at resolution have occurred,
and what the consequences have been. For the second phase,

identify the solution, establish initial ground rules, determine the interests of the individuals involved, develop alternative approaches and criteria for choosing among those approaches, and weigh possible solutions against the criteria. Finally, implementing the solution is the final phase and includes a concrete action plan and determining how to actually respond to the conflict. Attending to the process is important because "regardless of the initial source of the dispute . . . the outcomes of the conflict (either positive or negative) often hinge on the way the dispute is handled" (Warters, 2000, p. 3). When addressing a conflict between two leaders of a student organization, it is important to determine the true course of any interpersonal conflict that is creating difficulties for them and the organization. This might entail talking with them separately and then together. If necessary, gathering information from other members of the organization might help clarify any ambiguities. Setting ground rules is necessary so that the discussion can be productive and civil. Then brainstorming and discussing possible solutions and determining the basis or criteria for deciding among those solutions are essential. It is important to remember that conflict is rarely one sided; typically, each member contributes something to the conflict.

In addition to the specific steps involved in addressing conflict, the literature discusses various available approaches and theories. Decisions about conflict management are influenced by student development, organization development, and community development theories (Creamer, 1993). Student growth is linked to organization well-being, and focusing on that can further help the organization meet its goals. Creamer specifically identified two approaches to conflicts—conflict management and conflict resolution—while Warters (2000) described an additional approach: conflict transformation. Conflict management conceptualizes conflict as a fact of life with the ultimate goal being to manage it constructively. Conflicts provide the opportunity for growth; the goal is to "maximize the benefits and minimize the disruptive effects" (Creamer, p. 320). A common example occurs when intervening in a roommate conflict. The second approach, conflict resolution, typically focuses on addressing and resolving underlying causes rather than symptoms (Warters). If student organizations typically experience conflict because they are continually fighting over resources, it is more prudent to address this underlying financial stress than addressing each conflict as it erupts. Three types of interventions are often used within the conflict resolution approach: negotiation, mediation, and arbitration. Each of these interventions has its own goals and strategies for resolving conflict. More and more, these techniques are being used on campuses, either through specific positions like an ombudsperson or through programs like peer mediation. According to Creamer, conflict management involves "actions taken for the benefit of the organization as a whole," while conflict resolution is focused on "actions taken for the benefit of the individual" (p. 322). Conflict transformation, the third approach, offered by Warters, is a more recent conceptualization and views conflict as being socially constructed and offering opportunities for learning and exploration. Overall the approaches and procedures for addressing conflict have varied over time, based on the available resources, theories, and norms. Complications resulting from increased regulation and legalizations on college campuses have brought forth additional layers, and sometimes complications, to the process of attending to conflicts.

Specific skills have been associated with these approaches. Conflict management skills include sensitivity to organization culture and insight into the process of change (Creamer, 1993). Having an understanding of how organizations work and knowing how to be an effective leader increases the likelihood of a win-win solution. This emphasis on finding solutions that accept the reality of conflict, value change, and demonstrate respect for fairness can contribute to organizational well-being. According to Creamer, "Conflict management skills are anchored in building an effective social system or culture for the organization" (p. 325).

Creamer (1993) suggested that mediation and negotiation skills, as part of conflict resolution, have overlapping skills. Negotiation, which is based in joint decision making, uses conferencing, discussion, and compromise to bring about an acceptable solution. Mediation provides third-party intervention focused on structured problem solving, especially when other methods have not worked. Mediation is typically a voluntary and confidential process that is used for highly visible disputes. Being an effective mediator requires confidence, patience, and knowledge about the situation and individuals involved. Warters (2000) emphasized that giving all invested parties the opportunity to express and listen to feelings and perceptions enhances communication, clarifies issues and concerns, and interrupts disruptive communication; it also helps individuals moderate their positions and power and strives for impartiality. To be an effective mediator, one must have facilitation and negotiation skills, be aware of the power differential, avoid blaming, focus on the present more than the past, and limit involvement to those individuals who are directly involved in the conflict. Creamer emphasized that "the foundation of conflict resolution skills lies in open dialogue, information sharing, and the exercise of fairness and good judgment" (p. 325). Regardless of the approach chosen, most experts on conflict agree that "a conflict left unmanaged will only grow and bring increasing hardship to the individuals, the departments, and the institutions" (Holton, 1995a, p. 89).

Addressing conflict on campus is one way for student affairs professionals to demonstrate leadership. According to Creamer (1993), "The ability of student affairs administrators to manage conflict may be a crucial determinant of their success and failure as leaders" (p. 313). Holton (1995c) suggested that acknowledging the reality and influence of community is a crucial aspect of dealing with conflict. Since conflict invariably influences the larger community, it is essential that the community have some say in the process and outcome of the conflict resolution and management process. Building an effective system or culture within an institution means modeling effective conflict resolution, not only for the students, but for the staff and faculty as well. This is especially important in addressing multicultural issues. Holton (1995b) suggested that the increasing diversity on campuses has contributed to the heightened prevalence of conflict. Rather than avoiding such conflicts and trying to minimize their negative effects, student affairs professionals have the opportunity to face conflicts without trepidation and work toward common ground—and, in the process, be models for the students they encounter.

Preparation and Training for Crisis and Conflict Management on Campus

Professional standards and guidelines for student affairs preparation programs suggest the importance of teaching a wide range of helping skills, including conflict and crisis management; however, they tend to set aside little time to address and emphasize these important and distinct skills. The majority of student affairs professionals most likely must rely on their actual work experience, professional training and conference programs, and supervision to prepare themselves to proactively and constructively address the inevitable crises and conflicts that occur daily on college campuses, just as they do when responding to students' mental health difficulties. Even with the lack of formalized training to manage conflict and crises, there are likely uneven and inconsistent training efforts used to assist practitioners in developing the necessary awareness, knowledge, and skills for conflict and crisis management (Findlen, 2000). Wilson (2007) emphasized the need for comprehensive training as part of campus crisis management.

Holton (1995c) emphasized the need for leaders in all parts of higher education institutions to be able to handle conflict and change effectively; however, such leadership needs to be cultivated. Many conflict management, mediation, emergency-preparedness, crisis intervention, and disaster-response programs already exist across college campuses. Typically, specific offices like an ombudsperson, counseling center, or employee assistance program provide such services without the complete involvement of the campus community (Warters, 2000). Without full involvement of the campus community, however, it is unlikely that such programs can be truly successful. Integrating training programs and evaluating their effectiveness is essential for a campus to respond successfully to crises and conflicts. Such training can instill the positive expectation that the community can withstand any trauma and is ready to mobilize all the necessary resources to effectively respond to crises and conflicts (Dunkel et al., 1998). Institutional planning for crises or disasters without campuswide training can leave a campus vulnerable when the community is most in need.

Using or adapting preexisting training models or creating new approaches is essential to the crisis and conflict response efforts and overall success of student affairs divisions. Such programs already exist in other educational environments, such as K–12 schools (e.g., Stevahn, Johnson, Johnson, & Schultz, 2002), or within higher education (Warters, 2000), and some are based in sound research and practice. Providing leadership that leads to innovative and constructive training programs can have a lasting impact on the campus environment. Such efforts undoubtedly benefit individual students, the student body as a whole, and the entire college or university institution.

Summary

Conflict and crises are a natural and healthy part of campus life. While they create challenges for student affairs professionals, they also provide opportunities for growth for the individuals involved as well as for the institution. However, crisis intervention and conflict resolution and management require unique helping skills that not all practitioners possess. Learning how to intervene and respond in constructive ways that lead to growth and development is essential. Even more important is developing the tools and strategies necessary to prevent potential crises and ameliorate the potentially negative and traumatic effects of these life-changing events. Student affairs professionals are uniquely positioned to deal with campus crisis: "We have support services in place; we work in communities with shared values; and our ongoing communication and relationships with students, faculty, and staff provide a positive context for dealing with crises well" (Duncan, 1993, p. 347). This chapter focused on the various types of conflicts and crises that can occur on a college campus and the specific awareness, knowledge, and skills necessary to effectively address these events. It also explored specific strategies and ways to cope with campus crises and conflicts.

Chapter Eight

Group Dynamics and Skills

When considering the importance of helping skills within student affairs, many practitioners first think about individual interactions or interventions, like sitting down with a student and assisting her/him with a specific problem or concern. And while it is true that student affairs professionals are often in the position to help individual students and coworkers on a one-on-one basis, participating in groups is also a common occurrence in student affairs work. However, higher education tends to underuse and underappreciate group interventions (Winston, Bonney, Miller, & Dagley, 1988). This relegation of group interventions to a secondary status is common within the counseling field as well (Kincade & Kalodner, 2004; Slocum, 1987).

In reality, not only are group interventions viewed as one of the five core areas of study within the *Council for the Advancement of Standards in Higher Education Master's-Level Graduate Program for Student Affairs Professionals Standards and Guidelines* (Council for the Advancement of Standards in Higher Education [CAS], 2003), but they are also a frequent delivery method for helping skills in higher education. There are countless daily opportunities for helping to occur on a group level, whether it is facilitating staff or student organization meetings, implementing a group intervention like a structured group workshop, or leading staff training. To be prepared for many of these situations, student affairs professionals need to gather the unique awareness, knowledge, and skills necessary to effectively intervene within a group;

however, unfortunately, student affairs professionals are rarely given the proper training necessary to be effective group leaders.

Despite the limited training opportunities, there are many reasons why expanding student affairs professionals' helping skills repertoire to include group skills and interventions is good. According to Winston et al. (1998), groups are an ideal mechanism for promoting student development. They identified nine reasons for using group interventions: (1) groups are an efficient use of resources; (2) groups can be less intimidating because students don't feel as alone; (3) groups can have a synergetic outcome with students feeling that there is more to gain from groups than from an individual helping interaction, and interacting with their peers has an added benefit for behavioral change; (4) groups by their very design draw attention to important areas that need to be addressed; (5) outcome data shows that students report having positive group experiences that lead them to want to participate in more groups; (6) group interventions are easily adaptable and can focus on a variety of issues, goals, developmental tasks, and groups of students; (7) groups provide safe spaces for students to take risks and try new ways of interacting with others; (8) when groups are well designed and implemented, they use teaching strategies based on developmental and learning style theories; and (9) college students are often highly motivated toward group affiliations with their peers. Winston et al. further state that "the power of the peer group to enhance the development of individual students makes groups an excellent strategy to consider" (pp. 4–5).

Other authors have highlighted additional advantages for group interventions. Ellsworth (2003) emphasized how group experiences take advantage of the social nature of human beings. Corey (1995) suggested that groups can be more effective for skills practice, allow participants to gain insight about themselves and their behavior from their peers, and provide opportunities for modeling; students can "learn to cope with their problems by observing others with similar concerns" (p. 4). Chen and Rybak

(2004) identified several underlying assumptions that help explain the value of groups. First, they believe that most difficulties are interpersonal by nature, so it makes sense that the foundation of group learning should be based on social relationships that occur in groups. A second assumption says that many of the interpersonal difficulties individuals experience are based in their family experiences. It follows, then, that the social experience in the group activates or reactivates those interpersonal difficulties: "group interaction provides a rich soil where members' interpersonal problems have a chance to show" (Chen & Rybak, p. 14). These new relationships that are based in the here and now grow and develop and provide the opportunity to reexperience some of the interpersonal difficulties in new and more constructive ways. This can lead to change and healing. The most effective learning needs to be experiential rather than intellectual. The more that group members focus on the immediate here and now, the less likely they are able to avoid and intellectualize their difficulties. Finally, the most hopeful assumption offered by Chen and Rybak is that even short-term group interventions can have a positive effect.

Yalom (2005) has long advocated the therapeutic effect of groups as being the basis for their effectiveness. While some of his therapeutic factors are best understood in the context of group therapy, they have meaningful application across other types of group experiences. For example, instillation of hope and universality are two core therapeutic factors that help explain how participating in groups makes individuals feel less isolated and alone and more hopeful about themselves and their future. The very nature of groups is based on altruism or the belief that individuals receive through giving to others. Yalom also highlighted the social learning that occurs in groups through imitation or modeling behavior and the ways in which groups re-create the interpersonal world that exists in members' daily lives. By interacting in that re-created environment, group members can learn to understand themselves better and possibly make changes. Group cohesion as a therapeutic factor creates the opportunity for group members to feel cared for and accepted. Finally, the emotional aspects of the group experience allow individuals to learn to handle their feelings in more effective ways, and the cathartic effect of emotional expression may encourage growth and understanding. These factors help highlight the value of the group experience and how even when groups are not oriented toward therapy or counseling, as is often the case in higher education, they can have positive, growth-enhancing, and therapeutic effects.

The purpose of this chapter is to explore the various group situations—such as training, workshops, or working with student groups—in which student affairs professionals participate. Since group experiences are a frequent form of intervention in higher education, practitioners need to fully understand the essential awareness, knowledge, and skills needed to work in groups. This chapter addresses the group competence that student affairs practitioners need to be effective in their work. Specific examples of the types of group competence—such as knowing about the various stages of group development, detecting group dynamics that affect the group experience, and learning about effective group interventions—are just a few of the areas that are further explored in this chapter. Specific strategies for addressing group issues in student affairs practice are also examined.

Illustrations of Group Work Across Functional Areas

Elsewhere in this book, specific functional areas within student affairs were identified to conceptualize the types of roles and responsibilities that practitioners may face: (1) counseling-oriented positions like career and personal counseling; (2) leadership development and educational positions (e.g., student activities, Greek affairs, campus life, health and wellness, and residence life); (3) administrative positions like dean of students, judicial affairs, and admissions; and (4) academic affairs positions (e.g., advisement and academic support services). Various examples will be identified to increase awareness of how and in what situations group interventions may occur.

Within the counseling functional area, student affairs professionals are very likely to use groups for a variety of reasons. Many counseling and career centers have active group programs that provide group therapy, support groups, and structured or psychoeducational groups. According to Corey (1995), groups can be therapeutic, educational, or a combination of both. Counselors or psychologists working in the counseling center typically provide group therapy experiences because of the need for more specialized training and the ability to address significant mental health issues, while other student affairs professionals more easily offer support or structured groups. Support groups provide members with the opportunity to have a shared experience with individuals facing similar concerns or issues; their focus is less on underlying therapeutic issues and more on providing support for problems with daily living. Group leaders may play a less defined role in these groups. Running support groups for specific underrepresented or underserved populations on campus is one way to provide an essential service. Connecting with others who face similar struggles—such as students of color at a historically white university, international students, or lesbian, gay, bisexual, and transgender (LGBT) students on any campus—through support groups is a way to support and empower those students. Structured or psychoeducational groups often deal with a specific theme or population; they are typically short-term groups with an emphasis on self-awareness or particular skills. According to Kincade and Kalodner (2004), psychoeducational groups are the most common groups offered on campuses. Examples of structured groups include stress management, career choice, nontraditional student, and women's self-esteem groups. Winston et al. (1988) provide an extensive model for offering intentionally structured groups within student affairs as a means to help students change behavior and attitudes within a supportive and educational environment. Within counseling-oriented student affairs positions, the only limitations to the groups being offered are the imagination of the individuals involved.

Within leadership development and educational positions, many student affairs professionals often deal with student groups such as those composed of student leaders, peer helpers, health educators, or residence assistants. These groups may run meetings, provide training, or offer workshops for the larger student body within settings such as the residence halls or campus center. While the behaviors needed to manage a group meeting or staff training might differ from the skills necessary to lead a therapy or support group, particular group awareness, knowledge, and skills are still needed. The dynamics present in an ongoing work group will likely need attention throughout the year as well as specific knowledge and skills regarding effective group strategies. Depending on the group involved and their issues, the student affairs practitioner may have to address some interesting dynamics. For example, imagine facilitating a fraternity council meeting when addressing complaints that some of the fraternities have been engaging in homophobic behavior during pledge time. How explicitly or whether to address such group dynamics and interpersonal processes will depend on the practitioner's comfort and skill level.

In many administrative positions, student affairs professionals may have the opportunity to work with groups outside their own staff in a more limited fashion, including dealing with particular student or staff committees or organizations or providing various informational and educational efforts for students, staff, or parents. In addition, there may be some student groups under the purview of student affairs administrators, such as student judicial boards or some student-run organizations. Learning about the leadership skills and personal characteristics to be an effective leader is still quite crucial to the successful provision of any group services.

Finally, like administrators, individuals in academic affairs positions may have more limited opportunities for group interactions. They are likely to work in groups for educational purposes or academic skill development in addition to closely advising or working with certain student groups like tutors or academic-major groups. While much academic advising occurs one-on-one, increasingly campuses are relying on group interactions during orientation and other regular advisement periods. Providing academic skills through various group activities or workshops can be a valuable way to impart knowledge and skills. Teaming up with offices across campus like the educational opportunity program can be a way to ensure that an underserved group gains access to important academic skills. Learning to manage the group process and address the unique needs of a particular student group as one furthers students' academic efforts is a necessary skill for any academic adviser or administrator.

Specific Group Competencies for Student Affairs Professionals

Given the significant amount of time that student affairs professionals work in groups, either as a member of a workgroup or committee or as a group leader, it is paramount that they develop the specific awareness, knowledge, and skills needed to accomplish their goals. Effective communication and interpersonal skills do successfully translate into group settings; however, there are some unique realities, such as the stages of group development, that affect how such interventions are perceived and received. Understanding the nuances and singular aspects of the group experience and how individuals behave and respond in groups in distinctive ways will enhance the success of student affairs practitioners.

In terms of the awareness needed to effectively work in a group context, the importance of being able to recognize the process or the subtext of communication cannot be overstated.

To work effectively in groups, it is vital that student affairs professionals be aware that there is always a group dynamic that may influence the experience and/or outcome of the group intervention. Whether that is sensing the tension between two members of one's student staff or identifying that a training participant is having an emotional reaction to a workshop on suicide, being aware of one's surroundings is essential. This awareness includes being conscious of nonverbal behaviors that may represent the underlying feelings or concerns of group members or participants. Having a highly attuned antenna that can pick up the feelings and words that are not being said is just as important as the behavior one is able to directly observe. In addition to being attentive to the underlying processes in others, it is paramount that helpers working in a group context be aware of their own reactions. Often, in a therapeutic situation, counselors in training are advised to use themselves and their reactions to what is occurring around them as an instrument. If a group interaction makes the group leader tense, uncomfortable, or confused, it is likely affecting others in a similar fashion. Developing and honoring one's intuitive self is an essential tool in the helping process, and being aware of or listening to that inner self is the first step. Such awareness allows a person to explore important knowledge later and, for example, assess the developmental stage and concerns of the group.

Basic knowledge that is vital to effective group interventions varies, depending on what type of group intervention is involved. Being knowledgeable about group dynamics, specific interventions, and the content involved with certain types of groups is critical. Working with groups is very different from individual helping, and even if one fully understands the process of one-on-one helping, such knowledge is not necessarily transferable to the group context. Gathering information about the various types of group interventions, such as support groups and structured groups, and when to use which type of group is important. And since most student affairs professionals are not trained in group theory, it is incumbent on the practitioner to proactively seek out such knowledge. Outside reading, attending conference presentations, and consulting with other student affairs professionals who have developed some group competence are ideal ways to enhance and expand one's knowledge base. This content knowledge is pivotal to the effective implementation of group interventions.

There are many concrete and specific skills that can assist student affairs professionals in implementing group interventions or responding in group settings. Many of these build on the basic microcounseling or helping skills discussed previously in this book. There is no substitution for good listening, effective paraphrasing, empathic responding, being culturally sensitive, and the other foundational helping skills, whether it is one-on-one or in a group context. However, it is also true that what you listen for and how you respond will vary in a group setting. The importance of providing good feedback in a group setting—whether it is a training workshop, staff meeting, or structured group—is a basic helping skill (Bunker, 1982; Porter, 1982a). Being comfortable with straight talk that enhances communication is also viewed as a vital skill (Jamison, 1987). Establishing productive norms that support meaningful and effective communication among members is particularly salient in all group settings (Porter, 1982b). Attending to the process dynamics or how individuals relate to each other, often in unspoken ways, is also essential to effective group leadership (Hulse-Killacky, Killacky, & Donigian, 2001). Ellsworth (2003) identified basic communication, conflict resolution, and community building as core skills for group leaders. Although these are just a few of the fundamental skills needed to be an effective group leader, it is important to remember that leadership skills can be easily learned and refined with practice (Corey & Corey, 1997).

Integrating multicultural awareness, knowledge, and skills into the core competencies of group work is essential. Group leaders need an appreciation and understanding for the ways in which groups members' cultural similarities and differences may have an effect on how they relate to one another (Merta, 1995). The impact that cultural differences has on groups and group members can be profound and unspoken. It is important that such a responsibility not fall on the underrepresented group member; if tension or other dynamics exist, it is up to the student affairs practitioner to ensure that such differences are addressed. For example, if there are students who embrace a religious viewpoint that is intolerant of LGBT individuals and LGBT students or allies are on the same resident adviser staff, conflict is inevitable. An effective and multiculturally competent group leader will set ground rules for difficult dialogues and assist the student staff members in addressing their differences.

There is actually much written in the group literature on group leadership and how to be an effective group leader. Many group experts suggest that beginning leaders should expect to have some doubts and concerns about their ability to be effective (Corey & Corey, 1997; Yalom, 2005). A practitioner only needs to have one experience with a group gone astray—whether it is a training that is unproductive, a workshop that bombs, or a meeting that is full of conflict—to truly understand the demands of being a group leader. Corey & Corey identified over twenty leadership skills that group leaders need to be effective. This list includes such skills as clarifying, summarizing, confronting, reflecting feelings, facilitating, initiating, setting goals, suggesting, disclosing, modeling, linking, and terminating the group experience. Ultimately, the goal is to enhance the group experience and help members reach their individual goals (Corey & Corey).

DeLucia-Waack (2006) explored some of the core categories of leadership behaviors necessary for successful groups. Caring as displayed by empathy, acceptance, genuineness, and support helps set the stage for group development. Meaning attribution, or the ability to help members understand or make sense of group dynamics and their own behaviors, is accomplished through a variety of behaviors, such as processing, and is essential for learning to occur. Emotional stimulation behaviors encompass those actions displayed by the leader that assist members in connecting their feelings and behaviors to better understand what is happening in the group. This often influences the meaning that members make of group dynamics. Finally, executive functions include the leadership behaviors that provide structure to the group, like goal setting, defining norms, managing time, and suggesting activities that are necessary for a group to be productive. All these leadership behaviors take time to develop and are often honed through group experiences that professionals face during their own training and work experience.

Leading groups is challenging, demanding both specific skills and personality characteristics that deepen and enrich the group experience (Corey, 2004). When considering what type of group leader they want to be, student affairs professionals need to consider their personality, their knowledge base, their view of and expectations for groups, and their talents. Being an effective group leader requires some minimum leader knowledge, skills, and experience. According to Winston et al. (1988), those important and basic leadership competencies include the following: (1) developmental and group dynamics theory, (2) group facilitation and process skills, (3) diagnostic skills, (4) content knowledge for a given intervention, (5) supervised practice, (6) experience as a participant, and (7) self-awareness. Developing one's unique personal style of group leadership is also essential: "As a group leader, you bring your background of experiences and your personality, value systems, biases, and unique talent and skills" (Corey, 1995, p. 81), which will shape the group experience for all individuals involved.

Strategies and Approaches for Addressing Group Issues in Student Affairs Practice

Group work is a well-established specialty within the counseling field with many books, manuals, and journal articles that specify the necessary strategies and most effective approaches to working with all sorts of groups (cf. Cooper, Robinson, & Ball, 2004; Corey, 2004; DeLucia-Waack, 2006; DeLucia-Waack & Donigian, 2004; Winston et al., 1988; Yalom, 2005). Most of the literature and available resources are targeted toward group counseling and psychotherapy rather than a broader range of group interventions focused on college students. The breadth and depth of the literature make fully exploring this literature beyond the scope of this chapter. However, this chapter does explore some of the most essential tenets and approaches within group work that apply to the higher education setting to further our understanding of the use of groups on a college campus.

Essential to being an effective group leader is a thorough understanding of group dynamics and the various stages that groups experience as they evolve and change. It is vital that group leaders have the knowledge and the ability to manage these dynamics to be successful (Winston et al., 1988). Such forces exist in every group, although how they are manifested and expressed will certainly vary depending on the personality of the group members, the skills of the group leader, and the purpose of the group. Without an understanding of group dynamics, group leaders are inherently limited in their ability to anticipate and react to the internal environment within the group.

According to Armstrong and Yarbrough (1996), "A collection of individuals is not necessarily a group. The collection must become a group" (p. 34). The internal environment is shaped by the group leader and influenced by the group members. Groups are complex living entities that take on a personality and presence just as individuals do (Weber, 1982). If managed effectively, groups provide the opportunity for individuals to learn about themselves not only through the content explored but through the interpersonal interactions (Carroll & Wiggins, 1997). One way for a group leader to learn to manage the group process and facilitate maximum growth is to understand the stages of group development so s/he can anticipate and react to how members interact with each other and how the group as an entity progresses. While these stages of development were created for understanding the process within therapy groups, it is possible to apply some of the concepts to other types of groups, including ongoing work groups, such as resident assistant staffs or student government, or other longer-term structured group experiences.

Much has been written about the group cycle within the counseling literature, and while many of the terms and descriptions may slightly differ, the basic concepts are similar (Ellsworth, 2003). Such a developmental process has been applied to school settings, college classrooms, community groups, and counseling groups. Ellsworth described group development as being sequential and cyclical so that issues are typically apparent in a particular order and the issues are often revisited throughout the group's life span. According to Moosbruker (1987), small groups, whether they are T-groups (counseling groups) or task groups, should be viewed as a social system. He identified four stages: orientation, conflict, solidarity, and productivity. Weber (1982) suggested that there were three major stages that corresponded to developmental growth: infant, adolescent, and adult. He viewed each stage as having four dimensions: group behavioral patterns, group tasks/issues, interpersonal issues, and leadership concerns. Corey (1995) labeled his four stages as initial stage, transition stage, working stage, and final stage. The similarity of the developmental patterns might be best depicted in the common descriptions of these stages: forming, storming, norming, performing, and adjourning. At the beginning of this life cycle, group members often have a tentative and superficial connection. Over time, with effective support and intervention from a group leader, many groups evolve; and as members become more connected, disclose more, and take more risks, they are less likely to encounter conflict and tension. Ellsworth suggested that trust building is essential for a group to evolve and be productive. If the group conflict is effectively addressed and individuals learn from those interactions, then the group can continue to evolve. Without the formation of trust and the opportunity to face conflict in a constructive manner, groups will likely remain somewhat superficial. If conflict between group members or possibly between the group and its leader is addressed and explored, the group may be able to set up new norms and become cohesive and productive. Finally, a closing stage that focuses on consolidation of learning and saying good-bye is an ideal way to end a group.

In addition to trust, Ellsworth (2003) suggested that promoting tasks, especially during a group's working stages, is central to healthy group functioning. Signs that a group is developmentally task oriented included members responsibly accomplishing assigned tasks, limited game playing and testing of limits, direct communication, honest and constructive feedback, motivation toward work tasks, and cohesion. Winston et al. (1988) emphasized that for a group to be successful, its members must see the benefit of membership, have similar goals, trust and accept each other, have an established identity as a member, and share an informal network of relationships. Anyone who has ever worked with a student or professional staff group has experienced groups that have worked and those that never quite gelled or achieved their full potential. To be an effective leader of a structured group or work/task group, student affairs professionals need to fully appreciate these important dynamics and know how to facilitate development.

Winston et al. (1988) identified several dynamic forces that help form and maintain a group. Cohesiveness is the first force, and it can vary within the same group at different times. Cohesion typically begins with common interests, concerns, or identity, or some shared experiences. This can be established during the early team building that often occurs as part of staff training. Whether implementing such training during student government, resident adviser, or Greek-affiliated leadership training, it is essential to the group's later productivity. According to Winston et al., "A cohesive group tends to be productive, with group members willing to be influenced by the leader and each other, and their experiences tend to be perceived as personally satisfying" (p. 42). The second force influencing group development is group norms, which are the rules that a group operates by and the expectations its members have about the group. These norms may come from the group leader, who may express what is expected of members. They also originate from the group members themselves, although they may not be explicitly expressed. Once group members know what acceptable behaviors are, they are more able to move toward cohesion and productivity. This pressure to conform is an inevitable aspect to group development, and reaching a proper balance is essential to group success. Too much pressure on conformity makes for an unproductive group because it undermines the unique nature and perspective of individual members. Without some conformity, a group never truly becomes a group.

While attending to the developmental stages of groups is an essential strategy for group leaders, there are other approaches and strategies necessary for building effective groups. Hulse-Killacky et al. (2001) identified some basic assumptions about the necessary behaviors for an effective group, regardless of the type of group. Groups must have a clear purpose and be able to develop a culture that values differences within the group. Part of that culture must also embrace collaboration and mutual respect. This includes being open to conflict and being able to give and receive feedback. Balancing content (which is often the purpose) and process (which is how members relate to each other and how things happen) is essential to meaningful group exploration—that is, the group's commitment to and ability to address the here-and-now moments that invariably occur. While content, or what the group discusses, is important, it is often the process that illuminates how the group handles communication, conflict, and emotion (Schein, 1982). A leader must also learn to be a follower and encourage group members to be influential; this leads to a healthy level of interdependence and mutuality for the group. This interdependence means it is no longer solely the leader's responsibility to ensure that the group is successful. Members need to come to the group ready to contribute to the goals and not just rely on the leader to facilitate change and/or the interpersonal process. For all this learning to occur, it is vital that group members have time to reflect on themselves and the work that they are doing.

Armstrong and Yarbrough (1996) suggested that creating a culture that facilitates group learning is essential to all groups. To create such a learning group, leaders must facilitate development through the previously described stages. It is not enough for group members to learn some new content or skill; they must learn about themselves, others, and the group as an entity. In addition, all groups occur within a social milieu that influences their task, function, and development. The culture of a student affairs division and how professionals relate to each other within that division will influence the relationships and functions of the various groups that occur. If a division or department is oriented toward growth and learning, then it is likely that the group experiences that occur as either task/work groups or structured experiences, such as psychoeducational groups, will also be oriented toward growth. Finally, how members perceive the group and how outsiders view the group and its performance invariably influence the group dynamic and its ability to function as a learning group. As stated by Armstrong and Yarbrough, "Learning groups do not occur in a vacuum. They are socially and institutionally situated" (p. 39). As such, effective leaders must attend to the larger social and work environment when creating group experiences. The diversity of the members and how they perceive that diversity and each other can also have a profound impact on the group process.

While this chapter's introductory nature does not allow for a thorough exploration of the various strategies or approaches frequently used in groups, it is important to highlight potential models for effective group efforts in higher education. Three such efforts are briefly highlighted here as illustrations of ways to approach group solutions to various issues affecting college students. Hulse-Killacky et al. (2001) provide a model for task groups that is especially constructive for student affairs professionals who engage in many task groups as part of their work. Rather than relying on more interpersonally and experientially based groups as a primary source of important learning, Hulse-Killacky et al. suggest that there is extensive potential for intrapersonal insight and interpersonal risk. They provide concrete examples of specific task groups through which the reader can apply and make meaning of their principles and assumptions. DeLucia-Waack (2006) offers an extensive guide for providing psychoeducational groups for children and adolescents. She gives concrete suggestions for how to set up psychoeducational groups and explains what typically happens in such groups, including specific plans and related training activities. While this resource does not provide a one-size-fits-all approach to psychoeducational groups, it does furnish the reader with examples and resources to implement groups within a campus environment. Finally, Winston et al. (1988) wrote a text that gives suggestions about how to create meaningful and intentionally structured group (ISG) experiences within a higher education context. From highlighting the purposes of these groups to describing how to implement them, the authors provide the tools needed to implement ISGs, including an extensive sample manual for creating such a group. The tools and resources provided by these three models offer a range of group opportunities that any student affairs professional can apply to her/his own campus. Using these and other group resources will create opportunities for practitioners to consider how, where, and when to implement meaningful and productive group experiences that can positively influence students' college experiences.

Challenges and Benefits of Conducting Groups

There are many challenges and benefits to using group interventions on a college campus. Probably one of the biggest challenges to developing effective groups comes from finding the time and resources to make them work. Whether starting a new structured or psychoeducational group from scratch or wanting to focus more on group processes in an ongoing task group or preestablished staff group, there are many important considerations. The first question that needs to be asked is whether the leader has the knowledge and skill to be effective. If not, s/he likely needs more training. One simple way to get such training is to colead a group with a more experienced professional who can model effective group skills and provide meaningful feedback.

Starting a psychoeducational or support group takes substantial planning and effort. Kincade and Kalodner (2004) identified some of the nuts-and-bolts issues to consider, such as recruitment and screening of prospective group members, and other preparation or pregroup activities, such as determining the group's focus and goals or the length and number of sessions. DeLucia-Waack (2006) emphasized the importance of planning in order to be prepared to address the various concerns that can arise in running groups. This includes having the proper materials available for activities, such as handouts, games, books, or videos. Planning can be time consuming because it occurs not only before the group begins but between group meetings.

Another challenging aspect of group work is managing the diversity of opinions, values, worldviews, cultural backgrounds, and experiences. This requires a commitment to exploring one's own underlying assumptions and values about human behavior. DeLucia-Waack and Donigian (2004) emphasized the importance of examining one's cultural values and beliefs about group work and learning about how one's culture and cultural worldview may affect the group process. Whether one addresses diversity issues within a heterogeneous group or one creates a homogeneous group focused on meeting the needs of an underserved population on campus, developing multicultural competence in a group context is vital for effective and efficacious practice. More and more literature, resources, and recommendations address how to incorporate multicultural sensitivity into group practice (cf. D'Andrea, 2004; Garrett, 2004; Horne & Levitt, 2004; Seligman & Marshak, 2004; Yau, 2004).

Finally, managing the group dynamics that occur when members engage in unproductive and problematic behaviors can be complicated and draining. Some of these behaviors include anger, attention-seeking behavior, shyness, resistance, monopolizing the conversation, and group cliques. In addition, dealing with tension and group conflict can be a potentially thorny issue for many group leaders (Chen & Rybak, 2004). The positive side to those challenges is that "these situations present unique opportunities for everyone to learn something about interpersonal relationships, how they work, and how to improve them" (Smead, 1995, p. 68).

In terms of the benefits of being involved in group interventions, the potential to have a positive impact on more college students is much greater than if their concerns and issues were addressed one student at a time. When groups are managed effectively, they offer ample opportunity for all involved to learn and grow from the experience. And unlike the type of learning and self-awareness that occurs within individual helping, group learning replicates the day-to-day interpersonal situations that many students face. This means that what students learn in groups can be both practical and immediately applicable to their lives. This is true for both structured group experiences as well as membership in ongoing groups, such as student staffs or student organizations.

Preparation and Training for Addressing Group Issues on Campus

The CAS (2003) standards and guidelines and the Council for the Accreditation of Counseling and Related Educational Programs (2001) standards specifically emphasize the importance of incorporating both individual and group interventions as part of the curriculum. Counseling or helping skills are consistently offered as a core course in graduate preparation programs, although such courses focus almost exclusively on individual interventions. Group training standards are quite minimal and understated (Carroll & Wiggins, 1997). While many graduate students may have access to group courses as part of an affiliated counseling program, these courses are typically electives and are specifically geared toward developing group therapy skills. Rarely do preparation programs offer specific group courses targeting the unique needs and circumstances of the higher education setting.

Group counseling training is often structured in very unique and specific ways within graduate-level counseling programs. In addition to providing content about group therapy, these programs often offer an experiential component that involves participating as a member of a structured group. These training groups are often run by advanced graduate students and provide trainees with an opportunity to experience a group firsthand. Such an opportunity is considered essential in the training of group counselors. It fully exposes future leaders to the group experience, which includes learning what it takes to lead and be a member of a group. According to Yalom (2005), "Such an experience may offer many types of learning not available elsewhere. You are able to learn at an emotional level what you may previously have known only intellectually. You experience the power of the group" (p. 553). In addition, some training programs provide advanced courses that allow graduate students to actually lead groups with faculty member supervision. Unfortunately, since many group courses are highly intensive and resource dependent, there are not always adequate or properly skilled faculty available to teach them (Carroll & Wiggins, 1997).

Yalom (2005), with his experience as a group clinician and researcher, strongly advocates for an extensive training program that moves beyond the theoretical and includes observation experiences, close clinical supervision, personal group experience, and personal therapy. He provides important detail about how to structure such a training program and how to effectively prepare group leaders. Jaques (1991) views experiential groups as only one of several methods for improving group skills and behavior. He suggests three approaches as possible means to develop effective group leaders: (1) training groups, (2) teaching groups, and (3) task groups.

According to Jaques (1991), the training group provides the environment for individuals to learn effective group behaviors as well as unlearn those behaviors and expectations that may be counterproductive to the group experience. He suggests that such experiences are not meant to focus on the intrapersonal; rather, the goal of training groups is to examine the social behavior of group members. In other words, the focus is less on the *why* of behavior and more on *how* people act. Teaching groups, which are much more risk-free than training groups, are designed as a more cognitive and less experiential learning experience. These groups typically involve more of a seminar or tutorial approach that give trainees the opportunity—through didactic instruction, role plays, and other training activities—to learn how to be a leader. This type of training can easily be used to train student affairs professionals who are working directly with students either in an academic context (e.g., tutoring groups) or in a more leadership-oriented context (e.g., peer educators, presidents of Greek organizations). The final approach for learning comes within a task group whose members want to focus on their ability to work as a team in addition to their assigned task. Such a model would seem ideal for the many groups that occur within higher education that have specific goals and tasks yet could also use the task group as a laboratory in which to further their understanding of the group process. For example, the members of a resident adviser staff in a residence hall, an executive committee for a student organization, or an ad hoc planning committee could, with proper support and leadership, easily turn their work into an opportunity for learning about themselves and the group process. To facilitate the training process, Jaques provides examples of activities that can be used within any of these approaches to enhance group skills.

Jaques (1991) suggested some training assumptions and principles that are central to developing an effective training program regardless of the method chosen. Focusing on the whole person (thinking, feeling, behaving) is key to developing effective leaders. This means accepting people's unique needs, styles of behavior, and worldview. Such understanding is important; however, the training approach needs to primarily focus on people's social self rather than their inner self. Sanford (1967) advocated many years ago that if learning was to occur, there needed to be a balance of challenge and support. And finally, practice accompanied by guided experience and constructive feedback is essential in training group leaders.

Without an opportunity for specific group training, student affairs professionals are left to develop the appropriate awareness, knowledge, and skills as part of their work experiences. It is only through actually participating in, and eventually leading, group experiences such as meetings, trainings, and structured workshops and groups that practitioners begin to develop the essential competencies to effectively incorporate groups as part of their helping repertoire. Such on-the-job training without meaningful supervision makes learning group skills all the more difficult. Graduate preparation programs would be well advised to consider adopting some type of group training program. This course could be designed as an expanded version of a helping skills course that focuses on group competencies and interventions. Given the continual demand for services and lack of resources in most student affairs divisions, it is disappointing that the profession underutilizes such an effective and efficient use of resources as group interventions.

Summary

Group interventions are a much needed and often overlooked technique in the repertoire of student affairs professionals. Whether they are used in leading structured group experiences, training staffs, or managing the dynamic that occurs within a student organization or paraprofessional staff meeting, group competencies are essential for all practitioners. Being able to address group dynamics and provide services to a group of students creates additional opportunities for promoting student growth and development. Understanding the various stages of development, as well as the unique strategies and skills essential to creating effective and meaningful group experiences, needs to become an essential component of student affairs preparation. This chapter explored the specific awareness, knowledge, and skills needed to work with groups across various student affairs functional areas and provided illustrations of specific tools and strategies needed for group interventions.

Chapter Nine

Supervision

When considering helping skills as a central component to student affairs work on campus, it is common for most professionals to envision the myriad ways that they assist students. However, supervision and related activities, such as mentoring and coaching, that typically focus on enhancing the awareness, knowledge, and skills of other practitioners are also essential helping skills. Winston and Creamer (1998) described supervision as a "helping process provided by the institution to benefit or support staff" (p. 29). Too often within student affairs, our attention and energy are so strongly focused on providing direct services to students that the care, development, and supervision of staff are almost forgotten (Janosik & Creamer, 2003).

In reality, supervision is one component of a much larger student affairs competency: leadership and management (Dalton, 2003). Managing human resources involves a full spectrum of activities that can be classified as staff and talent development. "As educators and leaders no outcome is more important for us to achieve in our relationships with others than to recognize, cultivate, and encourage the gifts of those with whom we lead, learn, and collaborate" (Roper, 2002, p. 26). The realities of staff selection and training, performance appraisal, delegation of tasks, and motivation of staff are just a few of the responsibilities facing the typical student affairs manager (Mills, 1993). Such management occurs at all levels of the student affairs organizational chart, from the graduate resident director working with resident advisers, to program directors supervising their staff members, to the vice president for student affairs overseeing the work of the departmental directors.

Without a commitment to these important work relationships, it is difficult to find ways to motivate and challenge each person, which is probably why some believe that "supervision is one of the most difficult tasks of student affairs leadership" (Dalton, 2003, p. 412). According to Roper (2002), the ability to create and manage important relationships is the key to success: "The challenge before us as student affairs professionals is to develop an approach that places relationships with others at the center of both our personal and professional life" (p. 11). Supervision, mentoring, and other related behaviors focused on staff growth and development are meaningful ways to connect with others and respond to their personal, professional, and career-related needs and interests.

Supervision is a means to achieve those important relational and motivational goals, and more and more it is vital because of the diversifying workforce and the increasing complexity of roles and responsibilities within student affairs. Despite the significant need for supervision as a core competence, it is rarely addressed within the student affairs literature (Cooper, Saunders, Howell, & Bates, 2001; Janosik & Creamer, 2003; Stock-Ward & Javorek, 2003). Professional development programs on supervision at conferences are limited, and in terms of coursework in professional preparation programs, supervision as a topic is likely incorporated into courses on administration and management (Janosik & Creamer). Winston and Creamer (1997) reported that only 50 percent of staff surveyed received training in supervision and that only half of those trained experienced any training since their graduation. And any discussions of supervision often focus on common issues and challenges supervisors face, rather than the awareness, knowledge, and skills they need to be effective.

The purpose of this chapter is to explore the roles and responsibilities that student affairs professionals face as supervisors across the various functional areas where they work.

Practitioners need information on the specific supervision awareness, knowledge, and skills needed to be effective in most jobs, so this chapter examines these core competencies, including concrete examples. Tangible strategies for addressing supervision issues in student affairs practice are also explored. In addition, the related competency of mentoring is briefly explored as another skill that is needed on college campuses, which can contribute positively to a professional development focus on campus. Finally, preparation and training concerns for supervision and mentoring issues are examined.

Role of Supervision on Campus

There are common characteristics of student affairs work that heighten the need for supervision and guidance (Winston & Hirt, 2003): "The pace of the work is hectic and unrelenting," and the type of work is "varied and fragmented" (p. 44). The types of decisions that need to be made daily in student affairs vary from "urgent and strategic to routine and trivial" (p. 44). The immediacy of these conditions can often cause supervision to be neglected. And yet the type of demands and decisions required within student affairs is exactly why supervision is so necessary. Senior professionals within student affairs are responsible for ensuring that newer and less experienced staff have the necessary knowledge and skills and are aware of new developments and practices in the profession (Janosik & Creamer, 2003). There is certainly a trickle-down effect within every organization; the quality and type of supervision that occurs at the top levels likely will have an effect on the supervision that occurs at every other level. Supervision provides new professionals and those who are new to a particular institution with "expectations of performance, institutional culture, goals and objectives of the assignment, skills required, institutional values, essential relationships, and vital constituencies" (Janosik & Creamer, p. 1). Ultimately, supervision is an extension of the training and professional development function within student affairs and has the potential to create a culture in which individuals seek out learning opportunities, request feedback, and desire personal growth. Having the awareness, knowledge, and skills to develop such supervisory environments is essential to becoming an effective student affairs professional.

Illustrations of Supervision Across Functional Areas

Student affairs practitioners use supervision at every level of the organization, and examining the different situations and contexts in which supervision occurs can increase practitioners' awareness and readiness. Previously in this book, specific functional areas within student affairs were identified to conceptualize the types of roles and responsibilities that practitioners may face: (1) counseling-oriented positions like career and personal counseling; (2) leadership development and educational positions (e.g., student activities, Greek affairs, campus life, health and wellness, and residence life); (3) administrative positions like dean of students, judicial affairs, and admissions; and (4) academic affairs positions (e.g., advisement and academic support services). Various examples will be identified to increase awareness of how and in what situations supervision is likely to occur.

Within the counseling functional area, student affairs professionals are very likely to engage in supervision because it is seen as an essential tool for ethical practice. Clinical supervision has an extensive literature, complete with supervision theories and strategies to assist counselors in their work as supervisors (cf. Bernard & Goodyear, 1998; Stoltenberg & Delworth, 1987). Although counseling centers have directors who provide leadership and guidance, supervision is not typically viewed as a management task in a clinical environment. Newly trained counselors are required to seek out clinical supervision before they can become licensed. When counselors relocate to a new state, they may need to fulfill additional supervision requirements to transfer their license. However, even without those requirements, peer supervision, in which counselors consult and discuss their clinical work with each other as a way to improve their counseling competence, is a common occurrence. Within counseling centers, the opportunity for supervision occurs on an individual and group basis and is especially common when counselors are working on challenging cases. Directors also provide supervision to counselors for the many nonclinical tasks that college counselors engage in, such as outreach, training, and programming. While the professional mandate for supervision does not exist in the same way in career centers, it is also very common for career counselors to consult and discuss with each other their work with students. In addition, directors of career centers provide administrative supervision for their staff members. Both sites may have graduate and undergraduate student staff (practicum students or peer counselors) or employees who also require supervision.

Within leadership development and educational positions, much of the supervision that occurs is done with students. Within student life and residence life, there are many layers of students who work with student affairs staff (such as elected leaders of student government, Greek, and other student organizations) and paid student staff (such as resident advisers, peer health advocates or educators, or computer consultants). In addition to the multiple levels of professional staff to be supervised, certain environments—such as residence life, student unions, and athletics facilities—have custodial and housekeeping staff members who also need supervision. "Supervising such a diverse work force requires an understanding of the policies, rules, and procedures that apply to different classes of employees and an understanding of the needs and expectations of individuals who work in such diverse job roles" (Dalton, 2003, p. 412).

Student affairs practitioners need a well-grounded understanding of supervision to be able to apply it differentially across various work groups.

In many administrative positions, student affairs professionals provide supervision to a variety of professional and secretarial staff. Providing support for the daily challenges of administering a diverse array of programs and personnel is a significant task for most student affairs practitioners. Depending on the level of their administrative position, administrators typically supervise some students, including student employees, graduate assistants, or possibly student leaders within student government or the student judicial board. Similar to administrators, staff in academic affairs positions may have more limited opportunities for supervision unless they work with student employees, such as tutors or work-study students. As in all the previous types of positions, the more seniority practitioners have within their area, the more likely they are to supervise other professional staff. Regardless of the role and responsibility of the individuals such practitioners supervise, "supervision implies directing others, overseeing their work, or inspecting their performance in order to ensure that quality services are being provided" (Stock-Ward & Javorek, 2003, p. 77).

Specific Competencies for Student Affairs Professionals as Supervisors

With supervision composing one of the most central roles of student affairs practitioners, it is vital that those practitioners develop the specific awareness, knowledge, and skills needed to be effective supervisors. Like most helping interactions, a key component to meaningful and productive supervision is the relationship formed; however, there are some unique features to supervisor-supervisee relationships that need to be considered. In addition, the goals of a supervisory relationship differ

from those of a traditional helping relationship between a practitioner and student. Understanding the distinct competencies
needed to address the specific and unique realities of supervision
will better prepare student affairs professionals to assist in the
personal and professional development of the students and staff
they supervise.

Much of the same self-awareness suggested for other helping relationships and tasks is also necessary when considering
how to be an effective supervisor. Being sensitive to nonverbal
interactions and unspoken messages is an example of the level
of communication and microskills needed to be a successful
supervisor. It is important that supervisors be keenly aware of
one of the most unique features of supervision: the power differential. Unlike other helping relationships, supervisory relationships typically contain an evaluative component; supervisors
usually are required to conduct formal performance appraisals or
assessments that automatically change the way that both individuals approach the supervision process. At times this power
differential may cause the supervisee to approach supervision
in a very tentative fashion, for fear of appearing weak (Roper,
2002). Anticipating this type of reaction, especially with new
professionals, and, when necessary and appropriate, addressing
it in supervision will likely lead to increased openness and trust.
Another important awareness has to do with gathering insight
into viewing supervision as "a cumulative process, not an event"
(Winston & Hirt, 2003, p. 43). By attending to the process of
supervision and the dynamics of the relationship, rather than
the specific outcomes of the actual supervision and appraisal,
supervisors will be able to respond more effectively to the constantly evolving supervision relationship.

Taking the time to study the supervision literature and
expand one's knowledge of the unique dynamics of that relationship is an important part of preparing to be a supervisor. Being
a self-directed learner is especially necessary given the limited

attention to supervision theory, models, and strategies within graduate preparation programs. Using resources from the clinical supervision and management literature, attending professional development and conference programs, and talking with senior professionals are just some of the ways supervisors can expand their knowledge and be more prepared to be successful supervisors. Stock-Ward and Javorek (2003) encouraged the application of clinical supervision models as a way to enhance the practice of supervision within student affairs. Specifically, they recommend using the Integrated Developmental Model (IDM) as part of supervision practice in student affairs (Stoltenberg & Delworth, 1987; Stoltenberg, McNeill, & Delworth, 1998). According to Stock-Ward and Javorek, supervision likely will be more successful when the developmental level of the supervisee is considered. Understanding how development occurs allows supervision to be individualized to meet the supervisee's specific needs.

There are three main developmental levels within the IDM that warrant further description. Helpers at level 1 typically are limited in their work experience, lack confidence in their ability, and are unsure of the expectations and rules in their work environment and the supervision relationship. They often focus on their own performance, worry about evaluation, and want approval from students and their supervisor. As a result, they may depend on their supervisor for direction and be eager for information, guidance, and encouragement. Level 2 helpers are more capable of focusing on others—in particular, the students with whom they are working. They are more able to empathize; however, this can lead to overidentifying with others. Helpers at this level may be confused about how much independence they want and how able they are to handle challenges on their own. Sometimes this may lead them to rely less on their supervisors, but other times they may become needy and dependent. Helpers who are at level 3 are more confident and comfortable in their role as helper. They are developing their personal style yet are comfortable consulting with others for feedback and support. They are more aware of and accepting of their strengths and weaknesses. Stock-Ward and Javorek (2003) suggested that this "developmental progression from novice to expert professional can be applied to professional development in student affairs" (p. 80). Using this model to assess the developmental level of one's supervisees and then structuring supervision to address those individual concerns and needs is just one way that increased knowledge can enhance one's supervision skills. There is more and more literature on the unique supervision needs of graduate students and new professionals (cf. Cooper et al., 2002; Janosik, Creamer, Hirt, Winston, & Saunders, 2003) that provides essential content for practitioners.

In addition to expanding one's knowledge base, it is vital to develop new skills and expand one's repertoire of available tools and strategies to be an effective supervisor. There are many basic skills that can help student affairs professionals be more effective supervisors. Many of the fundamental helping skills discussed previously in this book are just as relevant to a supervisory context. Supervision based on good communication skills with an emphasis on a positive working relationship is a solid foundation for learning. Winston and Hirt (2003) stressed the "vital performance of open, frequent communication between the supervisor and new practitioner" (p. 50). This includes sharing information, asking questions, and listening to the ideas and concerns of one's supervisee without judgment. Adding specific skills necessary for the evaluation component of supervision, such as the ability to provide constructive feedback, is also very important. Writing skills, especially good grammar and a well-developed vocabulary, are necessary for productive and effective written evaluations, which serve a central role in employee evaluations. Being able to assess the developmental and skill level of one's supervisee and then use developmentally appropriate and effective interventions are other skills that are essential to being a good supervisor. Armino and Creamer (2001) suggest that "high-quality supervisors engage in commonsense, ordinary supervision activities such as listening, role modeling, setting the cultural context, motivating, teaching, giving direction, and caring" (p. 14).

Like all helping interactions, there are important multicultural considerations that need to be incorporated into the unique nature of the supervision process. First, supervision is an extension of training, and as such, it is essential that supervisors integrate multicultural issues and set an example for the staff and/or students whom they supervise. In addition, the power differential inherent in this relationship is based on the performance evaluations process. Therefore, it is vital that supervisors be the ones who acknowledge any cultural realities that may be occurring in their supervisees' work life; they must take the lead and the risk (Reynolds, 2005). If the coordinator of sorority and fraternity affairs believes that racial profiling is occurring during the pledging process but is afraid to bring it up with her supervisor because she doesn't have proof, then the supervision process is not working. The dynamic of the relationship and the meaning of the concerns may change depending on the racial membership of the individuals involved. Attending to multicultural dynamics within the supervisory relationship can be challenging for many supervisors, especially if they have not been trained in multicultural supervision or helping. Effective supervisors need to have the multicultural competence to anticipate and address such issues in the workplace.

Strategies and Tools for Addressing Supervision Issues in Student Affairs Practice

Supervision is a vital competency for any student affairs practitioner, and specific strategies and tools are known to be effective in building effective and constructive supervisory relationships.

Winston and Hirt (2003) reported that supervisees want certain characteristics and traits in their supervisors. They want "supervisors who are organized and can teach them how they can organize and manage their responsibilities efficiently and effectively" (p. 48). This ability to provide structure should be accompanied by trust and support that allows supervisees to become independent practitioners who are confident and comfortable in what they know. Opportunities for frequent feedback, including an emphasis on early success, are essential (Stock-Ward & Javorek, 2003). Dalton (2003) underscored the importance of consistent and intentional supervision to facilitate such feedback. Saunders, Cooper, Winston, and Chernow (2000) found that supervision is not typically used to foster staff development but rather to just "get the job done" (p. 188). Without an opportunity to get feedback, practitioners have a limited view of their strengths and weaknesses and are unable to improve their performance. Supervisees have reported that positive feedback and support help them be successful in their work (Winston & Hirt). Role modeling is also an important component to supervision. By leading through example, supervisors expand the opportunities and options for other practitioners to consider. Being familiar with new research and literature and being current in the field, self-disclosing one's own struggles in the past and present, and otherwise providing new professionals with a window into the life of a senior practitioner can sometimes provide a new paradigm that facilitates growth in others.

Cooper and Saunders (2003) identified some important supervisor attributes that can assist graduate students and new professionals in their development, including interpreting office and institutional culture and politics, learning from mistakes, clarifying expectations, creating opportunities for autonomy, being a positive role model, avoiding micromanaging, and behaving in an open, fair, and consistent manner. Dalton (2003) suggested some additional motivational strategies, such as noticing good work and maintaining a personal touch. Getting to know one's staff on a personal level can make a supervisee feel valued and builds loyal and caring connections with staff. Communicating institutional and personal values helps supervisees see how senior professionals blend their own ideas and values with the institution's. Providing opportunities for staff to renew and regenerate through nontraditional staff development programs and personal mentoring can help prevent burnout (Dalton). Providing mutually acceptable structure and goals is also essential to the supervision relationship (Winston & Creamer, 1998).

In an effort to simplify the many strategies available to supervisors, Stock-Ward and Javorek (2003) broke it down into two primary approaches: building rapport and structuring the supervisory relationship. "Creating the optimal training environment in an evaluative atmosphere" (p. 84), while challenging, is not impossible. Research on clinical supervision has proved that the supervision relationship is one of the most important factors in successful supervision. One of the most compelling aspects of effective supervision is a supervisor's ability to be a genuine, three-dimensional person rather than a detached expert. Well-timed and appropriate self-disclosure can be especially useful in humanizing a supervisor. Stock-Ward and Javorek also suggested that confronting problematic behavior early on also helps build rapport because it fosters trust and an understanding that the supervisor can be counted on to be honest and direct. Structuring the supervisory relationship is the supervisor's task and responsibility. Finding the appropriate level of structure given the supervisee's developmental needs as well as the supervisor's personal style is a balancing act. Using the correct mixture of challenge and support will help supervisees take risks and grow at a pace that is comfortable for them. Helping supervisees understand the institutional chart and the diverse working relationships among the various student affairs departments and professionals is essential. This means realizing that a chain of command and established flow of communication exists. Creating a weekly agenda that balances administrative tasks and details with personal attention can provide supervisees with an ideal mix of structure and support. There are many strategies to consider when cultivating a productive and meaningful supervision relationship. According to Dalton (2003), "The best supervisors seem to be those who have developed a collegial relationship with staff, who respected staff competency and participation but actively led and guided, usually through collaborative leadership styles" (p. 411).

Dalton (2003) and others have emphasized the value in adopting the Winston and Creamer (1997) Synergistic Supervision Model as a method of effective supervision. According to Saunders et al. (2000), "This approach is called synergistic because through the cooperative efforts of staff and supervisor the total effect is greater than the sum of their individual efforts" (p. 183). There are six characteristics to consider: dual focus, joint effort, two-way communication, competence, growth orientation, and systematic and ongoing process. Maintaining a dual focus within supervision is one component that makes that working relationship unique. The supervisor needs to balance her/his attention between her/his needs, values, and expectations and those of the institution. Meeting the institution's goals is no more important than facilitating the supervisee's personal and professional development. The challenge for supervisors is finding that balance. Of course, within this dynamic it is vital to remember that the reality of students' needs is always at the root of the work. Joint effort, the second characteristic, means that the success of supervision depends on the work of both the supervisor and the supervisee. Both need to invest time and energy and to commit to the tasks at hand as well as to the relationship. However, because of experience, power, and position in the institutional structure, the supervisor has more responsibility to make the relationship work and to accomplish the work that has to be done. Research has shown that multicultural issues are more likely to be addressed when initiated by the supervisor (Miklitsch, 2006) and that attention to multicultural issues in supervision leads to heightened multicultural competence. A third characteristic of the Synergistic Supervision Model is an emphasis on two-way communication. This means that communication must be open and honest so that a "genuine, respectful, personal relationship" (Dalton, p. 30) is formed.

A focus on competence is also essential to a mutual supervisory relationship. In this context competence means an emphasis on knowledge, work-related skills, personal and professional skills (such as time management and writing), and attitudes. An emphasis on growth as the goal and product of supervision is key. Finally, viewing supervision as a systematic, intentional, and ongoing process rather than merely a functional work relationship is a powerful part of the definition. Synergistic supervision has been found to have the potential to "enhance staff productivity, perceptions of organizational effectiveness, satisfaction with the work environment, and staff morale" (Saunders et al., 2000, p. 183).

Challenges and Benefits to Working Effectively as a Supervisor

There are many challenges and benefits to being an effective supervisor on a college campus. Winston and Creamer (1998) highlighted the most insidious barrier to supervision: the assumption that if individuals are well meaning, functional, and competent at their job, then they do not need supervision or professional development. This type of attitude is dangerous and leads to a lack of respect for the value of supervision in a learning organization. An equally destructive corollary suggests that supervision is only needed when there is a problem or a new employee (Winston & Hirt, 2003). Although such attitudes do not prevent supervision from occurring on campuses, they inevitably relegate supervision to a reactive and unproductive intervention.

One reason why negative attitudes toward supervision exist is because supervision and its related responsibilities, such as performance appraisals, are often implemented poorly. Ineffective supervision occurs in myriad ways. Intense micromanagement may cause resentment because supervisees don't have autonomy. Supervisors who abuse their power, try to catch their staff making mistakes, or do not know how to positively motivate individuals reinforce negative attitudes toward supervision (Winston & Creamer, 1998). Supervisors need to be aware of the impact of their dual relationships with supervisees especially because of the power differential inherent in the supervision relationship. Too much focus on negative feedback (Saunders et al., 2000) can cause supervisees to devalue supervision as a method of enhancing their performance and, thus, their career opportunities. Supervisors who do not individualize their approaches to supervision based on their supervisees' developmental needs and personality style are less likely to make growth-oriented interventions (Stock-Ward & Javorek, 2003).

Taking the time to learn how to be an effective supervisor is no small undertaking. Many management models used in student affairs do not value individual professional development, but rather focus more on the outcome of the work (Stock-Ward & Javorek, 2003). And yet research in the business, education, and counseling fields has shown that effective supervision and opportunities for employees' professional development lead to enhanced performance not only for individuals but for the organization as well. The limited literature and discussion within the student affairs profession makes it difficult for managers and administrators to obtain the necessary awareness, knowledge, and skills to become good leaders and supervisors.

Of course, the benefit and payoff to becoming an effective supervisor is potentially endless. Good supervision can be a gift that keeps on giving in its ability to increase motivation, loyalty, and ultimately, effective performance. Since supervision is meant both to promote institutional goals and to enhance individual performance, it provides a win-win scenario for all involved. The Synergistic Supervision Model suggested by Winston and Creamer (1997) encourages cooperation, communication, and collaboration, which ultimately lead to improved productivity, work satisfaction, and staff morale. Having a positive impact on another's personal and career development has the potential to enhance the supervisor's confidence, creativity, and energy as well. Forming open, honest, and mutual relationships that provide support, autonomy, and consistency creates work environments that benefit the students, too.

Mentoring on Campus

Similar to supervision, mentoring is viewed as an essential component of professional development (Campbell, 2001). Mentoring has been viewed as an aspect of supervision as well as its own unique and essential skill and professional development tool within many major fields and occupations (Benishek, Bieschke, Park, & Slattery, 2004). Both provide opportunities to attend to the personal and professional development of a peer or protégé. In addition, the literature for both emphasizes the creation of an affirming, mutual, growth-oriented relationship as a foundation for this personal and professional development. However, there has been little attempt to examine these two related constructs in any integrated fashion (Campbell, 2001). Although supervision and mentoring do share some similar skills, their underlying goals and approaches are unique. The distinctive aspects of mentoring and its application in a student affairs context is briefly explored here.

Descriptions of mentoring date back to ancient times (Summers-Ewing, 1994). Despite this longevity, there is no commonly accepted definition of what constitutes mentoring (Benishek et al., 2004; Campbell, 2001; Jacobi, 1991). Mentoring is viewed as a "process whereby two people are engaged in a mutually beneficial relationship. A mentor provides emotional support, information, and advice; shares values; facilitates access to key networks; motivates; is a role model; protects; and provides the type of interactions that allow for transfer of knowledge and skills" (Beyene, Anglin, Sanchez, & Ballou, 2002, p. 90). Benishek et al. suggested that both individuals need to be personally and professionally invested in the mentoring relationship. Zachary (2000) conceptualizes mentoring as primarily a learning relationship.

The research has identified two types of mentoring relationships: formal and informal (Kram, 1985). Formal mentoring relationships are often assigned and intended to facilitate the development of a younger or less experienced adult. Such programs are often found in communities and schools. Informal mentoring occurs because both individuals gain personal satisfaction out of that unique type of relationship (Summers-Ewing, 1994). Kram, who developed one of the most frequently cited mentoring models, identified two primary functions that occur within a mentoring relationship: career and psychosocial. Mentors engage in behaviors that enhance or support their protégé's career advancement by sharing their work experience and sponsoring the protégé in the work world. The psychosocial function of mentoring is more focused on the protégé's interpersonal development through the role modeling, advising, and friendship that are often part of a mentoring relationship. Jacobi (1991), in her compilation of the mentoring literature, found fifteen functions or roles given to mentors, including advice/guidance, coaching, role modeling, training, visibility/exposure, values clarification, sponsorship/advocacy, and acceptance/encouragement, among others. Expanding the traditional two-function model by Kram, Jacobi suggested that there were three primary functions: emotional and psychological support, direct assistance with career and professional development, and role modeling. In addition to this focus on functions, other models—such as ones offered by Kram, Zachary (2000), and others—have identified specific developmental phases that occur within a mentoring relationship.

Many configurations of mentoring relationships occur within the higher education community. The most common ones include graduate students and advisers, entry-level staff and supervisors, advisers and advisees, and instructors and students. Traditionally, a mentoring relationship was viewed as more commonplace between a graduate student and faculty adviser because of the emphasis on professional development and career advancement. However, mentoring "is increasingly looked to today as a retention and enrichment strategy for undergraduate education" (Jacobi, 1991, p. 1). The research in the past twenty years has established that students who feel connected to at least one adult on campus, be it a faculty or staff member, are more likely to persist and even graduate (Astin, 1984, 1993; Pascarella and Terenzini, 2005; Tinto, 1994). This effect is particularly true for first-year students, who make a major life transition when they come to college. Martin and Samels (1993) recommend using administrators as student mentors in addition to the faculty-student connections that often occur on campus. Jacobi stated that despite the growing emphasis on such mentoring programs, the available empirical research has not been well developed and the results of the limited studies have offered only partial support. A research agenda that investigates the effect of academic mentoring programs on undergraduate students' success is greatly needed.

In addition to the focus on providing mentoring for undergraduate students, there have also been research studies on mentoring as a complementary component to supervision within student affairs. Blackhurst (2000) highlighted the research that examines mentoring as a means of enhancing women's opportunities for professional mobility and career advancement in the face of many barriers (cf. Hamrick & Carlisle, 1990; Twale & Jelinek, 1996). The effect of race and gender on the mentoring relationship has been explored in higher education and elsewhere based on the assumption that it is more effective to match students with mentors of the same gender or race; however, the research is actually quite mixed (Jacobi, 1991). Despite the mixed research results, many mentoring programs continue to emphasize the need for same-race and same-gender pairings. Because of the unequal numbers in higher education in terms of race and gender, it is inevitable that the majority of mentoring relationships are likely to be cross-race or cross-gender. Therefore, Crutcher (2007) has emphasized the need for mentors to develop cross-cultural strategies as a means of addressing any differences in social or cultural backgrounds that may affect the mentoring relationship. Benishek et al. (2004) offered a multicultural feminist model as a means of addressing the cultural context that naturally occurs within mentoring relationships.

In addition to exploring the cultural context of mentoring, much of the mentoring literature has examined the types of skills and abilities necessary to be an effective mentor. And to the extent that mentoring is sometimes a component of the supervisory relationship, some of the same awareness, knowledge, and skills needed for supervision that were previously discussed will be highlighted here. Zachary (2000) highlighted important mentor skills needed to facilitate the learning that takes place in mentoring, such as coaching, encouraging, goal setting, guiding, managing conflict, problem solving, providing and receiving feedback, brokering relationships, and specific communication or microhelping skills (such as asking effective questions, paraphrasing, summarizing, and listening). She believes that providing challenge, support, and vision is critical to meaningful and productive mentoring relationships. Mentors assist their mentees in the socialization process with an institution or professional association, inform them of opportunities for their personal and professional development, and coach them on how to be successful (Summers-Ewing, 1994). According to Odiorne (1984), good mentors exhibit excellence and success in their own careers, are supportive, provide frequent and honest feedback, actively delegate to others, and are outstanding role models.

Attending to the relationship is a central component of the mentoring process (Beyene et al., 2002), just as it is for supervision. And while "each mentoring relationship is unique" (Zachary, 2000, p. 50), there are certain core issues that likely need attention. Discussing expectations and setting up appropriate boundaries that respect the needs and concerns of both individuals is important (Campbell, 2001). All work or supervisory relationships do not become mentoring relationships; the parties involved need to make a mutual decision for such a shift to occur. As in all relationships, a process focus in which individuals can share their feelings and concerns about the relationship is ideal. Successful mentoring relationships have "communication, trust, knowledge, connection (care), nurturance, mutual interest, open-mindedness, respect, and patience" (Beyene et al., p. 97).

Sutton (2006) has highlighted two different approaches to mentoring: instructional and developmental. Instructional mentoring programs often focus on changing and shaping behaviors. While some view this type of traditional effort as encouraging dependency, developmental mentoring focuses more on actively fostering the demands that supervisors take on, including their different roles such as teacher, guide, gatekeeper, and consultant.

The mentoring relationship has the potential to benefit both individuals. "A mentor's own growth and development are nurtured through reflection, renewal and regeneration" (Zachary, 2000, p. 161). Mentors are on their own journey in which, hopefully, they gain self-awareness and perspective. Beyene et al. (2002) found that mentees viewed mentor learning and growth as an important outcome; they truly wanted a reciprocal relationship that benefited both individuals. Mentoring has the potential to be a transforming experience for mentors and mentees and possibly for their institutions. Within higher education student affairs professionals have endless opportunities to provide mentoring and its benefits to many students and junior staff members. These relationships have the ability to create affirming growth- and learning-focused environments whose positive effects transcend the two individuals involved.

Preparation and Training for Supervision and Mentoring on Campus

One of the challenges of the preparation and training of student affairs professionals as supervisors is the lack of attention on supervision as a core competency within the profession. Most of the literature that has examined the core competencies has not focused on supervision as a foundational area needing attention (cf. Barr, 1993; Delworth & Hanson, 1989; Komives & Woodard, 2003). Lovell and Kosten (2000) identified supervision as one human facilitation skill necessary for success as a student affairs administrator. Wade (1993) described supervisory ability as one of the three most essential professional competencies needed for advancement.

Two studies—by Burkard, Cole, Ott, and Stoflet (2005) and Herdlein (2004)—examined the attitudes of mid- and senior-level student affairs professionals about the requisite skills needed for new professionals. Burkard et al. specified twenty-six responsibilities common to entry-level practitioners, and supervision of students as employees and paraprofessional staff were identified in the top eleven most common. When exploring significant competencies, the senior-level administrators viewed human relations skills (which included counseling, training, advising, crisis intervention, and supervision) as the second most important competence. However, Herdlein's survey of chief student affairs officers made no mention of supervision skills—even in the context of examining important human relations and management skills. This oversight reflects the field's current lack of appreciation of the centrality of supervision.

Some scholars—such as Miller and Winston (1991) and Pope and Reynolds (1997)—have suggested that administration, leadership, and management need to view supervision as a core competency. Waple (2006) found that supervision of staff was one of only four skills (out of twenty-eight core skills) professionals identified as being obtained at a low degree in their training but were needed to a high degree in their professional practice. In other words, many new professionals feel ill-prepared to manage the supervisory responsibilities and role in their work. These results led Waple to suggest that new professionals need additional training to be effective supervisors.

This need for additional training may result from the limited attention given to supervision within graduate preparation curricula (Janosik & Creamer, 2003). Neither the *Council for the Advancement of Standards in Higher Education Master's-Level Graduate Program for Student Affairs Professionals Standards and Guidelines* (Council for the Advancement of Standards in Higher Education, 2003) nor the Council for the Accreditation of Counseling and Related Educational Programs (2001) standards make any mention of the specific need for training in supervision. Rarely do courses within most preparation programs make more than a cursory reference to supervision. Schuh and Carlisle (1997) suggested that "few practitioners have received adequate preparation as supervisors" (p. 498). This absence is especially ironic given that accreditation standards place great importance on effective supervision as part of graduate students' training.

The result of this lack of graduate training is that these skills are learned on the job with no attention to supervision theory or other relevant content and limited opportunity for skill development. Janosik and Creamer (2003) suggest that the limited training opportunities available "seem woefully inadequate given the time student affairs professionals spend managing their human resources" (pp. 2–3). And while it is true that seasoned professionals do the majority of staff supervision, new professionals are still very much responsible for the supervision and training of undergraduate and graduate staffs and sometimes support custodial or housekeeping staff members. This on-the-job training without meaningful educational experiences makes learning supervision and related skills, such as performance appraisal, quite challenging. Exploring alternative ways within preparation graduate programs to assist students in developing supervision competencies, such as some additional advanced skills training, which could incorporate many of the helping skills identified in this book, would seem a very effective and efficient means of ensuring proper training of new professionals in the craft of supervision. Stock-Ward and Javorek (2003) strongly suggested the need to focus training on facilitating supervisory growth and development through coursework, conferences programs, and on-the-job professional development efforts that would make the link between human development skills on the one hand and management and supervision practice on the other. Such efforts would encourage supervision to become a "better-understood and better-practiced endeavor" (p. 90).

Summary

Given that "supervision in student affairs has the potential to facilitate individual growth, improve service, and change the nature of the entire field" (Stock-Ward & Javorek, 2003, p. 89), it is vital that the student affairs profession invest more resources and energy into supervision as a core competency within the field. Rather than relying on actual work experience as the primary training ground for supervisors, it would be worthwhile to develop an intentional and well-thought-out educational and professional development approach to creating effective supervisors. This chapter identified some of the specific supervision awareness, knowledge, and skills needed to be effective in most student affairs positions. It also explored tangible strategies for addressing supervision issues in student affairs practice. In addition, it briefly examined mentoring as a related competency and an additional skill worth developing to enhance one's contributions to a culture of personal and professional development on campus.

Chapter Ten

Looking to the Future

Integrating the Helping Role

Conceptualizing student affairs professionals as helpers is not a unique idea. However, the increasing demands placed on student affairs professionals to meet students' personal, academic, and interpersonal needs has made this helping role—and its requisite awareness, knowledge, and skills—more central to their work. Every day on a college campus, there are endless opportunities to provide compassion and solace, guidance and information, and challenges and support to college students. In addition, similar opportunities abound in our interactions with student affairs colleagues (both new and experienced), faculty members, other campus administrators, parents, and community members. Within each of these interactions, whether planned or spontaneous, practitioners have the opportunity to demonstrate their competence as helpers.

The purpose of this book has been to explore the specific and unique awareness, knowledge, and skills that student affairs and other higher education practitioners need to be effective and ethical helpers. Examining the assumptions and beliefs underlying the helping process has been central to that exploration. Since most student affairs professionals have limited exposure and opportunity to learn about being a helper, this book has attempted to synthesize and integrate important information from the counseling field and apply that to a student affairs context. With a more thorough understanding of what it means to be an effective helper and how those skills might be integrated differently across various student affairs positions, practitioners can have a greater appreciation of the demands and limits of their work. Expanding the concept of helping skills and applying those skills to every possible student affairs position and responsibility has been a significant undertaking. The sooner that student affairs practitioners embrace the broadest understanding and application of the helping skills required to be an effective and ethical professional, the easier it will be to ensure that everyone working in student affairs has an adequate level of competence. The final goal of this book has been to intentionally and purposefully integrate the latest literature and application of multicultural competence to every aspect of the helping endeavor. It is not possible to adequately discuss helping without fully integrating and emphasizing the power and impact of worldview, sociocultural identity, cross-cultural communication, oppression, and cultural assumptions that are potentially present in every human interaction.

Addressing the emotional demands of academic life and promoting personal development have always been central to the role of the student affairs professional (Creamer, Winston, & Miller, 2001). Addressing the personal concerns and issues of students who are experiencing difficulties while at college is taking up more and more of those professionals' time (Levine & Cureton, 1998b). In every nook and cranny of college student life and experiences are opportunities for practitioners to assist students with decision making, problem solving, and self-exploration. Student affairs practitioners are typically quite visible and are often the first adult on campus that students turn to, to help them understand and deal with their academic, social, and personal concerns. The importance of these relationships between students and student affairs professionals cannot be overstated. Not only do these supportive relationships contribute positively to college students' retention and academic success (Astin, 1977; Tinto, 1987), but they also have the potential to improve students' emotional well-being and prevent distress. While some in the higher education community would argue that it is not higher education's responsibility to provide for college students' emotional and mental health needs, since many of these students are academically viable and active members of the community, it remains our responsibility to provide support and interventions so they can continue to be academically successful (Kadison & DiGeronimo, 2004; McKinley & Dworkin, 1989).

Hopefully, this book has offered new ways to examine the role of student affairs in intervening in students' lives in productive, affirming, and appropriate ways. Through the active and meaningful exploration and integration of specific awareness, knowledge, and skills, student affairs professionals have the potential to become more effective helpers on campus. This final chapter briefly highlights the key points of the preceding chapters as well as some of the recurrent themes and needs that have emerged. Finally, it shares suggestions and resources to assist student affairs practitioners and the larger profession in their efforts to support students and build communities that help students develop and thrive personally, socially, and academically.

Summary of Key Points

This book is divided into two primary sections: "Understanding the Helper's Role" and "Essential Helping Skills." Both sections are vital to developing a new understanding of the importance of being a helper in higher education today, regardless of one's work title or responsibilities. By exploring student affairs practitioners as helpers, mental health issues on campus, ethical issues, and underlying helping theories, practitioners can establish a thoughtful framework for approaching students, faculty, staff, parents, and others in their daily work. In addition, a thorough examination of the various core skills necessary for effective helping in higher education—such as group work, supervision, crisis and conflict management, microcounseling, and multicultural counseling—will well equip student affairs professionals to integrate a helping perspective and mind-set into everything they do.

Student Affairs Practitioners as Helpers

Helping has been established as one of the core competence areas necessary for student affairs practitioners to fulfill their role on college campuses. This is true for all levels, from entry-level professionals to those in middle and upper management. Research studies have determined that specific helping skills are needed. These skill areas include human relations skills, interpersonal and communication skills, caring, empathy, collaboration, teamwork/team building, training, presentation and group facilitation, counseling/active listening, advising, conflict resolution and mediation, supervision, consultation, crisis intervention, problem-solving abilities, and assertiveness/confrontation. Advanced helping skills have become increasingly important, as working with college students has become more complex, nuanced, and challenging. Student affairs professionals are interacting with students who come from more diverse backgrounds, with less academic preparation and more emotional and psychological problems. And while student affairs practitioners are not trained as counselors, student mental health issues are so pervasive on campus that it is no longer feasible that these concerns remain the sole responsibility of campus counselors or psychologists. Because of how frequently practitioners interact with students on campus and because they are so student centered, they may often be the first professionals on campus who become aware that a student is struggling psychologically or academically. To do their job effectively, student affairs professionals need a specific set of helping awareness, knowledge, and skills. Their work with students, colleagues, faculty members, other administrators, parents, and community members require interpersonal sensitivity and specific communication skills. And while the specific awareness, knowledge, and skills needed may vary—depending on whether one works in a counseling, leadership development, educational, administrative, or academically oriented position—it is apparent that meaningful and productive human interaction is the cornerstone of effective and ethical student affairs practice. However, without proper and comprehensive training and supervision, one of the most challenging yet rewarding aspects of student affairs work is beyond the ethical scope of practice for most practitioners. Academic preparation and professional development that emphasize essential helping skills are paramount so that student affairs professionals may perform all aspects of their work more effectively.

Mental Health Needs and Realities on Campus

Addressing students' mental health concerns and the ramifications of those concerns on the campus environment has become an undeniable and unfortunate reality for student affairs professionals. More and more students are coming to college having received treatment for mental health symptoms and problems, and even more will develop psychological concerns—such as depression, anxiety, suicidal thoughts, and substance abuse—while attending. These concerns certainly can impair students' ability to be successful academically and socially and, ultimately, to graduate from college. In general, students use counseling services more often and present with more serious emotional, behavioral, and psychological issues. This reality, along with several significant national events in recent years where student mental health issues have led to suicide and mass shootings, has caused many college and university staff and faculty members to become uncomfortable and concerned. Student affairs professionals are likely to come in contact with students facing certain mental health issues, so it is vital that they are aware and knowledgeable. And while it is true that student affairs practitioners are not counselors and are not expected to help students deal with serious mental health issues, it is likely that they may be one of the first to observe or learn of these concerns because of their frequent daily interactions with students. Being aware of the many text and Web-based resources that exist can assist practitioners in their efforts to understand and be sensitive to the diversity of mental health issues facing college students today. Despite the increasing frequency of these concerns, student affairs preparation programs and professional development workshops rarely address mental health issues; this reality must change if practitioners are going to become competent in supporting students with psychological concerns, responding to their behaviors, and referring them to counseling services when necessary. To be effective, student affairs divisions need to have proactive, constructive, and coordinated policies and educational efforts to create effective services and procedures to meet the needs and address the impact of students with mental health issues on campus.

Ethical Implications

Working with students, especially in a helping role, places student affairs practitioners face-to-face with ethical dilemmas and challenges. These ethical challenges are increasingly complex and require that professionals be prepared and knowledgeable so that they are able to address these situations with forethought and integrity. Being aware of potential ethical concerns, having knowledge about professional standards and ethical codes, and identifying strategies to deal with ethical dilemmas that occur when helping, advising, or counseling students is essential. Applying ethical principles—such as respecting autonomy, doing no harm, benefiting others, being just, being faithful, and telling the truth—is inherent to the helping enterprise. Many ethical dilemmas result from the tension between various constituency groups and their expectations; for example, different individuals on campus have different perspectives on when information should be kept confidential and when it should be shared. One of the most significant ethical dilemmas currently centers on the rights and interests of individual students versus the interests and responsibility of the larger community. Full exploration of competence, dual relationships, confidentiality, and suicide and duty to warn as ethical issues is necessary for ethical student affairs practice. It is vital that student affairs practitioners understand the role of professional ethics and standards in their daily work. There are many resources and models available to assist practitioners in their ethical decision making. Being aware of common ethical concerns helps one anticipate such dilemmas. Scanning the environment for these challenges helps practitioners be proactive about the inherent ethical demands of student affairs work. Because ethical training in preparation programs is limited, student affairs professionals often accumulate effective and practical tools and strategies to address ethical concerns on campus through on-the-job experiences and training.

Underlying and Relevant Helping Theories

Theory has always been fundamental to understanding and improving the knowledge base and professional practice in student affairs. Historically, the use of student development theory in higher education has been used to explain the psychological and sociological influences on college students. As a wide-ranging and interdisciplinary field, student affairs professionals have used theories from a variety of fields, including management, supervision, leadership, and counseling. Comprehensive and thorough knowledge of relevant theories, as well as an understanding of the models and techniques for translating theory into practice, is necessary for effective practice. Part of developing a theory competency is critically examining the assumptions, biases, strengths, and liabilities of theories across myriad institutional and cultural contexts. As helpers, student affairs practitioners do not need to be experts on counseling theory; however, some familiarity with these important theories can inform and enhance their skills in the helping process. Understanding the core theories or forces within psychology determines how practitioners conceptualize and respond to student concerns. Some of these central theories include psychodynamic, behavioral, humanistic, multicultural/feminist, systems/family, and eclectic. Each of these theories has unique assumptions about human nature and how change occurs, as well as diverse philosophies, histories, goals, and techniques of therapy. These approaches also have differing strengths and limitations and are uniquely applicable to student affairs helping roles. In addition to understanding counseling theory, practitioners, as part of their helping roles, need to embrace the importance of the helping relationship and its impact on the process. Finally, developing a personal theory of helping can be a valuable component of working with students; this personal theory can act as a lens for making meaning of how students develop and change, which ultimately determines what interventions to use.

Becoming a Multiculturally Competent Helper

Multicultural competence has recently been described as one of the seven core competencies within student affairs. This competence is defined as the multicultural awareness, knowledge, and skills that enables practitioners to work more effectively and competently with diverse students and colleagues. Multicultural competence, which grew out of the counseling literature, is especially relevant to student affairs practitioners as part of their role as helpers. Multicultural awareness—which means being aware of how one's beliefs, attitudes, and assumptions affect our view of others and the relationships we form—is a core aspect of multicultural competence. Without such self-awareness, it is difficult to be open to other cultural worldviews and ways of being in the world. Multicultural knowledge, which is often not included as part of the traditional educational enterprise, needs to be incorporated so that our understanding of others' cultures is accurate and well informed. In addition, understanding key cultural constructs—such as racial identity, acculturation, and oppression—are essential to fully appreciating the reality of individuals who have been historically discriminated against and who continue to face ongoing prejudice and microaggressions in today's society. Having this important information about various cultural groups allows student affairs professionals to be aware of the impact of cross-cultural communication styles and identity development on the helping relationship so that they are able to more effectively meet the needs of students who have been historically underrepresented and underserved in higher education. Multicultural awareness and knowledge helps practitioners develop and implement culturally relevant and meaningful interventions. Although multicultural education has become more integrated into student affairs preparation programs, multicultural competence is still most frequently learned through on-the-job training and professional development. Through these educational efforts, student affairs professionals become more able to apply their multicultural awareness, knowledge, and skills to the real-life situations and challenges inherent in daily practice. While the challenges and benefits to becoming a multiculturally competent helper are many, the lifelong process of achieving multicultural competence is essential to helping practitioners learn how to best address the needs and concerns of all students.

Communication and Microcounseling Skills

There are often daily opportunities for student affairs professionals to enact their helping skills. Developing basic helping skills and knowledge to serve students effectively, both
individually and in groups, is essential to effective and ethical student affairs practice, but personal and institutional barriers often make it difficult for practitioners to learn and/or
incorporate helping skills into every facet of their work. Much
of the understanding of the essential helping skills comes from
the counseling field; however, it is important to apply such
behaviors in a higher education context. The helping process is
frequently conceptualized in three phases: establishing rapport
with the student and exploring the dilemma, gaining insight into
the dilemma and focusing, and taking action. Creating a caring
and responsive connection with others encourages them to open
up and share their concerns and feelings. Building that rapport
through empathy and effective listening often creates the safe
space that many individuals need to take interpersonal risks.
Through important microcounseling skills like active listening,
reflecting feelings, clarifying, and questioning, student affairs
professionals are able to gain insight into others' worldviews.
This awareness is necessary before one helps with problem solving, goal setting, and other action-oriented efforts. It is vital,
however, for practitioners to realize when they are not the best
one to provide assistance. Sometimes the most helpful thing a
student affairs professional can do is to make an appropriate and
effective referral so that students, colleagues, and other significant individuals receive the best help available. To be an effective helper, professionals need to do more than acquire helping
skills; they also must learn how and when to use those skills.
This will require that they face certain temptations, such as
advice giving and premature problem solving. Being concerned
about making mistakes or being uncomfortable with silence are
just a few of the fears that may inhibit practitioners from being

effective helpers. With extensive training and supervision that focuses on more advanced helping skills, all student affairs professionals have the ability to become effective helpers.

Conflict and Crisis Management

Managing conflict and crises on college campuses is a challenging and inevitable task facing all student affairs professionals. Because of their high visibility and the amount of time they interact directly with students where students live, work, and play, it is essential that practitioners are competent to effectively address interpersonal conflict and personal crises that are commonplace in higher education today. While different in many ways, crisis intervention and conflict resolution and management share overlapping awareness, knowledge, and skills. Campus crises include diverse intrapersonal, interpersonal, and societal events. Individual students face different types of crises every day of varying levels of severity, from a relationship breakup to the death of a parent. This adversity can lead to depression and suicidal feelings and behaviors or to intense, violent anger. Awareness of these potential realities helps prepare practitioners to address these concerns. In addition, institutional, community, or societal crises are also potential challenges, whether they are a hate crime on campus, a tornado in the local community, or terrorism fears. Addressing these realities demands personal insight, interpersonal skill, and community collaboration. The diverse conflicts that can occur on campus between individuals, between established groups, or between individuals and the larger institution also require vital awareness, knowledge, and skills. Having the important personal characteristics and skills needed to work in crisis and conflict situations will assist student affairs professionals in their daily jobs. Through shared professional values, ongoing communication, and relationships with students, faculty, and staff, practitioners are well situated to develop and use the strategies and resources for preventing potential crises and minimizing the negative effects of intense campus conflict and crises.

Group Dynamics and Skills

As helpers, most professionals typically consider the ways that they assist students and colleagues on a one-on-one basis, when in fact, working in groups is very common in student affairs. Running staff meetings, advising student organizations, conducting student staff trainings, and providing psychoeducational groups are just a few examples of important group work offered by practitioners. Despite their frequency of use, group interventions continue to be underutilized and underappreciated within higher education, but using groups to deliver services is ideal for many reasons. Besides the economy of staff time and resources, groups provide unique learning opportunities for all involved. Groups interventions can help individuals feel less isolated and can enhance collaboration. Ultimately, groups offer safe spaces for individuals to take risks, try new ways of interacting, and learn from others. When individual learning styles and developmental needs are accounted for, group interventions have the potential to be very powerful. Even when groups are not used for counseling purposes, they are known to have therapeutic effects when run effectively. While all communication and interpersonal skills apply to group settings, there are some unique awareness, knowledge, and skills that are needed. For example, being knowledgeable about group dynamics and their impact on group outcomes (e.g., staff cohesion, training program effectiveness) is an important group content area. Learning about leadership skills that create productive and meaningful group experiences is essential to developing competency. Using group experiences across the main functional areas within student affairs requires specific skills and learned personality/behavioral traits that work well with the actual group experience. Since many practitioners do not have specific group training, they must actively search for information and resources through outside reading, conferences, and consultation, which will help them develop as professionals.

Supervision

Supervision and the larger issues of training and mentoring are central to the duties and responsibilities of nearly every student affairs professional on campus. Whether it is working with student workers, clerical or custodial staff, or professional colleagues, most practitioners are engaged in staff selection and training, performance appraisal, delegation of tasks, motivation of staff, and other supervision-related work. And even though supervisory skills are often one of the most vital yet challenging interpersonal skills required, it is very uncommon for graduate students or new professionals to receive explicit training in supervision. This task is further complicated by the diversifying workforce and increasing complexity of roles and responsibilities within student affairs. Unfortunately, supervision is often neglected because there are so many other immediate tasks that require attention. And yet the need for professionals to ensure that newer and less experienced staff and student staff have the necessary knowledge and skills and are aware of new developments and practices in the profession is not diminished. As with all helping contexts, the relationship formed is key to meaningful and productive supervision. There are, however, some distinctive aspects to supervisor-supervisee relationships, such as the power differential that work evaluations introduce to the dynamic. Learning how to work with the varying developmental levels of trainees or supervisees introduces another unique component. Knowledge of various supervision models and theories from management and counseling are a necessary part of developing competence in supervision. Addressing the many challenges inherent in the supervision process is core to being a successful supervisor. To ensure that supervision is viewed as a key helping competence, more attention on individual professional development and the creation of effective supervisory models is needed in student affairs.

Themes

In writing about helping skills in student affairs, three important themes have emerged, requiring some final examination and integration before concluding this book. First is the centrality of how we view the helping role; this conceptualization has a strong influence on determining the awareness, knowledge, and skills that practitioners need. Next is the pivotal issue of training student affairs professionals; if job requirements and expectations continue to expand, then ensuring that the proper preparation occurs is paramount. Finally, there is the necessity of making a commitment to advocacy and integrating it fully into the philosophy and expectations of the field.

Conceptualizing the Helping Role More Broadly

All student affairs professionals are helpers, from the entry-level practitioner to the upper-level administrator. And yet somehow it is only the line staff, those responsible for meeting the everyday needs of students, who are typically viewed in that role. By not viewing all professionals as helpers who need helping skills, we affect the culture and expectations of how our divisions, departments, and professional associations operate. Supervision, advising, and mentoring are as much helping skills as counseling is. The target audience may be different (professional colleagues vs. students), and yet it would seem that both sets of interactions embrace similar goals: others' growth and development. If our daily tasks and responsibilities incorporated helping others as a goal, then perhaps our approach and interactions with everyone would be more effective. As the saying goes, "If the only tool you have is a hammer, then everything looks like a nail." So it may also be true that if we view ourselves as helpers, we will see opportunities to help and contribute to others' growth, development, and well-being. It is hard to conceive a scenario where that is a bad thing. Of course, a vice president's conceptualization of her/his role as a helper will differ from a career counselor's, residence hall director's, or academic adviser's. And yet a helping orientation will more likely lead to the development of a learning organization philosophy (Senge, 2006) that has unlimited potential to enhance an organization's effectiveness and value and its meaning and value for every member of it.

The roots of the student affairs profession are firmly embedded in the roles of educator, leader, and helper. In recent years the student affairs literature has emphasized the centrality of learning in the academy (e.g., *Learning Reconsidered,* American College Personnel Association & National Association of Student Affairs Administrators, 2004). This effort has been crucial because the history of the student affairs profession and the diverse roles we have played within our institutions are often overlooked. However, even in our efforts to reemphasize our unique contributions to our institutions, it is vital that we remember that student affairs' mission also has been rooted in addressing the needs of the whole student. So it is through broadening our conceptualization of the helping role and its centrality to the student affairs profession that we not only honor our past but create an opportunity to build better and stronger organizations that benefit everyone. Changing our expectations of our roles and responsibilities can make student affairs relevant in new ways. As campuses struggle to write policies and respond to students in distress, we can make a significant contribution through our role as helpers. Many campuses are struggling to meet the needs of the diverse and changing student body, and our understanding of student development and our knowledge about who college students are and what they need to learn, grow, and develop as students and human beings can help better humanize our institutions.

Training Student Affairs Professionals as Helpers

One of the underlying messages in the skills-based chapters of this book was the fact that the training of student affairs professionals as helpers has been quite limited. Graduate students in preparation programs may learn basic helping skills, such as microcounseling skills, but they are rarely taught more advanced helping skills and those skills' corollary competencies. Burkard, Cole, Ott, and Stoflet (2005) suggested that administrators need new professionals who have more advanced skills than are typically taught in graduate school. This includes skills like collaboration, conflict resolution/mediation, group facilitation, consultation, crisis intervention, supervision, and multicultural competency. These new requirements grow out of the perception of the changing needs of college students and how the role and responsibilities of student affairs professionals are becoming increasingly dynamic and demanding. In most instances, professionals at all levels of their institutions learn these skills on the job with limited formal training in graduate school or through professional development.

Therefore, it would seem that the current level and type of helping skills training in student affairs is inadequate and somewhat haphazard. What graduate students and new professionals learn is not based on an overall philosophy and approach to developing helping skills but rather left to the priorities of individual programs and administrators who want their students and professionals to have a broader set of skills. It would benefit the profession to gather together the learned leaders in the area of helping skills to create a document and imperative similar to the one offered by *Learning Reconsidered* (ACPA & NASPA, 2004). By being more intentional, this panel could explore more fully the helping skills needed by student affairs professionals and identify the most productive and effective ways to teach a broader and more advanced set of helping skills. This helping skills education doesn't have to occur in graduate preparation programs. Instead, creating institutes that offer more in-depth skill development, and possibly even provide seminars that focus on specific skills like supervision, may be a more beneficial model. Such seminars would be attended by professionals in the field who could bring their real-life work situations with them to enhance their learning and make it more relevant to their daily work.

Regardless of the method of instruction, it is vital that the student affairs profession rethink the current models and approaches to helping skills training. As more and more professionals require advanced skills, the profession needs to recommit itself to training and professional development. The complex and dynamic nature of our campuses and our students demand nothing less.

Making a Commitment to Advocacy

Historically, helping has focused on assisting individuals with their problems and concerns, and that conceptualization is no different in student affairs. Helping others—whether they are students, colleagues, parents, or faculty members—most often means identifying and meeting their individual needs. That type of assistance typically entails helping them—and possibly their feelings, thoughts, or behaviors—change to adjust to the difficulties or situations in their lives. The problem is that such individualistic helping is not always culturally relevant and meaningful to all (Sue & Sue, 2003). In addition, this type of helping does not always address the underlying issues, concerns, and causes. At times the source of an individual's problems and concerns is located in environmental, organizational, or societal realities. And while individualistic helping is essential and can absolutely make a difference in the lives of many, it is not sufficient. There needs to be another layer of helping that goes beyond the individual or even the particular group being served.

Helping implies that one person is the helper and one person or group needs to be helped. Such an approach puts the locus of power and importance with the helper. An alternative approach currently being explored within the counseling field is an emphasis on advocacy on the micro- and macrolevel (Lewis, Arnold, House, & Toporek, 2003). This advocacy approach is based on conceptualizing student or client empowerment and community collaboration as central to the helping enterprise. This orientation to helping focuses on empowerment approaches and systems change interventions that incorporate the influence of social, economic, and cultural factors on human growth and development. Exploring those broader factors, identifying the strengths and resources of students, and assisting them in self-advocacy fits with a commitment to social justice based in the historical and philosophical foundations of the field (Evans & Reason, 2001).

By making a commitment to advocacy and placing it as a primary goal of the helping enterprise, we are able to help others twice: once by addressing their individual concerns and needs and a second time by encouraging the development of self-advocacy skills whereby they are empowered to make meaning of their own world and create changes that will benefit them and the world around them. This speaks to the larger professional imperative of incorporating multicultural competence so that we are fully able to help all students. Advocacy, empowerment, and community collaboration are the tools of tomorrow; they are the gifts that keep on giving because they provide individuals the strategies and tools to affect their environment and create change. If helping is really going to make a difference, it is essential that it contribute to the larger social good.

Summary

Student affairs professionals play a central role in the development of college students and their campus environments. As campus leaders, it is essential that practitioners set a positive example of what it means to be a helper who places students' well-being and success above all other priorities. Having the awareness, knowledge, and skills to be effective helpers is essential to achieving that goal. In *Helping College Students: Developing Essential Support Skills for Student Affairs Practice*, readers have been challenged to broaden their view of the helping role and the diverse ways in which they are called up to intervene in the lives of students, their colleagues, and the larger institution. The opportunities are endless and the challenges are many. There is more need for help and support on the typical campus than student affairs professionals can effectively meet. However, by developing campus collaborations, practitioners can work together to provide a safety net to help students succeed. Creating supportive and affirming environments for all is essential for students' personal and academic success, and student affairs professionals have the potential to be the change agents on campus to help make that happen.

References

Abreu, J. M., Chung, R.H.G., & Atkinson, D. R. (2000). Multicultural counseling training: Past, present, and future directions. *The Counseling Psychologist, 28,* 641–656.

Alishio, K., & Hersh, J. (2005). Working with students in the medication era: Do we all have to know how to diagnose and treat mental conditions? *About Campus, 20,* 2–7.

American College Health Association. (2006). *Reference group executive summary.* Retrieved August 10, 2007, from http://www.acha-ncha. org/docs/ACHA-NCHA_Reference_Group_ExecutiveSummary_ Fall2007.pdf

American College Personnel Association. (1996). *The student learning imperative: Implications for student affairs.* Retrieved June 18, 2008, from http://www.acpa.nche.edu/sli/sli.htm

American College Personnel Association. (2006). *Statement of ethical principles and standards.* Retrieved August 7, 2007, from http://www.myacpa.org/ ethics/statement.cfm

American College Personnel Association & National Association of Student Affairs Administrators. (2004). *Learning reconsidered: A campus-wide focus on the student experience.* Washington, DC: Author.

American Counseling Association. (1992). *Cross-cultural competencies and objectives.* Retrieved June 12, 2007, from http://www.counseling. org/Publications

American Psychological Association. (2000). Guidelines for psychotherapy with lesbian, gay, and bisexual clients. *American Psychologist, 55,* 1440–1451.

American Psychological Association. (2003). Guidelines on multicultural education, training, research, practice, and organizational change for psychologists. *American Psychologist, 58,* 377–402.

American Psychological Association. (2007). Guidelines for psychological practice with girls and women. *American Psychologist, 62,* 949–979.

Archer, J., & Cooper, S. (1998). *Counseling and mental health services on campus: A handbook of contemporary practices and challenges.* San Francisco: Jossey-Bass.

Armino, J., & Creamer, D. G. (2001). What supervisors say about quality supervision. *College Student Affairs Journal, 21,* 35–44.

Armstrong, J. L., & Yarbrough, S. L. (1996). Group learning: The role of environment. In S. Imel (Ed.), *Learning in groups: Exploring fundamental principles, new uses, and emerging opportunities* (New Directions for Adult and Continuing Education, No. 71, pp. 33–49). San Francisco: Jossey-Bass.

Asante, M. (1987). *The Afrocentric idea.* Philadelphia: Temple University Press.

Astin, A. W. (1977). *What matters in college?* San Francisco: Jossey-Bass.

Astin, A. W. (1984). Student involvement: A developmental theory for higher education. *Journal of College Student Personnel, 25,* 297–308.

Astin, A. W. (1993). *What matters in college? Four critical years revisited.* San Francisco: Jossey-Bass.

Baker Miller, J. (1986). *Toward a new psychology of women* (2nd ed.). Boston: Beacon.

Baldwin, D. R., Chambliss, L. N., & Towler, K. (2003). Optimism and stress: An African-American college student perspective. *College Student Journal, 37,* 276–285.

Baron, R. A. (1990). Introduction. In M. A. Rahim (Ed.), *Theory and research in conflict management.* New York: Praeger.

Barr, D. J., & Strong, L. J. (1988). Embracing multiculturalism: The existing contradictions. *NASPA Journal, 26,* 85–90.

Barr, M. J. (1993). Becoming successful student affairs administrators. In M. J. Barr (Ed.), *The handbook of student affairs administration* (pp. 522–529). San Francisco: Jossey-Bass.

Bazelon Center for Mental Health Law. (2007). *Supporting students: A model policy for colleges and universities.* Retrieved August 12, 2007, from http://www.bazelon.org/pdf/SupportingStudents.pdf

Benishek, L. A., Bieschke, K. J., Park, J., & Slattery, S. M. (2004). A multicultural feminist model of mentoring. *Journal of Multicultural Counseling and Development, 32,* 428–442.

Benton, S. A. (2006). The scope and context of the problem. In S. A. Benton & S. L. Benton (Eds.), *College student mental health: Effective services and strategies across campus* (pp. 1–14). Washington, DC: National Association of Student Personnel Administrators.

Benton, S. A., & Benton, S. L. (Eds.). (2006a). *College student mental health: Effective services and strategies across campus.* Washington, DC: National Association of Student Personnel Administrators.

Benton, S. A., & Benton, S. L. (2006b). Responding to the campus student mental health problem. In S. A. Benton & S. L. Benton (Eds.), *College student mental health: Effective services and strategies across campus* (pp. 233–244). Washington, DC: National Association of Student Personnel Administrators.

Benton, S. A., Benton, S. L., Newton, F. B., Benton, K. L., & Robertson, J. M. (2004). Changes in client problems: Contributions and limitations from a 13-year study. *Professional Psychology: Research and Practice, 35,* 317–319.

Benton, S. A., Robertson, J. M., Tseng, W., Newton, F. B., & Benton, S. L. (2003). Changes in counseling center client problems across 13 years. *Professional Psychology: Research and Practice, 34,* 66–72.

Bernard, J. M., & Goodyear, R. (1998). *Fundamentals of clinical supervision.* Needham Heights, MA: Allyn & Bacon.

Berry, J. W. (1996). On the unity of the field: Variations and communalities in understanding human behavior in a cultural context. *Interamerican Journal of Psychology, 30,* 85–139.

Beyene, T., Anglin, M., Sanchez, W., & Ballou, M. (2002). Mentoring and relational mutuality: Protégés' perspectives. *Humanistic Counseling, Education, and Development, 41,* 87–102.

Bishop, J. B., Gallagher, R. P., & Cohen, D. (2000). College students' problems: Status, trends, and research. In D. C. Davis & K. M. Humphrey (Eds.), *College counseling: Issues and strategies for a new millennium* (pp. 89–110). Alexandria, VA: American Counseling Association.

Black, L. L., Suarez, E. C., & Medina, S. (2004). Helping students help themselves: Strategies for successful mentoring relationships. *Counselor Education and Supervision, 44,* 44–55.

Blackhurst, A. (2000). Effects of mentoring on the employment experiences and career satisfaction of women student affairs administrators. *NASPA Journal, 37,* 573–586.

Blimling, G. S. (2001a). Diversity makes you smarter. *Journal of College Student Development, 42,* 517–519.

Blimling, G. S. (2001b). Uniting scholarship and communities of practice in student affairs. *Journal of College Student Development, 42,* 381–396.

Blocher, D. (1978). Campus learning environments and the ecology of student development. In J. Banning (Ed.), *Campus ecology: A perspective for student affairs* (pp. 17–24). Cincinnati, OH: National Association of Student Personnel Administrators.

Boswinkel, J. P. (1987). The college resident assistant (RA) and the fine art of referral for psychotherapy. *Journal of College Student Psychotherapy, 1,* 53–62.

Brammer, L. M. (1993). *The helping relationship: Process and skills* (5th ed.). Boston: Allyn & Bacon.

Brammer, L. M., & MacDonald, G. (1999). *The helping relationship: Process and skills* (7th ed.). Needham Heights, MA: Allyn & Bacon.

Broido, E. M. (2000). The development of social justice allies during college: A phenomenological investigation. *Journal of College Student Development, 41*, 3–18.

Brown, D., & Srebalus, D. (2003). *Introduction to the counseling profession* (3rd ed.). Boston: Allyn & Bacon.

Brown, L. L., & Robinson Kurpius, S. E. (1997). Psychosocial factors influencing academic persistence of American Indian college students. *Journal of College Student Development, 38*, 3–12.

Brown, R. D. (1985). Creating an ethical community. In H. Canon & R. Brown (Eds.), *Applied ethics in student services* (New Directions for Student Services, No. 30, pp. 67–80). San Francisco: Jossey-Bass.

Brown, V. L., & DeCoster, D. A. (1989). The disturbed and disturbing student. In U. Delworth (Ed.), *Dealing with the behavioral and psychological problems of students* (New Directions for Student Services, No. 45, pp. 43–56). San Francisco: Jossey-Bass.

Bruce, S., & Keller, A. E. (2007). Applying social norms theory within affiliation groups: Promising interventions for high-risk drinking. *NASPA Journal, 44*, 101–122.

Bunker, B. B. (1982). Using feedback to clear up misunderstandings in important relationships. In L. Porter & B. Mohr (Eds.), *Reading book for human relations training* (pp. 39–41). Arlington, VA: NTL Institute.

Burkard, A., Cole, D. C., Ott, M., & Stoflet, T. (2005). Entry-level competencies of new student affairs professionals: A Delphi study. *NASPA Journal, 42*, 283–309.

Burns, D. D. (1999). *Feeling good: The new mood therapy revised and updated*. New York: Harper.

Campbell, L. F. (2001). *The role of mentoring in supervision*. Greensboro, NC: ERIC Counseling and Student Services. (ERIC Document Reproduction Service No. 460 323)

Canon, H. J. (1993). Maintaining high ethical standards. In M. J. Barr (Ed.), *The handbook of student affairs administration* (pp. 327–339). San Francisco: Jossey-Bass.

Carkhuff, R. R. (2000). *The art of helping in the 21st century* (8th ed.). Amherst, MA: HRD Press.

Carkhuff, R. R., & Anthony, W. A. (1979). *The skills of helping: An introduction to counseling skills*. Amherst, MA: HRD Press.

Carpenter, S., & Stimpson, M. T. (2007). Professionalism, scholarly practice, and professional development in student affairs. *NASPA Journal, 44*, 265–284.

Carroll, M. R., & Wiggins, J. D. (1997). *Elements of group counseling: Back to the basics* (2nd ed.). Denver: Love.

Carter, G. C., & Winseman, J. S. (2003). Increasing numbers of students arrive on college campuses on psychiatric medications: Are they mentally ill? *Journal of College Student Psychotherapy, 18,* 3–10.

Carter, R. T. (1995). *The influence of race and racial identity in psychotherapy: Toward a racially inclusive model.* New York: Wiley.

Carter, R. T. (Ed.). (2001). *Addressing cultural issues in organizations: Beyond the corporate context.* Thousand Oaks, CA: Sage.

Chang, J., & Sue, S. (2005). Culturally sensitive research: Where have we gone wrong and what do we need to do now? In M. G. Constantine & D. W. Sue (Eds.), *Strategies for building multicultural competence in mental health and educational settings* (pp. 229–246). Hoboken, NJ: Wiley.

Chao, R. (2006). Counselors' multicultural competencies: Race, training, ethnic identity, and color-blind racial attitudes. In G. R. Walz, J. C. Bleuer, & R. K. Yep (Eds.), *Vistas: Compelling perspectives on counseling* (pp. 73–76). Alexandria, VA: American Counseling Association.

Cheatham, H. E. (1991). *Cultural pluralism on campus.* Alexandria, VA: American Association for Counseling and Development.

Cheek, D. (1976). *Assertive black . . . puzzled white.* San Luis Obispo, CA: Impact.

Chen, M., & Rybak, C. J. (2004). *Group leadership skills: Interpersonal process in group counseling and therapy.* Belmont, CA: Brooks/Cole.

Chickering, A. W., & Reisser, L. (1993). *Education and identity* (2nd ed.). San Francisco: Jossey-Bass.

Choi-Pearson, C., Castillo, L., & Maples, M. F. (2004). Reduction of racial prejudice in student affairs professionals. *NASPA Journal, 42,* 132–146.

Choudhuri, D. D. (2005). Conducting culturally sensitive qualitative research. In M. G. Constantine & D. W. Sue (Eds.), *Strategies for building multicultural competence in mental health and educational settings* (pp. 269–284). Hoboken, NJ: Wiley.

Clark, R. (2004). Interethnic group and intraethnic group racism: Perceptions and coping in black university students. *Journal of Black Psychology, 30,* 506–526.

Constantine, M. G., & Gainor, K. A. (2001). Emotional intelligence and empathy: Their relation to multicultural counseling knowledge and awareness. *Professional School Counseling, 5,* 131–137.

Constantine, M. G., & Sue, D. W. (2007). Perceptions of racial microaggressions among black supervisees in cross-racial dyads. *Journal of Counseling Psychology, 54,* 142–153.

Contrada, R. J., Ashmore, R. D., Gary, M. L., Coups, E., Egeth, J. D., Sewell, A., et al. (2001). Measures of ethnicity-related stress: Psychometric properties, ethnic group differences, and associations of well-being. *Journal of Applied Psychology, 31,* 1775–1820.

Coomes, M. D., & DeBard, R. (Eds.). (2004). *Serving the millennial generation* (New Directions for Student Services, No. 106). San Francisco: Jossey-Bass.

Cooper, D. L., & Saunders, S. A. (2003). Supervising student affairs internships: A special case. In S. M. Janosik, D. G. Creamer, J. B. Hirt, R. B. Winston, & S. A. Saunders (Eds.), *Supervising new professionals in student affairs: A guide for new professionals* (pp. 175–206). New York: Brunner-Routledge.

Cooper, D. L., Saunders, S. A., Howell, M. T., & Bates, J. M. (2001). Published research about supervision in student affairs: A review of the literature, 1969–1999. *College Student Affairs Journal, 20,* 82–92.

Cooper, D. L., Saunders, S. A., Winston, R. B., Hirt, J. B., Creamer, D. G., & Janosik, S. M. (Eds.). (2002). *Learning through supervised practice in student affairs.* New York: Brunner-Routledge.

Cooper, J., Robinson, P., & Ball, D. (Eds.). (2004). *Small group instruction in higher education.* Stillwater, OK: New Forums Press.

Cooper, S. E. (2000, August). *Clinical services in the new millennium: Expanding targets, limited ammunition.* Paper presented at the annual conference of the American Psychological Association, Washington, DC.

Corey, G. (1995). *Theory and practice of group counseling* (4th ed.). Pacific Grove, CA: Brooks/Cole.

Corey, G. (2001). *Theory and practice of counseling and psychotherapy* (6th ed.). Belmont, CA: Brooks/Cole.

Corey, G. (2004). *Theory and practice of group counseling* (7th ed.). Pacific Grove, CA: Brooks/Cole.

Corey, M. S., & Corey, G. (1997). *Groups: Process and practice* (5th ed.). Pacific Grove, CA: Brooks/Cole.

Corey, M. S., & Corey, G. (1998). *Becoming a helper.* Pacific Grove, CA: Brooks/Cole.

Cornish, J. A., Kominars, K. D., Riva, M. T., McIntosh, S., & Henderson, M. C. (2000). Perceived distress in university counseling center clients across a six-year period. *Journal of College Student Development, 41,* 104–109.

Council for the Accreditation of Counseling and Related Educational Programs. (2001). *Standards.* Retrieved June 7, 2007, from http://www.cacrep.org/2001Standards.html

Council for the Advancement of Standards in Higher Education. (2003). *Council for the Advancement of Standards in Higher Education master's-level graduate program for student affairs professionals standards and guidelines.* Retrieved July 17, 2007, from http://www.myacpa.org/comm/profprep/facressub/cas.htm#Anchor-Part-47857

Crafts, R. (1985). Student affairs response to student death. In E. S. Zinner (Ed.), *Coping with death on campus* (New Directions for Student Services, No. 31, pp. 29–38). San Francisco: Jossey-Bass.

Creamer, D. G. (1993). Conflict management skills. In M. J. Barr (Ed.), *The handbook of student affairs administration* (pp. 313–326). San Francisco: Jossey-Bass.

Creamer, D. G., Winston, R. B., & Miller, T. K. (2001). The professional student affairs administrator: Roles and functions. In R. B. Winston, D. G. Creamer, & T. K. Miller (Eds.), *The professional student affairs administrator: Educator, leader, and manager* (pp. 3–38). New York: Brunner-Routledge.

Creamer, D. G., Winston, R. B., Schuh, J. H., Gehring, D. D., McEwen, M. K., Forney, D. S., et al. (1992). *Quality assurance in college student affairs: A proposal for action by professional associations*. Washington, DC: American College Personnel Association and National Association of Student Personnel Administrators.

Cress, C. M., & Ikeda, E. K. (2003). Distress under duress: The relationship between campus climate and depression in Asian American college students. *NASPA Journal, 40*, 74–97.

Crutcher, A. N. (2007). Mentoring across cultures. *Academe, 93*. Retrieved September 23, 2007, from http://www.aaup.org/AAUP/pubsres/academe/2007/JA/Feat/crut.htm

Dainow, S., & Bailey, C. (1988). *Developing skills with people: Training for person to person client contact*. New York: Wiley.

Dalton, J. C. (2003). Managing human resources. In S. R. Komives & D. B. Woodard (Eds.), *Student services: A handbook for the profession* (4th ed., pp. 397–419). San Francisco: Jossey-Bass.

D'Andrea, M. (2004). The impact of racial-cultural identity of group leaders and members: Theory and recommendations. In J. L. DeLucia-Waack, D. A. Gerrity, C. R. Kalodner, & M. T. Riva (Eds.), *Handbook of group counseling and psychotherapy* (pp. 265–282). Thousand Oaks, CA: Sage.

D'Andrea, M., Daniels, J., Arredondo, P., Ivey, M. B., Ivey, A. E., Locke, D. C., et al. (2001). Fostering organizational changes to realize the revolutionary potential of the multicultural movement: An updated case study. In J. G. Ponterotto, J. M. Casas, L. A. Suzuki, & C. M. Alexander (Eds.), *Handbook of multicultural counseling* (2nd ed., pp. 222–253). Thousand Oaks, CA: Sage.

D'Andrea, M., Daniels, J., & Heck, R. (1991). Evaluating the impact of multicultural counseling training. *Journal of Counseling and Development, 70*, 143–150.

D'Augelli, A. R., D'Augelli, J. F., & Danish, S. J. (1981). *Helping others*. Monterey, CA: Brooks/Cole.

Davis, D. C., & Humphrey, K. M. (Eds.). (2000). *College counseling: Issues and strategies for a new millennium*. Alexandria, VA: American Counseling Association.

Davis, D. C., & Markley, B. L. (2000). College counselors' well being. In D. C. Davis & K. M. Humphrey (Eds.), *College counseling: Issues and strategies for a new millennium* (pp. 267–288). Alexandria, VA: American Counseling Association.

Deloria, B., Foehner, K., & Scinta, S. (1999). *Spirit and reason: The Vine Deloria, Jr. reader*. Golden, CO: Fulcrum.

DeLucia-Waack, J. L. (2006). *Leading psychoeducational groups for children and adolescents*. Thousand Oaks, CA: Sage.

DeLucia-Waack, J. L., & Donigian, J. (2004). *The practice of multicultural group work: Visions and perspectives from the field*. Belmont, CA: Brooks/Cole.

DeLucia-Waack, J. L., Gerrity, D. A., Kalodner, C. R., & Riva, M. T. (Eds.). (2004). *Handbook of group counseling and psychotherapy*. Thousand Oaks, CA: Sage.

Delworth, U. (1989). The AISP model: Assessment-intervention of student problems. In U. Delworth (Ed.), *Dealing with the behavioral and psychological problems of students* (New Directions for Student Services, No. 45, pp. 15–30). San Francisco: Jossey-Bass.

Delworth, U., & Aulepp, L. (1976). *Training manual for paraprofessionals and allied professionals programs*. Boulder, CO: Western Interstate Commission for Higher Education.

Delworth, U., & Hanson, G. R. (Eds.). (1989). *Student services: A handbook for the profession* (2nd ed.). San Francisco: Jossey-Bass.

Dickerson, D. (2006). Legal issues for campus administrators, faculty, and staff. In S. A. Benton & S. L. Benton (Eds.), *College student mental health: Effective services and strategies across campus* (pp. 35–120). Washington, DC: National Association of Student Personnel Administrators.

Duncan, M. A. (1993). Dealing with campus crisis. In M. J. Barr (Ed.), *The handbook of student affairs administration* (pp. 340–348). San Francisco: Jossey-Bass.

Dunkel, N. W., Griffin, W., & Probert, B. (1998). Development of coordinated mental health counseling resources in times of disaster. *NASPA Journal, 35,* 147–156.

Duran, E. (2006). *Healing the soul wound: Counseling with American Indians and other native peoples*. New York: Teachers College Press.

Eddy, J. (1981). A counseling stage model for methods training. In J. Eddy, M. Altekruse, & G. Pitts (Eds.), *Counseling methods: Developing counselors* (pp. 44–46). Washington, DC: University Press of America.

Egan, G. (1975). *The skilled helper: A model for systematic helping and interpersonal relating*. Belmont, CA: Wadsworth.

Egan, G. (2002). *The skilled helper: A problem-management and opportunity-development approach to helping* (7th ed.). Pacific Grove, CA: Brooks/Cole.

Ellsworth, J. D. (2003). *ABC's of group work: Building community in schools. A workbook for high school and college.* (ERIC Document Reproduction Service No. 474 075)

Enos, M. (1998). *Study guide for Schultz and Schultz's theories of personality* (6th ed.). Pacific Grove, CA: Brooks/Cole.

Epstein, B. H. (2004). Crisis intervention on campus: Current and new approaches. *NASPA Journal, 41,* 294–316.

Evans, D. R., Hearn, M. T., Uhlemann, M. R., & Ivey, A. E. (1998). *Essential interviewing: A programmed approach to effective communication* (5th ed.). Pacific Grove, CA: Brooks/Cole.

Evans, N. J., Forney, D. S., & Guido-DiBrito, F. (1998). *Student development in college: Theory, research, and practice.* San Francisco: Jossey-Bass.

Evans, N. J., & Reason, R. D. (2001). Guiding principles: A review and analysis of student affairs philosophical statements. *Journal of College Student Development, 42,* 359–377.

Faiver, C., Eisengart, S., & Colonna, R. (1995). *The counselor intern's handbook.* Pacific Grove, CA: Brooks/Cole.

Fenske, R. H. (1989). Historical foundations of student services. In U. Delworth & G. R. Hanson (Eds.), *Student services: A handbook for the profession* (2nd ed., pp. 5–24). San Francisco: Jossey-Bass.

Findlen, R. (2000). Conflict: The skeleton in academe's closet. In D. Robillard, Jr. (Ed.), *Dimensions of managing academic affairs in the community college* (New Directions for Community Colleges, No. 109, pp. 41–49). San Francisco: Jossey-Bass.

Flowers, L. A. (2003). National study of diversity requirements in student affairs graduate programs. *NASPA Journal, 40,* 72–82.

Fox, M. T., Lowe, S. C., & McClellan, G. S. (Eds.). (2005). *Serving Native American students* (New Directions for Student Services, No. 109). San Francisco: Jossey-Bass.

Frances, P. C. (2000). Practicing ethically as a college counselor. In D. C. Davis & K. M. Humphrey (Eds.), *College counseling: Issues and strategies for a new millennium.* Alexandria, VA: American Counseling Association.

Freire, P. (1972). *Pedagogy of the oppressed.* New York: Continuum.

Fried, J. (1995). *Shifting paradigms in student affairs: Culture, context, teaching and learning.* Washington, DC: American College Personnel Association.

Fried, J. (Ed.). (1997). *Ethics for today's campus: New perspectives on education, student development, and institutional management* (New Directions for Student Services, No. 77). San Francisco: Jossey-Bass.

Fried, J. (2003). Ethical standards and principles. In S. R. Komives & D. B. Woodard (Eds.), *Student services: A handbook for the profession* (4th ed., pp. 107–127). San Francisco: Jossey-Bass.

Fuertes, J. N., Stracuzzi, T. I., Bennett, J., Scheinholtz, J., Mislowack, A., Hersh, M., et al. (2006). Therapist multicultural competency: A study of therapy dyads. *Psychotherapy: Theory, Research, Practice, Training, 43*, 480–490.

Furr, S. R., Westefeld, J. S., McConnell, G. N., & Jenkins, J. M. (2001). Suicide and depression among college students: A decade later. *Professional Psychology: Research and Practice, 32*, 97–100.

Gallagher, R. P. (1989). *Counseling center survey.* Unpublished manuscript, University of Pittsburgh, PA.

Gallagher, R. P. (2006). *National survey of counseling center directors.* Alexandria, VA: International Association of Counseling Services. Retrieved June 10, 2007, from http://www.iacsinc.org

Garrett, M. T. (2004). Sound of the drum: Group counseling with Native Americans. In J. L. DeLucia-Waack, D. A. Gerrity, C. R. Kalodner, & M. T. Riva (Eds.), *Handbook of group counseling and psychotherapy* (pp. 169–182). Thousand Oaks, CA: Sage.

Gayles, J. G., & Kelly, B. T. (2007). Experiences with diversity in the curriculum: Implications for graduate programs and student affairs practice. *NASPA Journal, 44*, 193–208.

Gehring, D. D. (1993). Understanding legal constraints on practice. In M. J. Barr (Ed.), *The handbook of student affairs administration* (pp. 274–299). San Francisco: Jossey-Bass.

Gehring, D. D. (2001). Legal parameters for student affairs practice. In R. B. Winston, D. G. Creamer, & T. K. Miller (Eds.), *The professional student affairs administrator: Educator, leader, and manager* (pp. 107–152). New York: Brunner-Routledge.

George, R. L., & Cristiani, T. S. (1995). *Counseling: Theory and practice.* Boston: Allyn & Bacon.

Gerda, J. J. (2006). Gathering together: A view of the earliest student affairs professional organizations. *NASPA Journal, 43*, 147–163.

Gibson, J. (1995). "Can't we settle this?" Student conflicts in higher education and options for resolution. In S. A. Holton (Ed.), *Conflict management in higher education* (New Directions for Higher Education, No. 92, pp. 27–34). San Francisco: Jossey-Bass.

Goldstein, E. B. (1994). *Psychology.* Pacific Grove, CA: Brooks/Cole.

Grayson, P. A. (2006). Overview. In P. A. Grayson & P. W. Meilman (Eds.), *College mental health practice* (pp. 1–20). New York: Routledge.

Grayson, P. A., & Cooper, S. (2006). Depression and anxiety. In P. A. Grayson & P. W. Meilman (Eds.), *College mental health practice* (pp. 113–134). New York: Routledge.

Grayson, P. A., & Meilman, P. W. (Eds.). (2006). *College mental health practice.* New York: Routledge.

Greenspan, M. (1983). *A new approach to women and therapy.* New York: McGraw-Hill.

Grieger, I. (1996). A multicultural organizational development check-list for student affairs. *Journal of College Student Development, 37,* 561–573.

Grieger, I., & Greene, P. (1998). The psychological autopsy as a tool in student affairs. *Journal of College Student Development, 39,* 388–392.

Hage, S. M. (2005). Future considerations for fostering multicultural competence in mental health and educational settings: Social justice implications. In M. G. Constantine & D. W. Sue (Eds.), *Strategies for building multicultural competence in mental health and educational settings* (pp. 285–302). Hoboken, NJ: Wiley.

Hall, E. (1983). *Psychology today: An introduction* (5th ed.). New York: Random House.

Halpern, J., & Tramontin, M. (2007). *Disaster mental health: Theory and practice.* Belmont, CA: Brooks/Cole.

Hamrick, F. A., & Carlisle, L. W. (1990). Gender diversity in student affairs: Administrative perceptions and recommendations. *NASPA Journal, 27,* 306–311.

Harmon, A. (2005, November 16). *Young, assured, and playing pharmacist to friends.* Retrieved on November 16, 2005, from http://www.nytimes.com/2005/11/16/health/16patient.html

Harper, S. R., & Hurtado, S. (2007). Nine themes in campus racial climates and implications for institutional transformation. In S. R. Harper & L. D. Patton (Eds.), *Responding to the realities of race on campus* (New Directions for Student Services, No. 120, pp. 7–24). San Francisco: Jossey-Bass.

Hayman, P. M., & Covert, I. A. (1986). Ethical dilemmas in college counseling centers. *Journal of Counseling and Development, 64,* 318–320.

Henggeler, S. W., Sallis, J. F., & Cooper, P. F. (1980). A comparison of university mental health need priorities identified by professionals and by students. *Journal of Counseling Psychology, 27,* 217–219.

Heppner, P. P. (2006). The benefits and challenges of becoming cross-culturally competent counseling psychologists: Presidential address. *The Counseling Psychologist, 34,* 147–172.

Heppner, P. P., Kivlighan, D. M., Good, G. E., Roehlke, H. J., Hills, H. I., & Ashby, J. S. (1994). Presenting problems of university counseling center clients: A snapshot and multivariate classification scheme. *Journal of Counseling Psychology, 41,* 315–324.

Heppner, P. P., & Neal, G. W. (1983). Holding up the mirror: Research on the roles and functions of counseling centers in higher education. *The Counseling Psychologist, 11,* 81–98.

Herdlein, R. J. (2004). Survey of chief student affairs officers regarding relevance of graduate preparation of new professionals. *NASPA Journal, 42,* 51–71.

Heron, J. (2001). *Helping the client: A creative practical guide* (5th ed.). London: Sage.

Hill, C. E., & O'Brien, K. M. (1999). *Helping skills: Facilitating exploration, insight, and action*. Washington, DC: American Psychological Association.

Hodges, S. (2001). University counseling centers at the twenty-first century: Looking forward, looking back. *Journal of College Counseling, 4*, 161–173.

Holton, S. A. (1995a). And now . . . the answers! How to deal with conflict in higher education. In S. A. Holton (Ed.), *Conflict management in higher education* (New Directions for Higher Education, No. 92, pp. 79–90). San Francisco: Jossey-Bass.

Holton, S. A. (1995b). It's nothing new! A history of conflict in higher education. In S. A. Holton (Ed.), *Conflict management in higher education* (New Directions for Higher Education, No. 92, pp. 11–18). San Francisco: Jossey-Bass.

Holton, S. A. (1995c). Where do we go from here? In S. A. Holton (Ed.), *Conflict management in higher education* (New Directions for Higher Education, No. 92, pp. 91–96). San Francisco: Jossey-Bass.

Horne, S. G., & Levitt, H. M. (2004). Psychoeducational and counseling groups with gay, lesbian, bisexual, and transgendered clients. In J. L. DeLucia-Waack, D. A. Gerrity, C. R. Kalodner, & M. T. Riva (Eds.), *Handbook of group counseling and psychotherapy* (pp. 224–238). Thousand Oaks, CA: Sage.

Hulse-Killacky, D., Killacky, J., & Donigian, J. (2001). *Making task groups work in your world*. Upper Saddle River, NJ: Prentice-Hall.

Humphrey, K. M., Kitchens, H., & Patrick, J. (2000). Trends in college counseling for the 21st century. In D. C. Davis & K. M. Humphrey (Eds.), *College counseling: Issues and strategies for a new millennium* (pp. 289–306). Alexandria, VA: American Counseling Association.

Hyman, R. E. (1985, March). *Do graduate preparation programs address competencies important to student affairs practice?* Paper presented at the annual conference of the National Association of Student Personnel Administrators, Portland, OR.

Inman, A. G. (2006). Supervisor multicultural competence and its relation to supervisory process and outcome. *Journal of Marital and Family Therapy, 32*(1), 73–85.

Ivey, A. E., D'Andrea, M., Bradford Ivey, M., & Simek-Morgan, L. (2007). *Theories of counseling and psychotherapy: A multicultural perspective* (6th ed.). Boston: Allyn & Bacon.

Ivey, A. E., Ivey, M. B., & Simek-Morgan, L. (1993). *Counseling and psychotherapy: A multicultural perspective* (3rd ed.). Needham Heights, MA: Allyn & Bacon.

Jacobi, M. (1991). Mentoring and undergraduate academic success: A literature review. *Review of Educational Research, 61*, 505–532.

Jamison, K. (1987). Straight talk: A norm-changing intervention. In W. B. Reddy & C. C. Henderson (Eds.), *Training theory and practice* (pp. 209–223). Arlington, VA: NTL Institute.

Janosik, S. M. (2005). Anticipating legal issues in higher education. *NASPA Journal, 42*, 401–414.

Janosik, S. M. (2007). Common issues in professional behavior. *NASPA Journal, 44*, 285–306.

Janosik, S. M., & Creamer, D. G. (2003). Introduction: A comprehensive model. In S. M. Janosik, D. G. Creamer, J. B. Hirt, R. B. Winston, & S. A. Saunders (Eds.), *Supervising new professionals in student affairs: A guide for new professionals* (pp. 1–16). New York: Brunner-Routledge.

Janosik, S. M., Creamer, D. G., Hirt, J. B., Winston, R. B., & Saunders, S. A. (Eds.). (2003). *Supervising new professionals in student affairs: A guide for new professionals*. New York: Brunner-Routledge.

Janosik, S. M., Creamer, D. G., & Humphrey, E. (2004). An analysis of ethical problems facing student affairs administrators. *NASPA Journal, 41*, 356–374.

Jaques, D. (1991). *Learning in groups* (2nd ed.). London: Kogan Page.

Jenkins, Y. M. (1999). Salient themes and directives for college helping professionals. In Y. M. Jenkins (Ed.), *Diversity in college settings: Directives for helping professionals* (pp. 217–238). New York: Routledge.

Johnson, S. C., & Arbona, C. (2006). The relation of ethnic identity, racial identity, and race-related stress among African American college students. *Journal of College Student Development, 47*, 495–507.

Kadison, R., & DiGeronimo, T. F. (2004). *College of the overwhelmed: The campus mental health crisis and what to do about it*. San Francisco: Jossey-Bass.

Keeling, R. (2000, December 11). Psychological diversity and the mission of student affairs. *NetResults, XX*.

Kincade, E. A., & Kalodner, C. R. (2004). The use of groups in college and university counseling centers. In J. L. DeLucia-Waack, D. A. Gerrity, C. R. Kalodner, & M. T. Riva (Eds.), *Handbook of group counseling and psychotherapy* (pp. 366–377). Thousand Oaks, CA: Sage.

Kinzie, S. (2006, March 10). GWU suit prompts questions of liability: School barred depressed student. *Washington Post*, p. A01. Retrieved March 13, 2007, from http://www.washingtonpost.com/wp-dyn/content/article/2006/03/09/AR2006030902550.html

Kitchener, K. (1985). Ethical principles and ethical decisions in student affairs. In H. Canon & R. Brown (Eds.), *Applied ethics in student services* (New Directions for Student Services, No. 30, pp. 17–30). San Francisco: Jossey-Bass.

Kitzrow, M. A. (2003). The mental health needs of today's college students: Challenges and recommendations. *NASPA Journal, 41*, 167–181.

Knefelkamp, L. L., Golec, R. R., & Wells, E. A. (1985). *The practice-to-theory-to-practice model*. Unpublished manuscript, University of Maryland, College Park.

Knefelkamp, L. L., Widick, C., & Parker, C. A. (1978). *Applying new development findings* (New Directions for Student Services, No. 4). San Francisco: Jossey-Bass.

Kochman, T. (1981). *Black and white styles in conflict*. Chicago: University of Chicago Press.

Kolek, E. A. (2006). Recreational prescription drug use among college students. *NASPA Journal, 43*, 19–39.

Komives, S. R., & Woodard, D. B. (Eds.). (1996). *Student services: A handbook for the profession* (3rd ed.). San Francisco: Jossey-Bass.

Komives, S. R., & Woodard, D. B. (Eds.). (2003). *Student services: A handbook for the profession* (4th ed.). San Francisco: Jossey-Bass.

Kram, K. E. (1985). *Mentoring at work: Developmental relationships in organizational life*. Glenview, IL: Scott Foresman.

LaFromboise, T. D., Coleman, H.L.K., & Hernandez, A. (1991). Development and factor structure of the cross-cultural counseling inventory—Revised. *Professional Psychology: Research and Practice, 22*, 380–388.

Landrine, H., & Klonoff, E. A. (1996). The schedule of racist events: A measure of racial discrimination and a study of its negative physical and mental health consequences. *Journal of Black Psychology, 22*, 144–167.

Lazarus, A. A. (1986). Multimodal therapy. In J. C. Norcross (Ed.), *Handbook of eclectic psychotherapy* (pp. 65–93). New York: Brunner/Mazel.

Levine, A., & Cureton, S. (1998a). What we need to know about today's college students. *About Campus, 20*, 4–9.

Levine, A., & Cureton, S. (1998b). *When hope and fear collide: A portrait of today's college student*. San Francisco: Jossey-Bass.

Lewis, J., Arnold, M. S., House, R., & Toporek, R. (2003). *Advocacy competencies*. Retrieved April 22, 2008, from http://www.counseling. org/Files/FD.ashx?guid=680f251e-b3d0-4f77-8aa3-4e360f32f05e

Liebert, R. M., & Spiegler, M. D. (1982). *Personality: Strategies and issues*. Homewood, IL: Dorsey Press.

Linehan, M. (1993). *Cognitive-behavioral treatment of borderline personality disorder*. New York: The Guilford Press.

Lloyd-Jones, E. M., & Smith, M. R. (1954). *Student personnel work as deeper teaching*. New York: Harper.

Lopez, J. D. (2005). Race-related stress and sociocultural orientation among Latino students during their transition into a predominantly white, highly selective institution. *Journal of Hispanic Higher Education, 4*, 354–365.

Love, P. G., & Estanek, S. M. (2004). *Rethinking student affairs practice*. San Francisco: Jossey-Bass.

Lovell, C., & Kosten, L. (2000). Skills, knowledge, and personal traits necessary for success as a student affairs administrator: A meta-analysis of thirty years of research. *NASPA Journal, 37*, 553–572.

Lowery, J. W. (1998). Institutional policy and individual responsibility: Communities of justice and principle. In D. L. Cooper & J. M. Lancaster (Eds.), *Beyond law and policy: Reaffirming the role of student affairs* (New Directions for Student Services, No. 82, pp. 15–27). San Francisco: Jossey-Bass.

Malley, P., Gallagher, R., & Brown, S. M. (1992). Ethical problems in university and college counseling centers: A Delphi study. *Journal of College Student Development, 33*, 238–244.

Manese, J. E., Wu, J. T., & Nepomuceno, C. A. (2001). The effect of training on multicultural counseling competencies: An exploratory study over a ten-year period. *Journal of Multicultural Counseling and Development, 29*, 31–40.

Manning, K., & Coleman-Boatwright, P. (1991). Student affairs initiative toward a multicultural university. *Journal of College Student Development, 32*, 367–374.

Martin, J., & Samels, J. E. (1993). Training administrators to serve as student mentors: An untapped resource in retention planning. *College and University, 69*, 14–21.

Martin, S. (2005). A pragmatic exploration of the multicultural competence of community college student affairs practitioners (Doctoral dissertation, George Washington University, 2005). *Dissertation Abstracts International, 65*, 4491.

Mattox, R. (2000). Building effective campus relationships. In D. C. Davis & K. M. Humphrey (Eds.), *College counseling: Issues and strategies for a new millennium* (pp. 221–238). Alexandria, VA: American Counseling Association.

McEwen, M. K. (2003). The nature and uses of theory. In S. R. Komives & D. B. Woodard (Eds.), *Student services: A handbook for the profession* (4th ed., pp. 153–178). San Francisco: Jossey-Bass.

McEwen, M. K., & Roper, L. D. (1994). Incorporating multiculturalism into student affairs preparation programs: Suggestions from the literature. *Journal of College Student Development, 35*, 46–53.

McKinley, D. L., & Dworkin, D. S. (1989). The disturbed college student. In U. Delworth (Ed.), *Dealing with the behavioral and psychological problems of students* (New Directions for Student Services, No. 45, pp. 31–42). San Francisco: Jossey-Bass.

Megivern, D. M. (2001). *Educational functioning and college integration of students with mental illness: Examining the roles of psychiatric symptomatology and mental health service use.* Unpublished doctoral dissertation, University of Michigan, Ann Arbor.

Meier, S. T., & Davis, S. R. (1997). *Elements of counseling* (3rd ed.). Pacific Grove, CA: Brooks/Cole.

Meier, S. T., & Davis, S. R. (2005). *The elements of counseling* (5th ed.). Belmont, CA: Brooks/Cole.

Merta, R. J. (1995). Group work: Multicultural perspectives. In J. G. Ponterotto, J. M. Casas, L. A. Suzuki, & C. M. Alexander (Eds.), *Handbook of multicultural counseling* (2nd ed., pp. 567–585). Thousand Oaks, CA: Sage.

Miklitsch, T. A. (2006). The relationship between multicultural education, multicultural experiences, racial identity, and multicultural competence among student affairs professionals (Doctoral dissertation, State University of New York at Buffalo, 2005). *Dissertation Abstracts International, 66/08,* 2859.

Miller, T. K., & Winston, R. B. (Eds.). (1991). *Administration and leadership in student affairs: Actualizing student development in higher education* (2nd ed.). Muncie, IN: Accelerated Development.

Mills, D. B. (1993). Role of middle manager. In M. J. Barr (Ed.), *The handbook of student affairs administration* (pp. 121–134). San Francisco: Jossey-Bass.

Mintz, L. B., & Betz, N. E. (1988). Prevalence and correlates of eating disordered behaviors among undergraduate women. *Journal of Counseling Psychology, 35,* 463–471.

Moore, L. V., & Upcraft, M. L. (1990). Theory in student affairs: Evolving perspectives. In L. V. Moore (Ed.), *Evolving theoretical perspectives on students* (New Directions for Student Services, No. 51, pp. 3–23). San Francisco: Jossey-Bass.

Moosbruker, J. (1987). Using a stage model to understand and manage transitions in group dynamics. In W. B. Reddy & C. C. Henderson (Eds.), *Training theory and practice* (pp. 83–92). Arlington, VA: NTL Institute.

Mueller, J. A., & Pope, R. L. (2001). The relationship between multicultural competence and white racial consciousness among student affairs practitioners. *Journal of College Student Development, 42,* 133–144.

Mueller, J. A., & Pope, R. L. (2003). The relationship of demographic and experience variables to white racial consciousness among student affairs practitioners. *NASPA Journal, 40,* 149–171.

Nash, R. J. (1997). Teaching ethics in the student affairs classroom. *NASPA Journal, 35,* 3–19.

Nash, R. J., Bradley, D. L., & Chickering, A. W. (2008). *How to talk about hot topics on campus: From polarization to moral conversation*. San Francisco: Jossey-Bass.

National Association of Student Personnel Administrators. (1937). *The student personnel point of view*. Washington, DC: Author.

National Association of Student Personnel Administrators. (1990). *NASPA standards of professional practice*. Retrieved August 7, 2007, from http://www.naspa.org/programs/standards.cfm

Neville, H. A., Heppner, P. P., & Wang, L. (1997). Relations among racial identity attitudes, perceived stressors, and coping styles in African American college students. *Journal of College Student Development, 75,* 303–311.

Newton, F. B. (2006). Mental health consultation for urgent and emergent campus issues. In S. A. Benton & S. L. Benton (Eds.), *College student mental health: Effective services and strategies across campus* (pp. 139–150). Washington, DC: National Association of Student Personnel Administrators.

Norcross, J. (2002). *John Norcross explains how to establish a powerful therapeutic relationship*. Retrieved October 5, 2007, from http://www.nj-act.org/norcross.html

Nuss, E. M. (1998). Redefining college and university relationships with students. *NASPA Journal, 35,* 183–192.

Nuss, E. M. (2003). The development of student affairs. In S. R. Komives & D. B. Woodard (Eds.), *Student services: A handbook for the profession* (4th ed., pp. 65–89). San Francisco: Jossey-Bass.

Nystul, M. S. (2006). *Introduction to counseling: An art and science perspective* (3rd ed.). Boston: Pearson.

O'Connor, E. M. (2001). *Student mental health: Secondary education no more*. Retrieved July 12, 2007, from http://www.apa.org/monitor/sep01/stumental.html

Odiorne, G. S. (1984). *Strategic management of human resources*. San Francisco: Jossey-Bass.

Okun, B. F. (1997). *Effective helping: Interviewing and counseling techniques* (5th ed.). Thousand Oaks, CA: Brooks/Cole.

Okun, B. F. (2002). *Effective helping: Interviewing and counseling techniques* (6th ed.). Pacific Grove, CA: Brooks/Cole.

O'Malley, K., Wheeler, I., Murphey, J., & O'Connell, J. (1990). Changes in the levels of psychopathology being treated at college and university counseling centers. *Journal of College Student Development, 31,* 464–465.

Osfield, K. J., & Junco, R. (2006). Support services for students with mental health disabilities. In S. A. Benton & S. L. Benton (Eds.), *College student mental health: Effective services and strategies across campus* (pp. 169–188). Washington, DC: National Association of Student Personnel Administrators.

Owen, J. J., Tao, K. W., & Rodolfa, E. R. (2006). Distressed and distressing students: Creating a campus community of care. In S. A. Benton & S. L. Benton (Eds.), *College student mental health: Effective services and strategies across campus* (pp. 15–34). Washington, DC: National Association of Student Personnel Administrators.

Parrott, L. (2003). *Counseling and psychotherapy* (2nd ed.). Pacific Grove, CA: Brooks/Cole.

Parsons, R. D. (2004). *Fundamentals of the helping process*. Long Grove, IL: Waveland Press.

Pascarella, E. T., & Terenzini, P. T. (2005). *How college affects students: A third decade of research* (Vol. 2). San Francisco: Jossey-Bass.

Patterson, C. H. (1980). *Theories of counseling and psychotherapy* (3rd ed.). New York: Harper & Row.

Pavela, G. (2007). *Questions and answers on college student suicide: A law and policy perspective*. Asheville, NC: College Administration Publications.

Pederson, P. B. (Ed.). (1999). *Multiculturalism as a fourth force*. Castleton, NY: Hamilton.

Pedersen, P. B. (2002). Ethics, competence, and other professional issues in culture-centered counseling. In P. B. Pedersen, J. G. Draguns, W. J. Lonner, & J. E. Trimble (Eds.), *Counseling across cultures* (5th ed.). Thousand Oaks, CA: Sage.

Pedersen, P. B., & Ivey, A. E. (1993). *Culture-centered counseling and interviewing skills*. Westport, CT: Praeger.

Peterson, J. V., & Nisenholz, B. (1995). *Orientation to counseling*. Boston: Allyn & Bacon.

Pledge, D. S., Lapan, R. T., Heppner, P. P., Kivlighan, D., & Roehlke, H. J. (1998). Stability and severity of presenting problems at a university counseling center: A six-year analysis. *Professional Psychology: Research and Practice, 29*, 386–389.

Ponterotto, J. G., Alexander, C. M., & Grieger, I. (1995). A multicultural competency checklist for counseling training programs. *Journal of Multicultural Counseling and Development, 23*, 11–20.

Ponterotto, J. G., Rieger, B. P., Barrett, A., Harris, G., Sparks, R., Sanchez, C. M., et al. (1996). Initial development and validation of the Multicultural Counseling Awareness Scale (MCAS-B). In G. R. Sodowsky (Ed.), *Multicultural assessment in counseling and clinical psychology* (pp. 247–282). Lincoln, NE: Buros Institute of Mental Measurements.

Ponterotto, J. G., Rieger, B. P., Barrett, A., & Sparks, R. (1994). Assessing multicultural counseling competence: A review of instrumentation. *Journal of Counseling and Development, 72*, 316–322.

Pope, R. L. (1995). Multicultural organizational development: Implications and applications for student affairs. In J. Fried (Ed.), *Shifting paradigms in student affairs: Culture, context, teaching, and learning* (pp. 233–249). Lanham, MD: University Press of America.

Pope, R. L., & Mueller, J. A. (2000). Development and initial validation of the multicultural competence in student affairs—Preliminary 2 scale. *Journal of College Student Development, 41*, 599–608.

Pope, R. L., & Reynolds, A. L. (1997). Student affairs core competencies: Integrating multicultural awareness, knowledge, and skills. *Journal of College Student Development, 38*, 266–277.

Pope, R. L., Reynolds, A. L., & Cheatham, H. E. (1997). American College Personnel Association (ACPA) strategic initiative on multiculturalism. *Journal of College Student Development, 38*, 62–67.

Pope, R. L., Reynolds, A. L., & Mueller, J. A. (2004). *Multicultural competence in student affairs*. San Francisco: Jossey-Bass.

Pope, R. L., & Thomas, C. D. (2000). Cultural dynamics and issues in higher education. In R. T. Carter (Ed.), *Addressing cultural issues in organizations: Beyond the corporate context* (pp. 115–130). Thousand Oaks, CA: Sage.

Porter, L. (1982a). Giving and receiving feedback: It will never be easy, but it can be better. In L. Porter & B. Mohr (Eds.), *Reading book for human relations training* (pp. 42–46). Arlington, VA: NTL Institute.

Porter, L. (1982b). Group norms: Some things can't be legislated. In L. Porter & B. Mohr (Eds.), *Reading book for human relations training* (pp. 78–80). Arlington, VA: NTL Institute.

Prochaska, J. O., & Norcross, J. C. (2003). *Systems of psychotherapy: A transactional analysis* (5th ed.). Pacific Grove, CA: Brooks/Cole.

Pruett, H. L. (1990). Crisis intervention and prevention with suicide. In H. L. Pruett & V. B. Brown (Eds.), *Crisis intervention and prevention* (New Directions for Student Services, No. 49, pp. 45–55). San Francisco: Jossey-Bass.

Pruett, H. L., & Brown, V. B. (1990). Crisis intervention and prevention as a campus-as-community mental health model. In H. L. Pruett & V. B. Brown (Eds.), *Crisis intervention and prevention* (New Directions for Student Services, No. 49, pp. 3–16). San Francisco: Jossey-Bass.

Reason, R. D., Broido, E. M., Davis, T. L., & Evans, N. J. (Eds.). (2005). *Developing social justice allies* (New Directions for Student Services, No. 110). San Francisco: Jossey-Bass.

Rendon, L. I. (1994). Validating culturally diverse students: Toward a new model of learning and student development. *Innovating Higher Education, 19*, 33–51.

Reynolds, A. L. (1995a). Challenges and strategies for teaching multicultural counseling courses. In J. Ponterotto, M. Casas, L. Suzuki, & C. Alexander (Eds.), *Handbook of multicultural counseling* (pp. 312–330). Thousand Oaks, CA: Sage.

Reynolds, A. L. (1995b). Multicultural counseling and advising as a learning process. In J. Fried (Ed.), *Shifting paradigms in student affairs: A cultural perspective* (pp. 155–170). Washington, DC: American College Personnel Association Media.

Reynolds, A. L. (1995c). Multicultural counseling and advising in student affairs. In J. Fried (Ed.), *Shifting paradigms in student affairs: Culture, context, teaching, and learning* (pp. 155–170). Lanham, MD: University Press of America.

Reynolds, A. L. (1997). Using the Multicultural Change Intervention Matrix (MCIM) as a counseling training model. In D. Pope-Davis & H.L.K. Coleman (Eds.), *Multicultural counseling competence: Assessment, education, and training and supervision* (pp. 209–226). Thousand Oaks, CA: Sage.

Reynolds, A. L. (1999). Working with children and adolescents in the schools: Multicultural counseling implications. In R. H. Sheets & E. R. Hollins (Eds.), *Aspects of human development: Racial and ethnic identity in school practices* (pp. 213–230). Mahwah, NJ: Lawrence Erlbaum.

Reynolds, A. L. (2001). Embracing multiculturalism: A journey of self-discovery. In J. Ponterotto, M. Casas, L. Suzuki, & C. Alexander (Eds.), *Handbook of multicultural counseling* (2nd ed., pp. 103–112). Thousand Oaks, CA: Sage.

Reynolds, A. L. (2005). Applications of racial-cultural supervision. In R. T. Carter (Ed.), *Handbook of racial-cultural psychology and counseling: Training and practice* (Vol. 2, pp. 189–203). New York: Wiley.

Reynolds, A. L., & Pope, R. L. (2003). Multicultural competence in counseling centers. In D. B. Pope-Davis, H.L.K. Coleman, W. M. Liu, & R. L. Toporek (Eds.), *Handbook of multicultural competencies* (pp. 365–382). Thousand Oaks, CA: Sage.

Reynolds, A. L., Sneva, J. N., & Beehler, G. P. (2008). *The influence of racism-related stress on the academic motivation, resilience, self-efficacy, and outcome expectations of black and Latino students.* Unpublished manuscript, University at Buffalo, NY.

Rhoads, R. A., & Black, M. A. (1995). Student affairs practitioners as transformative educators: Advancing a critical cultural perspective. *Journal of College Student Development, 36,* 413–421.

Ridley, C. R. (2005). *Overcoming unintentional racism in counseling and psychotherapy: A practitioner's guide to intentional intervention* (2nd ed.). Thousand Oaks, CA: Sage.

Robbins, S., May, T., & Corazzini, J. (1985). Perceptions of client needs and counseling center staff roles and functions. *Journal of Counseling Psychology, 32,* 641–644.

Roberts, D. C. (1998). Student learning was always supposed to be the core of our work—What happened? *About Campus, 20,* 18–22.

Robertson, J. M., Benton, S. L., Newton, F. B., Downey, R. G., Marsh, P. A., Benton, S. A., et al. (2006). K-State Problem Identification Rating Scale (K-PIRS) for college students. *Measurement and Evaluation in Education, 39*, 141–160.

Rogers, C. (1967). The necessary and sufficient conditions of therapeutic personality change. *Journal of Counseling Psychology, 21*, 95–103.

Rogers, R. F., & Widick, C. (1980). Theory to practice: Using concepts, logic and creativity. In F. B. Newton & K. L. Enders (Eds.), *Student development practice: Strategies for making a difference* (pp. 5–25). Springfield, IL: Thomas.

Rollo, J. M., & Zdziarski, E. L. (2007). Developing a crisis management plan. In E. L. Zdziarski, N. W. Dunkel, J. M. Rollo, & Associates, *Campus crisis management: A comprehensive guide to planning, prevention, response, and recovery* (pp. 73–96). San Francisco: Jossey-Bass.

Roper, L. (2002). Relationships: The critical ties that bind professionals. In J. C. Dalton & M. McClinton (Eds.), *The art and practical wisdom of student affairs leadership* (New Directions for Student Services, No. 98, pp. 11–26). San Francisco: Jossey-Bass.

Rosenstein, I. C. (2006). Personality disorders. In P. A. Grayson & P. W. Meilman (Eds.), *College mental health practice* (pp. 281–302). New York: Routledge.

Rudd, D. M. (2004). University counseling centers: Looking more and more like community clinics. *Professional Psychology: Research and Practice, 35*, 316–317.

Sabnani, H. B., Ponterotto, J. G., & Borodovsky, L. V. (1991). White racial identity development and cross-cultural counselor training: A stage model. *The Counseling Psychologist, 19*, 76–102.

Saddlemire, G. L., & Rentz, A. L. (Eds.). (1986). *Student affairs: A profession's heritage.* Alexandria, VA: American College Personnel Association.

Saidla, D. D. (1990). Competencies for entry level staff identified by professionals in different positions in eight student affairs areas. *College Student Affairs Journal, 10*, 4–14.

Sanford, N. (1967). *Where colleges fail.* San Francisco: Jossey-Bass.

Saunders, S. A., Cooper, D. L., Winston, R. B., & Chernow, E. (2000). Supervising staff in student affairs: Exploration of the synergistic approach. *Journal of College Student Development, 41*, 181–192.

Schein, E. H. (1982). What to observe in a group. In L. Porter & B. Mohr (Eds.), *Reading book for human relations training* (pp. 72–74). Arlington, VA: NTL Institute.

Schlossberg, N. K. (1989). Marginality and mattering: Key issues in building community. In D. C. Roberts (Ed.), *Designing campus activities to foster a sense of community* (New Directions for Student Services, No. 48, pp. 5–15). San Francisco: Jossey-Bass.

Schuh, J. H., & Carlisle, W. (1997). Supervision and evaluation: Selected topics for emerging professionals. In E. J. Whitt (Ed.), *College student affairs administration* (ASHE Reader Series, pp. 498–515). Boston: Pearson.

Schultz, D. P., & Schultz, S. E. (2001). *Theories of personality* (7th ed.). Belmont, CA: Wadsworth.

Seligman, M., & Marshak, L. (2004). Group approaches for persons with disabilities. In J. L. DeLucia-Waack, D. A. Gerrity, C. R. Kalodner, & M. T. Riva (Eds.), *Handbook of group counseling and psychotherapy* (pp. 239–264). Thousand Oaks, CA: Sage.

Senge, P. M. (2006). *The fifth discipline: The art and practice of the learning organization*. New York: Doubleday.

Sharf, R. S. (1996). *Theories of psychotherapy and counseling: Concepts and cases*. Pacific Grove, CA: Brooks/Cole.

Silverman, M. M. (2006). Suicide and suicidal behavior. In P. A. Grayson & P. W. Meilman (Eds.), *College mental health practice* (pp. 303–323). New York: Routledge.

Slocum, Y. S. (1987). A survey of expectations about group therapy among clinical and nonclinical populations. *International Journal of Group Psychotherapy, 37*, 39–54.

Smead, R. (1995). *Skills and techniques for group work with children and adolescents*. Champaign, IL: Research Press.

Sodowsky, G. R., Kuo-Jackson, P. Y., Richardson, M. F., & Corey, A. T. (1998). Correlates of self-reported multicultural competencies: Counselor multicultural social desirability, race, social inadequacy, locus of control racial ideology, and multicultural training. *Journal of Counseling Psychology, 45*, 256–264.

Sodowsky, G. R., Taffe, R. C., Gutkin, T. B., & Wise, S. L. (1994). Development of the Multicultural Counseling Inventory (MCI): A self-report measure of multicultural competencies. *Journal of Counseling Psychology, 41*, 153–162.

Soet, J., & Sevig, T. (2006). Mental health issues facing a diverse sample of college students: Results from the College Student Mental Health Survey. *NASPA Journal, 43*, 410–431.

Speight, S. L. (2007). Internalized racism: One more piece of the puzzle. *The Counseling Psychologist, 35*, 126–134.

Spooner, S. E. (2000). The college counseling environment. In D. C. Davis & K. M. Humphrey (Eds.), *College counseling: Issues and strategies for a new millennium* (pp. 3–14). Alexandria, VA: American Counseling Association.

Stevahn, L., Johnson, D. W., Johnson, R. T., & Schultz, R. (2002). Effects of conflict resolution training integrated into a high school social studies curriculum. *Journal of Social Psychology, 142*, 305–331.

Stimpson, R. F. (1993). Selecting and training competent staff. In M. J. Barr (Ed.), *The handbook of student affairs administration* (pp. 135–151). San Francisco: Jossey-Bass.

Stock-Ward, S. R., & Javorek, M. E. (2003). Applying theory to practice: Supervision in student affairs. *NASPA Journal, 40*, 77–92.

Stoltenberg, C. D., & Delworth, U. (1987). *Supervising counselors and therapists*. San Francisco: Jossey-Bass.

Stoltenberg, C. D., McNeill, B., & Delworth, U. (1998). *IDM supervision: An integrated developmental model for supervising counselors and therapists*. San Francisco: Jossey-Bass.

Strange, C. C., & Banning, J. (2001). *Educating by design: Creating campus learning environments that work*. San Francisco: Jossey-Bass.

Sue, D. W. (2001). Multiple dimensional facets of cultural competence. *The Counseling Psychologist, 29*, 790–821.

Sue, D. W., Arredondo, P., & McDavis, R. J. (1992). Multicultural counseling competencies and standards: A call to the profession. *Journal of Counseling and Development, 70*, 477–486.

Sue, D. W., Bernier, J. E., Durran, A., Feinberg, L., Pederson, P. B., Smith, E. J., et al. (1982). Position paper: Cross-cultural counseling competencies. *The Counseling Psychologist, 10*, 45–52.

Sue, D. W., Bingham, R. P., Porche-Burke, L., & Vasquez, M. (1999). The diversification of psychology: A multicultural revolution. *American Psychologist, 54*, 1061–1069.

Sue, D. W., Carter, R. T., Casas, J. M., Fouad, N. A., Ivey, A. E., Jensen, M., et al. (1998). *Multicultural counseling competencies: Individual and organizational development*. Thousand Oaks, CA: Sage.

Sue, D. W., Ivey, A. E., & Pedersen, P. B. (1996). *A theory of multicultural counseling and therapy*. Pacific Grove, CA: Brooks/Cole.

Sue, D. W., & Sue, D. (2003). *Counseling the culturally diverse: Theory and practice* (4th ed.). New York: Wiley.

Summers-Ewing, D. (1994). *Mentoring: A vital ingredient for career success*. (ERIC Document Reproduction Service No. 378 519)

Sundberg, D. C., & Fried, J. (1997). Ethical dialogues on campus. In J. Fried (Ed.), *Ethics for today's campus: New perspectives on education, student development, and institutional management* (New Directions for Student Services, No. 77, pp. 67–80). San Francisco: Jossey-Bass.

Sutton, E. M. (2006). Developmental mentoring of African American college men. In M. J. Cuyjet (Ed.), *African American men in college* (pp. 95–111). San Francisco: Jossey-Bass.

Talbot, D. M. (1992). *A multimethod study of the diversity emphasis in master's degree programs in college student affairs*. Unpublished doctoral dissertation, University of Maryland, College Park.

Talbot, D. M. (2003). Multiculturalism. In S. R. Komives & D. B. Woodard (Eds.), *Student services: A handbook for the profession* (4th ed., pp. 423–446). San Francisco: Jossey-Bass.

Talbot, D. M., & Kocarek, C. (1997). Student affairs graduate faculty members' knowledge, comfort, and behaviors regarding issues of diversity. *Journal of College Student Development, 38,* 278–287.

Talley, F. J. (1997). Ethics in management. In J. Fried (Ed.), *Ethics for today's campus: New perspectives on education, student development, and institutional management* (New Directions for Student Services, No. 77, pp. 45–66). San Francisco: Jossey-Bass.

Tinto, V. (1987). *Leaving college: Rethinking the causes and cures of student attrition.* Chicago: University of Chicago Press.

Tinto, V. (1994). *Leaving college: Rethinking the causes and cures of student attrition* (2nd ed.). Chicago: University of Chicago Press.

Toporek, R. L., Gerstein, L. H., Fouad, N. A., Roysircar, G., & Israel, T. (Eds.). (2006). *Handbook for social justice in counseling psychology: Leadership, vision, and action.* Thousand Oaks, CA: Sage.

Tori, C. D., & Ducker, D. G. (2004). Sustaining the commitment to multiculturalism: A longitudinal study in a graduate psychology program. *Professional Psychology: Research and Practice, 35,* 649–657.

Twale, D. J., & Jelinek, S. M. (1996). Protégés and mentors: Mentoring experiences of women student affairs professionals. *NASPA Journal, 33,* 203–217.

Upcraft, M. L. (1993). Translating theory to practice. In M. J. Barr (Ed.), *The handbook of student affairs administration* (pp. 260–273). San Francisco: Jossey-Bass.

Upcraft, M. L. (1998). Do graduate preparation programs really prepare practitioners? In N. Evans & C. E. Phelps-Tobin (Eds.), *The state of the art of preparation and practice in student affairs* (pp. 225–237). Lanham, MD: University Press of America.

Utsey, S. O., Chae, M. H., Brown, C. F., & Kelly, D. (2002). Effect of ethnic group membership on ethnic identity, race-related stress, and quality of life. *Cultural Diversity and Ethnic Minority Psychology, 8,* 366–377.

Utsey, S. O., Ponterotto, J. G., Reynolds, A. L., & Cancelli, A. A. (2000). Racial discrimination, coping, life satisfaction, and self-esteem among African Americans. *Journal of Counseling and Development, 78,* 72–80.

Vera, E., & Speight, S. L. (2003). Multicultural competence, social justice, and counseling psychology: Expanding our roles. *The Counseling Psychologist, 31,* 253–272.

Wade, R. W. (1993). *An analysis of beliefs of chief student affairs administrators regarding their professional development needs for the 1980s.* Unpublished doctoral dissertation, Ohio University, Athens, OH.

Waple, J. N. (2006). An assessment of skills and competencies necessary for entry-level student affairs work. *NASPA Journal, 43*, 1–18.

Warters, W. C. (2000). *Mediation in the campus community: Designing and managing effective programs*. San Francisco: Jossey-Bass.

Washington, J., & Evans, N. J. (1991). Becoming an ally. In N. J. Evans & V. A. Wall (Eds.), *Beyond tolerance: Gays, lesbians, and bisexuals on campus* (pp. 195–204). Alexandria, VA: American College Personnel Association.

Weber, R. C. (1982). The group: A cycle from birth to death. In L. Porter & B. Mohr (Eds.), *Reading book for human relations training* (pp. 68–71). Arlington, VA: NTL Institute.

Wechsler, H., Lee, J. E., Kuo, M., Seibring, M., Nelson, T. F., & Lee, H. P. (2002). Trends in college binge drinking during a period of increased prevention efforts: Findings from four Harvard School of Public Health study surveys, 1993–2001. *Journal of American College Health, 50*, 203–217.

Weigand, M. J. (2005). The relationships between multicultural competence, racial identity, and multicultural education and experiences among student affairs professionals responsible for first-year student orientation programs (Doctoral dissertation, State University of New York at Buffalo, 2006). *Dissertation Abstracts International, 66/03*, 926.

Westefeld, J. S., Maples, M. R., Buford, B., & Taylor, S. (2001). Gay, lesbian, and bisexual college students: The relationship between sexual orientation and depression, loneliness, and suicide. *Journal of College Student Psychotherapy, 15*, 71–82.

Wijeyesinghe, C. L., & Jackson B. W., III. (Eds.). (2001). *New perspectives on racial identity development: A theoretical and practical anthology*. New York: New York University Press.

Williams, L. B. (2005). My medicated students: I'm not that kind of doctor. *About Campus, 10*, 27–29.

Wilson, M. E. (2007). Campus training. In E. L. Zdziarski, N. W. Dunkel, J. M. Rollo, & Associates, *Campus crisis management: A comprehensive guide to planning, prevention, response, and recovery* (pp. 183–206). San Francisco: Jossey-Bass.

Winek, J. L., & Jones, D. L. (1996). Balancing legal and ethical issues in college and university counseling. *College Student Affairs Journal, 15*, 64–73.

Winston, R. B. (2003). Counseling and helping skills. In S. R. Komives & D. B. Woodard (Eds.), *Student services: A handbook for the profession* (4th ed., pp. 484–506). San Francisco: Jossey-Bass.

Winston, R. B., Bonney, W. C., Miller, T. K., & Dagley, J. C. (1988). *Promoting student development through intentionally structured groups: Principles, techniques, and applications*. San Francisco: Jossey-Bass.

Winston, R. B., & Creamer, D. G. (1997). *Improving staffing practices in student affairs*. San Francisco: Jossey-Bass.

Winston, R. B., & Creamer, D. G. (1998). Staff supervision and professional development: An integrated approach. In W. A. Bryan & R. A. Schwartz (Eds.), *Strategies for staff development: Personal and professional education in the 21st century* (New Directions for Student Services, No. 84, pp. 29–42). San Francisco: Jossey-Bass.

Winston, R. B., & Hirt, J. B. (2003). Activating synergistic supervision approaches: Practical suggestions. In S. M. Janosik, D. G. Creamer, J. B. Hirt, R. B. Winston, S. A. Saunders, & D. L. Cooper (Eds.), *Supervising new professionals in student affairs: A guide for new professionals* (pp. 43–84). New York: Brunner-Routledge.

Winston, R. B., & Saunders, S. A. (1998). Professional ethics in a risky world. In D. L. Cooper & J. M. Lancaster (Eds.), *Beyond law and policy: Reaffirming the role of student affairs* (New Directions for Student Services, No. 82, pp. 77–94). San Francisco: Jossey-Bass.

Wrenn, C. G. (1951). *Student personnel work in college: With emphasis on counseling and group experiences*. New York: Ronald Press.

Wrenn, C. G. (1962). The culturally encapsulated counselor. *Harvard Educational Review, 32*, 444–449.

Yalom, I. D. (2005). *The theory and practice of group psychotherapy* (5th ed.). New York: Basic Books.

Yau, T. Y. (2004). Guidelines for facilitating groups with international college students. In J. L. DeLucia-Waack, D. A. Gerrity, C. R. Kalodner, & M. T. Riva (Eds.), *Handbook of group counseling and psychotherapy* (pp. 253–264). Thousand Oaks, CA: Sage.

Young, R. B. (2001). Ethics and professional practice. In R. B. Winston, D. G. Creamer, & T. K. Miller (Eds.), *The professional student affairs administrator: Educator, leader, and manager* (pp. 153–178). New York: Brunner-Routledge.

Zachary, L. J. (2000). *The mentor's guide: Facilitating effective learning relationships*. San Francisco: Jossey-Bass.

Zdziarski, E. L. (2006). Crisis in the context of higher education. In K. S. Harper, B. G. Patterson, & E. L. Zdziarski (Eds.), *Crisis management: Responding from the heart* (pp. 3–24). Washington, DC: National Association of Student Personnel Administrators.

Zdziarski, E. L., Dunkel, N. W., Rollo, J. M., & Associates. (2007). *Campus crisis management: A comprehensive guide to planning, prevention, response, and recovery*. San Francisco: Jossey-Bass.

Index